Still Away
with the Ferries

Still Away with the Ferries

Ferry tales from years of
Island Hopping

STUART CRAIG

LINDSAY
PUBLICATIONS

First published in 2009 by
Lindsay Publications
Glasgow

ISBN 1 898169 37 3

A CIP record of this book is available from the British Library

Designed and typeset in 10/12 Sabon
by Eric Mitchell, Glasgow

Front Cover: Designed by C&R Graphics, Cumbernauld

Printed and bound in Great Britain by Bell & Bain Limited, Glasgow

CONTENTS

Stuart

Gibbie

Ian

Andy

Bob

Sparky

INTRODUCTION

THIS BOOK IS, in essence, a sequel to my previous book with the remarkably similar title - Away With The Ferries. If you read that then you will know what this one is likely to be about. If you didn't read it - why not? No matter, let me explain.

In May 1989 myself and friend Gibbie Anderson embarked on a three-day trip around the Hebrides, with the aim of sailing on as many ferries and to as many islands as possible - within the confines of three days. The following year we were joined by another ship-lover, Ian McLaren, for a similar trip. We had such fun that we just couldn't stop, and by 1998 we had completed ten separate trips. These were chronicled in Away With The Ferries. But we still couldn't stop Island Hopping. In May 1999 the three of us were off again, and the next year again. Now, in 2008, we have completed another ten trips around the beautiful islands of Scotland.

During the first few trips of Away With The Ferries none of us were sure for how long our May adventure would continue. But after the success of the book it became our intention to take another ten trips. Well my intention anyway. If the others opted out after a couple of years I would just have to make the rest up!

Reading this as a sequel to Away With The Ferries would, I reckon, be more intelligible. But this book is easily an entity of its own. However I do occasionally refer to previous Island Hops from the first book.

So here comes the second lot of three-day Hebridean adventures. Another ten. The trips were all undertaken in May of each year, continuously from 1999 to 2008. The same three protagonists dominate but there were one or two changes of personnel. In 2006 we were joined by Bob Barr, a former colleague of Gibbie from Canada who just happened to be in Scotland at the right time (or perhaps the wrong time). In 2007 Ian couldn't manage the trip and was 'replaced' by Gibbie's wee brother Andy - an act of unadulterated nepotism. In the final year we couldn't shake Andy off so when Ian returned the three stoogies became the gang of four.

Personally I feel that these ten trips were even better that the previous ten - I don't honestly know what my colleagues think about that. But the ships are ever changing, different routes evolve and the patter just gets better.

This time we gave greater theme to our annual trips. We had one Island Hop based purely on the Clyde. In another we visited Orkney. We had one trip in which the aim was to stay overnight on islands which we had never before stayed on.

Not surprisingly Caledonian MacBrayne dominate the following pages. It is they, of course, who service the islands of western Scotland with their fleet of black and white hulled ships. During these ten years there were the inevitable changes to their fleet. On the positive side we witnessed much modernisation with the arrival of new ships such as *Clansman*, *Hebrides*, *Lochnevis* and the next generation of Rothesay ferries *Argyle* and *Bute*. But some old favourites were pensioned off: *Claymore*, *Iona* and *Pioneer*.

Routes have changed also, although not greatly. 'Clyde Cruising' by CalMac disappeared during these years, but the services to Bute and Islay were stepped up to two ships. A direct route from Tiree to Barra evolved and there was a new route across the Sound of Barra to Eriskay. Sailings to other islands became more frequent.

It is not all CalMac, however. Orkney Ferries and Northlink Ferries get star billing one year. And the dear old *Waverley* pops up out of the blue on more than one occasion. No more so than in the first chapter.

The period covered by this book also coincides with the time in which the very future of ferry services in the west of Scotland was being deliberated over by politicians in Scotland, Westminster and Europe. But you'll be delighted to discover that there is no political debate in these pages.

One may be forgiven for thinking that we had exhausted all sailing possibilities during the first ten years. This isn't the case. As mentioned earlier there were always new ships to try out and changes to ferry routes which had to be experienced. Every year there was something new to try - and this will be pointed out at the introduction to each trip. We even managed 'new' islands. We managed thirty-five in the first book but added further islands in these ten Island Hops. You'll have to read on to discover which ones! The appendix at the end will summarise both the islands sailed to and the ships sailed upon.

I hope you enjoy reading about our second ten years of Island Hopping as much as we enjoyed experiencing them. And just as I tempted the reader in the Introduction of Away With The Ferries - go and savour these islands for yourself.

At the start of each chapter/year there is The Plan. This is a rough guide to the aims of that year's trip. It is deliberately concise so as not to give the 'game away' on whether we were successful in acheiving our aims.

1999 Here We Go Again!

The Plan

ISLAND HOP PLANS ARE USUALLY drawn up in January, and this trip was no exception. The trip would go ahead in the third week in May, our favoured time. However, this was probably the only year when the itinerary was changed at the last minute. Well maybe not the last minute, but just four weeks before we were due to go.

The main goal was to sail on the new *Clansman*. This fine ship had just taken over the sailings to Barra and Lochboisdale from Oban, thus reinstating three major ferries sailing out of Oban in the summer months. Ten years ago the Oban fleet had been reduced from three to two. So *Clansman* was a must; we would take her to Barra. On either side of this excursion we may be able to visit a new island and take a trip around the Uig triangle. But we would start on the Clyde.

CalMac were using one of their upper firth car ferries as a Clyde cruise ship. The vessels (*Jupiter*, *Juno*, *Pioneer* and *Saturn*) were employed on a week-about rotational basis, calling at various Clyde piers on a roster dove-tailed into their car-ferrying duties between Gourock-Dunoon and Wemyss Bay-Rothesay. We would take whichever ship was on the 'cruising' roster, from Largs to Tarbert. So the plan was drawn up.

Four weeks before the start of our trip the spring timetable for paddle-steamer *Waverley* dropped through my letter box, and it contained a gem of an opportunity.

In the third week in May the paddle-steamer does not normally cruise on the Clyde. But due to a forthcoming major refit, funded partly by the Lottery Heritage Fund, her schedule had been altered. On the same day that we were due to start our island Hop *Waverley* was due to give a very special cruise. The fact that it was taking place on the first day of our Island Hop was merely coincidence and good fortune. That day, for the first time ever, *Waverley* and her screw-driven consort *Balmoral* would meet on the Clyde - at Millport. We just had to be there! Could we sail on both vessels?

So the first day of our trip was hurriedly redrawn. The CalMac Largs-Tarbert cruise would vanish from the schedule, but it might just be possible to join the CalMac ship on her home leg from Largs to Dunoon or Gourock. Three cruise ships on the one day!

Day One - *The Glorious Day Of Clyde Steaming*

It is 09.25 on Sunday 16 May 1999, and Ian and I are standing on the quay-side at Anderston – Glasgow home of the paddle-steamer *Waverley*. The old ship herself is lying wheezing alongside, having arrived here just a few hours ahead of us. Like us, she is preparing for the long day of cruising which lies ahead.

Gibbie isn't with us. No we've not abandoned him. At this precise moment he should be leaning over the rail of the Gourock-Dunoon ferry on his lonely sojourn to position his car at the Cowal capital. He had volunteered for the less glamorous part at the start of our trip. Assuming he has made the 09.20 sailing from Gourock on time he should soon be driving off at Dunoon, finding a parking place and then rejoining the ferry as a foot passenger, all within the next ten minutes. On his return to Gourock he will then furnish himself with a taxi for the short ride to Greenock. There, in around one and a half hours from now, we will come paddling in to meet him, and the three Island Hoppers would be reunited. The car? Well it will all be apparent later.

I describe Gibbie's route as the less glamorous option but Gibbie himself would think otherwise. The sail down the upper reaches of the Clyde, past decaying buildings, rotting timbers and the abandoned sites of old shipyards and their associated industries depresses him. He is happy to give the first part of *Waverley*'s cruise a miss.

So off we splash at 10.00, Ian, myself and a couple of hundred others, aboard *Waverley* at the start of a convoluted circuit of coastal cruising. Well it's convoluted for us, hopefully the other two hundred are not coming with us.

A mere heaving-line's length down river lies *Glenlee*. *Glenlee* was built at Port Glasgow in 1896 and is a 245 feet long, steel built, three-masted barque. She is one of only five remaining Clydebuilt sailing ships in the world. Rescued in 1990 from the scrap yard after languishing in Seville Harbour she was lovingly restored by volunteers with the aid of Heritage Lottery money and is now owned by the Clyde Maritime Trust. Having circumnavigated the world four times she is unlikely ever to sail again but visitors can tread her wooden decks and imagine what it was like plunging through an Atlantic Ocean swell.

For Ian the first part of this trip will be like a sail down memory lane. He has not sailed down river from Glasgow since the late 1960s and the days of *Queen Mary ll*.

We glide through the open (thankfully) swing-bridge built for the 1988 Glasgow Garden Festival - the Bell's Bridge. I wonder if that poor chap operating the mechanism must now sit the rest of the day out in the middle of his bridge until the paddler returns.

Glasgow's river is now almost devoid of shipping and in danger of silting up. At Kaeverner Shipyard at Govan finishing touches are being applied to a new vessel. Further on, at Linthouse, we pass the site where Alexander Stephens (shipyard) once stood. This is where Ian served his engineering apprenticeship, as a lad, and where he met Gibbie, who it is difficult to believe was ever a lad, serving his time likewise. The shipyard closed in 1968 - they had no part in this!

Further on again, on the opposite bank, things are looking a little better. Three British naval frigates lie moored to the quayside: *HMS London, HMS Kent* and, launched only yesterday, *HMS Portland*. It seems that although merchant shipbuilding has steadily declined we still need state-of-the-art frigates and destroyers of which Yarrow's builds the best.

Waverley paddles on. Manoeuvring this way and that to avoid floating logs of wood which drift upriver with the tide towards us, like menacing crocodiles. It seems as though half a forest has been emptied into the Clyde ahead of us. Just as a tree trunk seems about to be sucked under our sponsons we steer away from it and it bobs past harmlessly.

On towards Greenock and on the left bank a major problem to our Island Hop suddenly materialises. A red, yellow and black CalMac funnel can be seen rising up from Garvel Dry Dock. There are no overhauls at this time of year, one of their bigger ships must have a problem. I grab my binoculars. It's *Clansman*. She should be at Oban preparing to take us to Barra tomorrow night! Why is she here? Obviously something has gone bust onboard her and she is in dock for repairs. This could have serious consequences for our plans. *Clansman* is a crucial target ship for us as we have not sailed on her yet. The long sail out and back to Barra is one of the highlights of this year's trip. Now we will have to sail out on something else - if we are able to sail out at all!

It dawns on me that things could get worse. Another ship must have been redeployed to fill in for *Clansman*, which probably means that the versatile and trusty *Pioneer* has been sent up to Oban. This would deprive the Clyde services of one of their ships and will almost certainly mean that today's cruise ship to Tarbert - which we planned to join on part of the inward leg - will be cancelled. Gibbie may well have taken his car to Dunoon in vain. We may need it at Largs instead! Island Hop 1999 is falling apart before it has even properly begun.

As all of these negative thoughts are racing through my mind *Waverley* is arriving at Greenock pier and Ian scans the crowds for Gibbie. There he is, with his camera bag slung over his left shoulder in his typical casual style. (My children now refer to camera bags as "Gibbie Bags"). Perhaps he can shed some light on the *Clansman* situation.

He cannot. But he can tell us that the Tarbert cruise ship today is *Jupiter* and she is definitely sailing. He saw her leave Gourock this morning with her bunting fluttering merrily. So it may be that his trip to Dunoon with the car isn't in vain after all. Gibbie had sailed over from Gourock to Dunoon aboard *Saturn* at 09.20 and had deposited his car beneath the approving eye of the statue of Heilin Mary. He had made it back to *Saturn* before the crew had even noticed he was gone.

"This ship is going to Gourock, you know," the crewman volunteered. He had obviously noted Gibbie's unusual behaviour. Most of the others standing on Dunoon pier were waiting for *Jupiter*. He probably thought Gibbie was delivering a *hot* car. At Gourock he jumped into a taxi and took it the three miles to Greenock. That is how he comes to be standing in front of us now, aboard *Waverley*, with palm out, looking for reimbursement of the taxi fare from our 'kitty'.

So we know now that we should be able to join *Jupiter* from Largs to Dunoon later in the day. But what about *Clansman*? A few familiar faces from the CRSC (Clyde River Steamer Club - of which we are all members) also came aboard at Greenock. One of them is sure to know what the problems are. After all, steamer nutters like these find out about ship breakdowns before even Caledonian MacBrayne do!

It transpires that *Clansman* has rudder problems and has been replaced on her Outer Isles sailings by *Lord of the Isles*. She in turn has been replaced on her Mallaig - Armadale route by *Claymore*, which has been chartered back to CalMac from the Argyll and Antrim Steam Packet Company, where she is the incumbent on the Campbeltown - Ballycastle route. So we will get to Barra after all, but not on *Clansman* unfortunately. We should also get to Dunoon today. Hurray! The only real losers were the tourists trying to get from Campbeltown to Northern Ireland, but hey, who cares about them?

A number of passengers are waiting for the ship at Helensburgh. Today is proving to be a popular day out. We turn south now towards Largs and ultimately Millport. *Balmoral*, meanwhile, should be heading north towards us from Brodick. We are all eagerly looking forward to the two ships meeting up. *Waverley* herself seems eager, for she arrives at Largs twenty minutes ahead of schedule, forcing the Cumbrae ferry *Loch Riddon* to vacate the face of the pier to let us in.

Heading now for Millport, the capital of Great Cumbrae, and as we turn round Keppel Point into the bay, there ahead of us, sitting out in that stretch of water between the two Cumbraes called The Tan is *Balmoral*. Despite our ship's eagerness to get there first, we have been beaten to it. But on doing so the diesel vessel has to sit it out while we tie up against Millport Pier.

Waverley is known to anyone reading these pages but perhaps less so is *Balmoral*. She was built in 1949 by J I Thornycroft of Southampton for service to the Isle of Wight. In 1969 she was sold to P & A Campbell Ltd for Bristol Channel services and cruises. She was laid up at the end of the 1981 season and subsequently sold to a Dundee company, Craig Inns, for use as a floating pub. This venture was unsuccessful and the *Balmoral* lay at Dundee until 1985 when she was bought by *Balmoral* Excursions Ltd. to act as a consort for the famous paddler. She was refitted and suitably altered at Govan Drydock during the winter of 1985-86 and has ever since had tremendous success in boosting the company's cruising earnings with her own extensive cruising program. Although lacking the glamour of the paddle-steamer, and being a bit on the noisy side, she is nevertheless a fine ship with ample passenger accommodation and deck space.

Balmoral had left Campbeltown at 06.30 this morning and headed to the Ayrshire coast to call at Girvan (09.30) and Ayr (11.15). Her destination was then Brodick (12.45) and finally Millport where the two ships were due to meet just after 14.00. I sailed on her several times before, memorably out of Fraserburgh in 1991, to Lamlash Pier in 1994, to Iona from Oban in 1994 and with Gibbie from Ayr to Millport in 1993, but this was the first time we had encountered her on an Island Hop.

We would be joining her shortly for her "Round Cumbrae Cruise" but for now we are intrigued as to how the ships will tie up and how they will coordinate their historic meeting with each other. We don't have to wait long. *Waverley* ties up and disembarks most of her passengers, including us. *Balmoral* then creeps up alongside *Waverley*'s port side and ropes are thrown across to tether the two ships. Some 250 passengers stream across *Waverley*'s decks from the motor vessel and the already busy Millport pier is now thronged. A pipe-band, stuck in the middle somewhere, is heralding the arrival of the vessels. It is an auspicious day for Millport too.

I scuttle round a couple of corners to get a better camera position. I can't linger. *Balmoral* is due to leave and I am supposed to be on her.

We cross *Waverley*'s decks and onto *Balmoral*. The captains are at their respective bridges ironing out the finer details of how they are going to synchronise their ships as they both prepare to circumnavigate Great Cumbrae Island. I move forward to just below the bridge and eavesdrop brazenly, like a nosey neighbour behind a garden wall.

"So Steve, which way round are you going?" Asks *Waverley*'s captain.

"I haven't a clue." Is the reply.

"Okay then, I'll just follow you."

The ropes and gangways are thrown aside and both ships slip out into Millport Bay. They pivot and begin a clockwise circuit of the island. *Balmoral* leads the way, which gives us a wonderful view of the paddle-steamer creaming along in our wake, her angular, rakish bow parting the water like a blade through butter.

The next fifty minutes or so are quite simply terrific and within minutes we realise that we have picked the right ship to be on, for the views of *Waverley* paddling along closely behind us are stunning. I have never sailed so close to another ship. She would allow *Balmoral* to stretch a couple of cables ahead, and then, like a seasoned athlete, put on a touch of pace to come up alongside. On the rear deck of *Balmoral* our cameras fire away - recording the closest shots of the paddler at speed that either of us have ever managed to record. Soon both ships are hoisting semaphore flags to each other:

Waverley to *Balmoral* -	"We've just lost a propeller!"
Balmoral to *Waverley* -	"Do you require a tow?"
Waverley to *Balmoral* -	"I've got yellow fever aboard!"

Around the north tip of Great Cumbrae and into the Largs Channel. Sirens and steam whistles shriek out and the passengers on both ships shout out "Hip hip hurrahs!" to each other.

Back at Millport *Balmoral* berths first and we get off - well pleased with ourselves. A waitress from a nearby cafe comes running up to the purser at the gangway clutching something in her hand. It turns out to be a pipe with its mouthpiece carefully wrapped in a napkin. She points at *Balmoral*. "Someone off the *Waverley* left his pipe in our cafe."

The purser replies coolly, "This isn't the *Waverley*, this is the *Balmoral*, the *Waverley* has two big paddle things stuck on either side."

We now have a choice between jumping on a bus up to the Cumbrae ferry slip or waiting for *Waverley* to return and sailing back to Largs on her. There is no comparison, so we watch *Balmoral* head off back to Brodick and Ayr and wait for the paddler to move onto the pier to take her place. The air is buzzing and both ships' crews and their masters deserve credit for making this historic meeting so much fun for both sets of passengers. A great start to another ten years of Island Hopping.

Back at Largs our days cruising is not yet over, however. As *Waverley* steams upriver back to Glasgow we take our fish suppers - which, by the way, must rank as the worst we've ever had to suffer on an Island Hop trip, or any other kind of trip for that matter - onto the Cumbrae ferry. This turns out to be *Loch Riddon*. So we sail to Cumbrae for the third time, and on the third vessel, today. Why? Because we have some time to kill and using our CalMac *Rover* tickets we are in the habit of jumping on and off ferries whenever one appears in front of us. Just for the fun of it.

As we sail across I feed most of my fish supper to a large intimidating herring gull. It wolfs it down greedily. But something else quite extraordinary happens. It doesn't keel over but instead throws its head back and screeches out a raucous cacophony to its colleagues in the manner in which gulls normally do. Nothing extraordinary in that, except that it is so engrossed while doing this that it does not notice my hand patting its back. Eventually it does notice and then it gets such a fright that it literally falls off its perch. From a higher vantage point it proceeds to afford me a look of extreme indignation. It is the first time I have patted a live sea-gull. I use the word "live" hesitantly for after devouring that fish-supper its future existence must surely be in danger.

Gibbie views the sea-gull incident with acute disdain. Several years ago at his workplace in Kilmarnock he had an altercation with a young gull which has left him deeply distrustful of anything of an ornithological nature. He had found the young gull hobbling across the staff car park clearly distressed. Like the caring chap he is, he placed the poor bird in a large shoe box and took it to the Ayrshire equivalent of a Rolf Harris animal welfare centre. The bird recovered and two weeks later Gibbie watched in silent disbelief as it returned to the car park, flew around for a couple of minutes and then defaecated (not Gibbie's word I have to say) on the bonnet of his car. Gibbie is certain it was the same bird.

We consider staying on the Cumbrae side in order to sail on the other ferry *Loch Alainn*, but decide against it as she is temporary out of service. We cannot risk waiting for her as we have *Jupiter* to catch from Largs, so we remain onboard *Loch Riddon* and head back across. Ironically just as we sail away from the island *Loch Alainn* comes back into service and is soon overtaking us.

Jupiter can now be seen coming across the firth from Rothesay. She has had a busy day sailing to Tarbert but is soon tying-up at Largs Pier, at 18.20. On we get - our third Clyde cruise ship today, a rare event. A day in which almost ever viable Clyde pier has been visited by a cruising ship. A reasonable crowd are aboard but the car deck is empty, except for two chaps wandering about aimlessly as if they have lost their vehicles. Perhaps they've forgotten which pier they're heading for now. It's Dunoon, of course. Now you know why Gibbie's car was put there.

As we approach the Gantocks most of the ship's complement are already queuing to get off. We are still several minutes from the pier and yet they are ten deep at the railings. Of course, they are all queuing at the wrong side of the ship. We cut inside the Gantocks and spin round leaving them all staring across at Gourock. The penny drops and they all shuffle round like gaggling geese. The difference is now the three of us are at the head of the gangway. sFrom Dunoon pier we can see Gibbie's car waiting for us below the statue of Mary. She has kept a watchful eye on it.

Gibbie drives us north towards Oban, around the northern end of a Loch Fyne that looks like a sheet of glass on this still and windless evening. We reach Oban just before nine o' clock and are treated to the welcoming sight of the training schooner *Sir Winston Churchill* moored at the North Pier. At the Railway Pier *Lord of the Isles* is arriving late from Colonsay- a sailing that should have been performed by *Clansman*.

Our second treat of the night is a really stylish sunset as the golden orb of the sinking sun slowly dips behind Kerrera leaving behind a marbled sky of greys and deep crimsons. It is a suitably serene end to a stunning day of Clyde steaming.

Day Two - *Kerrera "Re-visited"*

We have an easy start this morning. We could have made it more difficult by taking the early morning return sailing to Lismore. Hey - Island Hopping isn't just ferries and islands. We should know - we're experts at it now. Sometimes it's about long lie-ins and unrushed, hearty breakfasts. In any case we did the Lismore thing a year or two ago and we have other interesting plans for the day.

Firstly we want to ascend to the summit of the hill that Dunoillie Castle rests upon. This dangerously ruined castle sits at the northern entrance to Oban Bay, overlooking the tip of Kerrera and affording superb views of passing ships and ferries as they sail close to the shore, on their passage in and out of the Oban. With the weather conditions so good - downright perfect to be precise - we decide to set up cameras at the castle to record the 10.00 departure of *Isle of Mull* to Craignure.

I mentioned that Dunoillie sits on a hill. In which case it may come as a surprise to hear that Gibbie agreed to climbing it. In which case it will be astonishing to learn that it was actually his idea to go there in the first place. The hill turns out to be a mere bump about 150 feet high, but we have to lug our gear up there. The castle itself looks ready to fall down at a moment's notice and we decide to respect the 'DANGER' signs that are in evidence.

From our vantage point we have a great view of Kerrera, the island guarding Oban Bay and now stretched out in front of us like a map. Do I dare to suggest to my colleagues that we also have time to go there this morning. After the failure in the past to add it to our list we had vowed never to mention the word "Kerrera" again, as if it were in some way a blasphemous Island Hopping expletive. I decide to play it circumspectly. I'll go along with anything my colleagues want to do this morning, and wait until they are in a good mood before raising the subject of going to Kerrera delicately, as if I've just thought of it, and like a nervous schoolboy asking his teacher if he can go to the bathroom.

The woods around and below us at Dunoillie are full of bird song. Wrens, chaffinches, a redstart, blackbird and song thrush, and a passing goldcrest. It is a gorgeous spring morning. But the birdwatching is interrupted by *Isle of Mull* gliding past. Cameras click enthusiastically.

"Where now?" I ask expectantly.

"McCaig's Folly?" Suggests Gibbie. Another hill! Has he taken leave of his senses? I smile encouragingly and we head off to Oban's best known tourist attraction. We normally avoid tourist attractions but the view over the town is splendid. Kerrera still dominates the panorama. *Sir Winston Churchill*, devoid of any sails on her rigging, still sits at the North Pier.

"Look there's Kerrera!" I point out casually; but I am ignored. Instead I give thought to the video footage I've taken this morning. I have made a documentary-style video of each Island Hop from 1993. Not only composed of clips of the ships but with some monologue from Gibbie or Ian, and some footage of our surroundings, edited into something that resembles a film record of our trip. I want to take a linking shot to my video-camera, I hide it in a small bush next to me. Unfortunately a woman wanders by and looks at me in astonishment as I appear to be talking to myself. "Well here we are in Oban and it's a lovely day."

She smiles nervously and speeds up her pace, looking back at me.

"Look at that lovely view - later today we hope to go to Kerrera."

16

After McCaig's Folly I pop the question. "Why don't we have a quick trip over to Kerrera? After all, it will be a new island."

Moans and groans but they at least agree to go to the ferry slipway, a couple of miles south of Oban. I know that once they are there they will succumb when they see the boat coming across for us.

There lies the problem. There is no boat coming across for us. It is now 11.00 and we want to be on the 12.00 sailing to Mull. The solution comes in the shape of two cyclists, one of whom has a mobile phone with which she calls the ferryman. I've always known that a use for a mobile phone would become apparent to me one day - and here it is. The result is that the metal hulled motorboat is soon racing across the Sound towards us. After a bit of negotiation it is agreed that the ferryman will take us over to Kerrera, wait a few minutes and take us back again. There is no turning back for Ian and Gibbie. It is 11.10 - we still have time to get over there and back before the noon sailing of *Isle of Mull*.

We sit aboard *Gylen Lass* along with our two cyclist friends and their bikes. No doubt they think we're mad - the ferryman certainly does! After ten years of this kind of thing we are in no doubt - we know we are mad.

Ironically Ian and Gibbie seem actually quite pleased to have finally made it to Kerrera. It is a lush island with great swathes of green bracken criss-crossed by a few gravely tracks. Gibbie finds himself a Kerrera stone to add to his collection. It looks the same as any other kind of stone but he seems well pleased with it. Ian and I stroll up the first part of the track to the red telephone box which we have looked at many times from the decks of a Colonsay bound ship. It has taken us years to get to this spot.

The ferryman is loitering around with intent so we get back into his boat and are soon being speedily conveyed back to civilisation. A few minutes later we are boarding *Isle of Mull* for our return sailing to the third island of the trip, having illegally deposited Gibbie's car in our favourite Oban hide-away-hole. The location of this will remain a closely guarded secret lest anyone reading this will claim it as their own and we will be forced to actually pay to park the car in the future.

Why are we going to Mull, yet again? Because we can. Simple as that. We have time to kill before sailing out to Barra and it is a very pleasant wee sail. Nevermind that we've done it 55 times before. In any case each time we do it the view from the top deck is different.

On the deck of the ship Gibbie is embarrassing Ian and I by his antics. He has produced three sticks of sun-blocker in different shades and is applying cream to different parts of his face, like an old woman trying to put on lipstick without a mirror. His features are picked out and decorated in yellow, white and green. He thinks he looks like an Australian fast-bowler, in fact he looks more like the Irish version of Danny La Rue.

At Craignure the tide is exceptionally low. The lowest we've ever seen here and passengers are advised to disembark from a lower deck. We remain onboard.

On the return to Oban a middle-aged woman sits terrified on her deck seat frightened to move. A herring gull is hovering ten feet above her with a greedy eye on the Tunnocks Caramel Wafer that she has grasped in her hand. Can you blame it? It tastes better than a Largs fish supper, that's for sure. Despite her husband trying to console her that she is not in a scene from a Hitchcock film, and that the bird will not actually attack her, she sits clutching her biscuit unable to move with fear. I feel like suggesting that if she just eats the thing the gull will fly off in pursuit of something else that it can get its beak into. All of this gives us an appetite so we go down to the restaurant for a quick bite of lunch. When we return up on deck some time later she is still squirming in her seat, glancing alternatively between the biscuit and the attending gull.

The real business of the day, apart from Kerrera, begins when *Lord of the Isles* arrives at Oban. We join her for the five hour sail out to Barra. It is such a beautiful day that our disappointment that she is not *Clansman* is now forgotten. In fact the *Clansman* has even less open deck space than *LOTI* so perhaps we shouldn't complain.

We sail on time. Once past Dunoillie, and into the Sound of Mull, the three of us head for a seat in the bar. Here, a very old lady opposite us is trying Gibbie's lipstick trick - only with lipstick. She produces a tiny mirror from her capacious handbag and with a shaky hand squints at her reflection and dabs at her not inconsiderable lips. The end result is two squiggly lines of bright vermillion which almost, but not quite, coincide with her lips. I feel that Gibbie should get up and help her (by the way we wouldn't let him on the ship until he removed his make-up).

Another lady - we seem to be attracting them today - is lying supine on the seats next to us. A half empty glass of wine sits on the table next to her. "I'll have one of whatever she's got," says Ian.

Ian gets talking to a well dressed chap who is consuming a packet of Rolos meticulously and single-handedly. He is moaning about the length of time the ship takes on passage to Barra. "I went out last week to visit my sick mother. I'm having to go out today because she's died and I'll be back out again next week for the funeral."

There is a silence for an uncomforatble length of time while one of us thinks of a meaningful response to that. Ian eventually comes up trumps, "Can I have one of your Rolos, please?"

Up on deck to see what's happening. We are right out into the open sea now but the water is calm and the sea-breeze not cold. Why are there so few seats out on deck? I have to make do with a coil of thick rope - which actually turns out to be quite comfortable.

A group of people on an ornithological/archaeological expedition to the Western Isles are being tutored out on deck by a chap whom it turns out I've known for many years. Stuart Gibson, a keen ornithologist with an interest in archaeology, acts as a guide on trips such as this, and takes small parties, on minor expeditions to the Hebrides every year. Everyone seems to be having a good time, though I fail to see the connection between ornithology and archaeology - unless someone digs up a pre-historic chicken or something. Being aboard a ship it is obvious that the ornithology is in the ascendancy at the moment.

"Look at that group of gulls over there - they're obviously feeding on some small fish that are near the surface. This is just the type of situation where we find a marauding great skua."

Amazingly, right on cue, a large brown bird, a great skua, swoops past them and takes a belligerent peck at one of the gulls. "How did you do that, Stuart?" I ask. "Did you see it coming out of the corner of your eye?"

Stuart just smiles back. I suppose he has to get his timing right once in a while. If his luck continues like this his party will dig up an Egyptian pyramid on Barra tomorrow. We go back to the bar for a heat - the air is getting cooler. The supine lady is still supine - she's not moved an inch. We exchange anxious looks at each other.

Stroll around the deck - well, it's a long trip. Barra is approaching, looking rather inviting as the sun begins her descent behind the southern islands of the Western Isles archipelago. Soon we're there and our hotel is a mere hundred yard climb up from the pier. Gibbie winces in anticipation, "I've already climbed two mountains today."

I return to the bar to collect a jacket. The crew are manipulating half a dozen large bin-bags, and the seat which held the supine lady is now empty - not that I am connecting the two, of course.

It is nice to arrive in daylight. Ian suggests it's just nice to arrive. *Lord of the Isles* is heading off to South Uist now, but will be back for us in the morning. At the hotel Gibbie is in his element. The young girl attending us in the restaurant speaks perfect English with a heavy German accent.

"To tell if she's German or Austrian I'll order potatoes, and ask her how to translate them." Gibbie loves practising his Teutonic tongue. He whispers to us, "If she says kartoffel then she's German, and if she says erdappel then she's Austrian." His little ploy works, she turns out to be Austrian and is suitably impressed. Unfortunately our food order arrives with six large bowls of boiled spuds!

A stroll afterwards in the dark. Venus and a new moon are spectacular sights in the clear sky. The midnight weather report on the television - Barcelona had 35 mm of rain. Barra had none. Temperature tomorrow should be 17 C with a 5 mph SE breeze. The high pressure above the north of Scotland is building. Enough of the weather forecast, it's time for bed.

Day Three - *Hold That Ship!*

I have a close shave in the dining-room at breakfast (my second close shave of the morning). One of the ornithology/archaeology party, a sprightly, ample-bosomed woman of maturing years, accosts me over the grapefruit segments bowl. From her slightly sycophatic sentiments I can tell that she thinks I'm the hotel manager.

"More bird-watching today?" I ask, puting on my best Basil Fawlty inflection.

"Oh no it's archaeology today," say declares enthusiastically.

"Well maybe you'll find a stone curlew." From her reaction she either doesn't get the joke or has never heard of such a bird.

"This grapefruit is delicious, isn't it?"

"Yes Madam, I opened the tin myself."

Down at the pier I sling my "Gibbie Bag" carelessly over my left shoulder and tear a four inch long strip from my leather jacket. This is sad news. This jacket has shared every Island Hop experience with me since 1992. All those years of sea salt have doubtlessly weakened the very fabric of it. It is certainly beginning to look slightly the worse for wear (just like us) - a few frayed edges here, a rusty button there - but I had hoped it would make it to the millennium. That doesn't look likely now. I hadn't been looking forward to the day when I emptied its numerous pockets, tucked away cleverly in all sorts of places, for the last time of all the detritus that I have amassed over the years. Things that have never left the jacket: my *HMS Britannia* badge, my lump of Tiree pier, the book of matches from Rossini's Restaurant in Manhattan, my hip flask (that has left the pocket a few times), my CalMac timetable.

Lord of the Isles pulls away from Castlebay exactly on time at 09.20. We are very glad about that for on arriving at Oban we will have only two and a half hours to get to Mallaig for the next leg of our journey - a sailing to Skye. This fine timing may be wishful thinking. If we arrive late at Oban then we may have to re-think.

There is a hint of sadness as we leave Barra. It is such a nice island - the archetypal Hebridean Island. Just the right size and shape, with lovely sandy beaches, friendly folk and a remoteness to give the visitor that holistic Hebridean experience. That's what this visitor thinks.

To add to the scene the ornithologists, oops archaeologists today, are waving their shovels at us from the road above the pier as we sail off. They all seem to be having fun - which, after all, is what it's all about.

We have another five hour sail ahead of us now and none of us are complaining about that. I set off to find the bosun to see if he has some kind of adhesive that will stop the shoulder of my jacket from flying in the wind. He leads me down to a door on the side of the port funnel. Inside is an Aladdin's Cave of a workshop, with all manner of tools set out neatly on their racks. He applies some strong glue to my flap of jacket and I am decent again. Clever man - a pity he couldn't have fixed *Clansman* three days ago.

Back up on deck as we enter the Sound of Mull. I'm sitting on my coil of rope again, chairing a committee meeting of Island Hoppers. The agenda is singular: what are we going to do once we get to Oban?

Our itinerary says that we have time to get up to Mallaig for the last sailing to Skye - which is today's eventual destination. My two pals doubt the itinerary. Well they never wrote it - I did. In fact we all doubt whether we can get to Mallaig in time for the last ferry, in which case we should just drive to Kyle of Lochalsh and go over the Skye Bridge. The attraction of the Mallaig crossing is that it is now apparent that it is *Claymore* that is filling-in for *Lord of the Isles* there, and we had more or less assumed that we would never see her in the Hebrides again.

After discussion we decide we can make a go of it, but to make sure I ask the purser when we are likely to reach Oban, and if he can find out if *Claymore* is running to time. He is happy to oblige and kindly radios ahead to Mallaig, while we have lunch. He returns ten minutes later with some key information for us to digest along with our chicken korma.

We are due to arrive at Oban at 14.30 (instead of 14.10). And the skipper of *Claymore* is prepared to wait a few minutes for us on her 16.45 sailing to Skye. Too neat. Apparently *Clansman* is now repaired and sitting at Oban Railway Pier. This last bit is the most relevant of all. We don't fancy a mad dash to Mallaig and will instead head for the Skye Bridge. But this will allow us an opportunity for a photograph of *Clansman* and *Lord of the Isles* together at Oban at the same time! An unusual event, we reckon. The decision seems an easy one. We thank the purser for his help and tell him there is no need to hold up *Claymore* just for us. But wasn't that nice of him?

Normally it is just me who ascends Pulpit Hill above the Railway Pier for photo calls, but this time all three of us are up there. *Lord of the Isles* is heading out to Tiree now, and *Clansman*, moored with her bow visor gaping, is having some finishing touches applied to her before she takes up her usual sailings tomorrow. This will allow *LOTI* to return to Mallaig, and *Claymore* to head back to Campbeltown.

Photos over we bundle into the car and head north on the long journey to Kyle of Lochalsh. It is a warm and thirsty drive which seems to take hours. In fact it does take hours, and by the time we reach Fort William we recognise that there was never any chance that we could have caught the *Claymore* sailing from Mallaig on time. At Kyle we stop for a breather. It is still an unseasonally warm and still afternoon, and we sit out on the lawn of the Kyle of Lochalsh Hotel, feeling quite pleased with ourselves, looking over at Skye and its new toll bridge.

I think the bridge looks nice. Its thin arch blends well into the surrounding landscape of hills and islands as it hopscotches across the Sound of Sleat. It does make Skye seem that wee bit less of an island now that it is no longer necessary to take a ferry to get over to it. The most important factor is the opinion of the people who live on the island and they now find it easier, if just as expensive, to get over to the mainland. For Island Hoppers like us there will always be lots of islands that cannot be so easily bridged.

We continue onwards - through Skye towards Portree. The sky above the Cuillins is clear blue. At first they seem so distant, but the main road through Skye is now a fast one and we are soon in amongst their looming bulk. Portree beckons beyond them like a lush little oasis basking in the early evening sun. It has been a long drive but it we are in pole position now for tomorrow's sailings around the Uig Triangle - over to North Uist and Harris.

Over dinner at the hotel Gibbie's is buried in the wine list. "I have a good nose for wine," he says. Sure enough - when he raises his head his nose is sunburnt to the complexion and hue of a good Claret.

In the bar after dinner there is an impromptu piping display by a young local. He blasts out a pibroach or two with an enthusiasm that renders his audience silent. Not that anyone could have made him or herself heard anyway. A drummer rattles away with his sticks in accompaniment, keeping pace admirably considering he is half pissed and doesn't even have a drum. The counter of the bar becomes his makeshift kettledrum.

In my room not much later, I am drifting pleasantly off to sleep. The walls are very thin and the poor woman in the next room seems very upset about something - judging from all the sighing that's going on. It must be the Ecstasy.

Day Four - *Around the Triangle*

My pre-breakfast stroll is downhill from the hotel to the sleepy harbour. The sun is already warm and the only other person I meet is a white-bearded chap who looks distinctly like Ian. It is Ian. I really should get my eyes tested.

Breakfast consists of kippers of the size of an anchovy. Then it is a quick getaway in Gibbie's car to "do" the Triangle.

"Let's hope it's not the Bermuda Triangle," says Gibbie in an uncharacteristic pessimistic tone. Our route involves us sailing around the "Uig Triangle". This does not make geometric sense but consists of three ferry sailings and a couple of taxi journeys to link them up. Our ship will be *Hebridean Isles* and she will cross from Uig, at the north-western edge of Skye, to Lochmaddy in North Uist. Somehow we will get ourselves the six or so miles to Otternish where we cross to Berneray via the new causeway and catch the ferry from there across the Sound of Harris to Leverburgh on Harris, where, with similar invention, we will somehow get further up the road to Tarbert. There *Hebridean Isles* will materialise and take us back across to Uig. Well that's the rough idea.

Soon we are standing at the roadside above Uig Bay watching *Hebridean Isles* circle silently towards the pier. Her mirror image reflected below her in the calm, blue water is perfection. She looks just like a radio-controlled model upon a park pond. When we are standing next to her on the pier ten minutes later she looks more like the real thing. Ian and Gibbie are peering into the water at her rear end and talking the mystifying, esoteric 'engineer's speak', which they lapse into from time to time. I can only look on and nod occasionally and randomly, as if I know what they are talking about. Ian is almost bent double, pointing at something which is just below the surface.

"There! Look! See that rudder there."

When we eventually board a crewman asks us if we will be taking the bus tour. Bus tour? Our eyebrows rise in unison - we know nothing of this. It appears that taxis may not be required after all as our route is now a recognised tourist attraction, and has chartered buses completing the links between the ferry terminals. So we nod to the crewman.

"Yes - we'll be taking the bus tour."

Soon we are sitting at our favourite sheltered rear-deck spot aboard *Hebridean Isles* (see Away with the Ferries) with jackets and jumpers off and faces angled up to the sun - and it is not yet ten am. It is now officially agreed that this year's trip has been blessed with the best weather ever. We calculate (we do this kind of thing when nothing else much is happening) that out of a total of 38 Island Hopping days over the past eleven years we have only had rain on five of them.

The particular sheltered deck spot we are now sitting at is ideal for enjoying the view. Some clever, forward thinking naval architect (there must still be some around) designed wind shields jutting aft from the rear of the aft observation lounge which give shelter from winds blowing up from either side. That is clever in itself, creating such a sheltered seating area, but what was inspirational was puting windows in the shields so that those who have raced up on deck to occupy these prestigious seats can see the view on three sides at the same time. Amazingly, every time that we have wedged ourselves into this little corner, and it's a few times now, the sun has always put in a starring role. Put another way, none of our five days of rain has occurred when we have been on this ship. This, however, is likely to be our last sailing on the *Hebridean Isles* on this route; a new vessel is being built for the Uig Triangle and the Heb Isles will be sent elsewhere.

I look around me at our fellow passengers and try to catagorise them. There are some elderly ladies who look as though they come from the islands, wear headscarfs and look somewhat overdressed. They carry plastic bags with pictures of dogs on them.

There are the non-local, recently retired gentleman who have swapped their city suits for long, baggy, beige shorts covering very white, thin legs. This type are always carrying binoculars. There are the "workies" in their blue, oil stained overalls, who have a white van parked on the car deck. They always carry a bottle of Irn Bru and never seem the least bit interested in the passing scenery, or even where they are going.

Then there are the 'anoraks', like us, who can never sit still and are

23

always adorned with cameras and lenses of various specifications. These types are so caught up in trying to get a photograph from a fresh angle that they've forgotten what day of the week it is. Relax, we know it's Tuesday - eh Sunday. The views today from half way across the Little Minch are superb. The air is particularly clear and away to the south Barra, and the islands further south are visible.

My jacket is holding up well - not that I am wearing it. I make good use of the pockets though, stocking them up with packets of sandwiches, drinks and a couple of apples. Well, we don't know what the catering facilities will be like between now and when we rejoin *Hebridean Isles* at Tarbert later in the afternoon. For all we know the North Uist bus may dump us at Otternish an hour and a half before the Sound of Harris ferry sails - and we could practically starve to death in that time.

At Lochmaddy there is indeed a bus waiting for us - and a substantial bus at that. We are not the only ones joining it, half the complement of the ship seems to be heading for it as well. Our driver, Tom, welcomes us all aboard and we head away from Lochmaddy westwards to begin a clockwise circuit of North Uist.

Tom proves to be an excellent guide. Various places of interest are pointed out to us along the way and his leisurely pace makes us quickly realise that he is in no hurry to get us to Otternish. In fact this is a carefully planned tour of the island, and Tom is very enthusiastic about pointing out the attractions of his island. He is clearly proud of it. Our previous fleeting visits to North Uist have not done it credit but today we see it in a new light.

Salmon farming is now an important part of the island's economy and Tom shows us the numerous lochs where salmon are taken to by helicopter from their growing tanks. At £700 per hour for the hire of the chopper it must be considered a valuable means of conveying them. I had to wait until my fortieth birthday to get a ride in a helicopter but these lucky fish get a shot when they are just kids. Mind you, in a few weeks time they're going to be eaten!

Tom stops the bus close to a burial mound that dates from 4000 years ago and then on again to pause briefly at substantial peat diggings. "With peat you have three choices," explains Tom. "Dig it up and pile it where it is. Dig it up and truck it to your house and pile it up there. Or you can forget the peat and switch your central heating on." Further along the road he points out a postwoman emerging from her post van. "We have to stop here and wave, for that's my wife and if I don't wave I don't get any dinner tonight."

To we Island Hoppers, the most interesting stopping point of all was on the far western side of the island, at Balmartin where Tom pulls the bus to a stop and points out to sea. "If you look closely, out there in the haze, on the horizon, you can just make out the cliffs of St.Kilda."

I couldn't quite believe this, but he is absolutely correct. It took a few seconds to get the eyes into gear but there it is, like a blue-grey shark fin sticking out of the water, over 40 miles away, St Kilda. The first time any of us have set eyes on it - and we are lucky to be able to. Only in exceptionally good atmospheric conditions is it visible. Today they must be ideal. Will we ever reach there on an Island Hop? Gibbie is looking at it incredulously for he always thought St Kilda lay of the west coast of Islay! He dismisses the thought of us going there in a future Hop, because CalMac don't sail there and because, once there, there is nowhere to buy a 'bacon butty'.

We move on again with Tom pointing across to some tidal islands which were once inhabited. "Be careful of the tides if you ever cross over to there in the dark," he warns. But I can't imagine myself ever having to heed his caution.

Otternish, at the top end of North Uist, has changed considerably since our last visit here two years ago. A causeway has been built over to the nearby island of Berneray, thus removing the need for a ferry on this leg. This probably ensures that Prince Charles will be unlikely to return to seek the remoteness and solitude that he encountered there several years ago. The causeway was opened by Prince Charles just a month ago. His cheesy grin as he cut the ribbon probably belied his disappointment that his very own Hebridean 'escape' would never be the same again.

As causeways go I rather like it, not that I've ever studied them from an aesthetic point of view. It is constructed from very substantial looking, honey coloured blocks of stone (about the size of Gibbie's renal calculi). It stretches a mile over to Berneray. Tom takes us across.

At the north-eastern end of Berneray our ferry, Loch Bhrusda, awaits. Tom's timing is impeccable and his guided tour of North Uist has been perfectly delivered. He turns his bus around to head back to Lochmaddy, presumably where his dinner will be waiting for him. We wave goodbye to him (I would have waved in a slightly more animated fashion had I realised then that I had left my camera tripod on one of his overhead shelves!)

We board the ferry for the fifty minute sailing to Leverburgh on Harris. Gibbie doesn't like this crossing. He feels that the numerous tight manoeuvres the ship has to take to avoid hidden reefs and sandbanks are an inherent risk. Consequently he has one hand on the passenger safety leaflet, one hand on a life-jacket and one foot in a life-raft as we clear the northern end of Berneray. Don't know where his other leg is. However these changes of course by the ferry are made as it follows a carefully laid passage of buoys. The route has been meticulously planned out and precisely marked. Silly Gibbie!

At Leverburgh we are met by the other bus and an equally chirpy driver. Ally will take us to Tarbert, a distance of about twenty miles, by a route which follows the western shores of Harris. I have never seen the west coast of Harris but have read of the high mountains and the golden beaches. I am not disappointed - ten minutes into our journey we are passing a beach of the most exquisite beauty. Not much further on our driver stops the bus with the words:

"We've a long way to go yet - you can get out and stretch your legs for a bit." I get off with great trepidation, the last time I heard those words was in the movie 'The Great Escape'.

However he has stopped at yet another of the beautiful beaches and suggests we try it out. And so at last I get to walk along a Harris beach. If I had a towel I would have the shoes and socks off and be paddling in the refreshing sea. For 'refreshing' read - bloody freezing!

At Tarbert we pull up at the pier just as *Hebridean Isles* is tying up - that's what I call timing! We couldn't have done it better ourselves.

As we sail away on the final link of our circular triangle I notice that the two crewmen handling the bow ropes are greatly amused by something they see ashore. I follow their gaze. Two young women, backpackers by the look of them, are having an altercation with each other. In fact they are actually screaming at each other in German and gesticulating angrily at each other's face. I can only guess at what has gone wrong with their holiday. Maybe they're supposed to be in Canada or something, or perhaps they thought they were in Tarbert, Loch Fyne instead of Tarbert, Harris. Could be they've simply lost their winning lottery ticket.

Once out at sea we take to the bar where we try to organise a photograph of the three of us. The barmaid is very willing to help.

"What's all this in aid of?" She asks.

We explain Island Hopping to her. "And how long have you been doing this nonsense?"

"Eleven years," I reply.

Fearful of her response. "Well I can see you've aged better than the other two." I daren't tell my colleagues this, 'cause she's addressing me.

As we head back across to Skye we sail out of the shadow of a long ribbon of cloud that stretches out into the Little Minch from Harris. At Uig Bay the sea is still so incredibly calm and reflective. Its perfect surface is broken not only by the ship but by a half dozen porpoises who have popped up from its depths to say hallo.

We have taken our last sea crossing of the trip and now face a 225 mile drive home from the north-west corner of Skye to Glasgow. It has been a trip of considerable contrast. Let's hope the next nine years will be just as much fun.

PIONEER, Mallaig

2000 A Farewell to (CalMac) Clyde Cruising

The Plan

A T THE END OF EACH YEAR'S ISLAND HOP we always sit on the train or ship or in a car and ponder on what to do next year. Each year the aura of the Greek Islands briefly condenses upon us, only to evaporate back into the clouds again. A more serious concept materialised at the end of the 1999 trip. What about a trip on the English Channel or the Irish Sea? Ideas were bounced off each other. Gibbie and Ian were the instigators of these ideas, as they usually are. Yet when push comes to shove they are the ones who always say, "Let's go back to Oban again - we've not seen Mull now for six months." So then it is back to The Western Isles. Ian always says that Gibbie and I can easily jump in the car down to the Clyde coast anytime, but as he is entrenched down in Surrey it is not so easy for him, and he would miss the annual sojourn to the Isles. So it doesn't look as if we will be brave enough to pick a different area to fulfill the absurdities of Island Hopping in the millennium year. So any plans of criss-crossing the Irish Sea from Heysham to Isle of Man to Belfast to Stranraer in 2000 were effectively vetoed.

But to be honest, I don't really mind. After eleven years, however, it is as essential as ever to have a theme, to give the trip a sense of purpose. We still haven't sailed on *Clansman* but with not one but two new CalMac ships being built in 2000, but not in service until the late summer, it seemed sensible to postpone *Clansman* for yet another year until we can sail on all three new vessels. That could be our theme for 2001. Maybe *Clansman* will become a bogey ship, just like Kerrera was a bogey island. This all makes the prospects for the 2001 trip very exciting, but what about 2000!

Then an announcement triggered the strategist's grey matter (what's left of it). CalMac announced that 2000 would be the last year of Clyde Cruising by their upper Clyde vessels (*Jupiter*, *Juno*, *Saturn* or *Pioneer*). Perhaps we should embrace our own river, and its ships, before they disappear.

Gibbie wasn't keen to venture 'far away', such as the Irish Sea. In fact he wasn't even keen to leave the Clyde. I suggested that he spent the four days going back and forth on the Renfrew ferry to spare him any hassle, but the notion of a purely Clyde based Island Hop, using CalMac's Clyde cruising programme in every conceivable combination, seemed like a good idea. And so "Farewell To (CalMac) Clyde Cruising" was born. To inject a little pace into the itinerary I suggested that during the four days of the trip we try to get aboard every Clyde vessel sailing during that period. Yes - including Western Ferries and Clyde Marine Motoring vessels. At the end of the trip we would treat ourselves by having a sail over to Islay - one of our favourite islands.

There was a major risk with this concept, however. CalMac do not really have a spare vessel, so if anything should breakdown anywhere in the Western Isles or Clyde then the cruising programme would likely be cancelled, and we would be left high and dry. But fortune favours the brave and I sat down in January 2000 to devise a suitable route.

It would take a fair degree of planning and timetable scanning to get us easily onto every Clyde vessel. There were about sixteen in all, that would be in service of some kind on the river during May 2000. Firstly I wrote down their names and routes and then I tried to weave an intricate pattern with them, that would make each of our days enjoyable and not just a mad race back and forward across the Clyde estuary. We would also require a car in order to make some of the connections, and that would have to be strategically positioned (dumped in Dunoon) in such a way that it could be picked up when most needed. All this took some time to look at but a favourable itinerary (particularly endorsed by Ian) was eventually produced which satisfied all the requirements. Unfortunately it was so complicated and convoluted that even on the evening before our departure none of us could remember exactly where we were going. The printed itinerary which normally gets lost in the base of our bags for the duration of the trip, became an important fixture to Gibbie's forehead, so that we could tell on an hour by hour basis just what we were doing and where we were going next. Rather than confuse the reader the route shall therefore be explained as we go along.

There is nothing new about trying to set records for boarding as many Clyde steamers in a day. In the 1971 Clyde River Steamer Club Magazine John Wood, one of the founder members of the Club, wrote accounts of recording breaking over the decades, with regard to how many steamers have been boarded on one day. According to John Wood the record number of ships sailed upon on one day stands at 22 by Messrs Cuthbert, MacDonald and Paterson of Ayr in the summer of 1913. Many similar day trips were undertaken over the years, some by Mr Wood and friends in the 1930s. On 24 August 1963, when there were still some great 'steamers' to sail on, three Greenock enthusiasts, Messers N. Murray, A. Riddell and P. McCrorie, broke the post-war record by sailing on 15 ships on one day as follows:

Cowal	Gourock - Dunoon	dep 06.50	arr 07.10
Maid of Cumbrae	Kirn - Gourock	07.30	07.50
Duchess of Montrose	Gourock - Dunoon	08.40	09.10
Waverley	Dunoon - Rothesay	09.15	10.05
Duchess of Hamilton	Rothesay - Largs	10.15	10.50
Leven	Largs - Millport	11.15	11.50
Ashton	Millport - Largs	12.00	12.35
Countess of Breadalbane	Largs - Wemyss Bay	12.45	13.20

Maid of Argyll	Wemyss Bay - Rothesay	dep 13.45	arr 14.15
Lochfyne	Rothesay - Gourock	15.40	16.50
Maid of Ashton	Gourock - Blairmore	17.00	17.30
Maid of Skelmorlie	Blairmore - Dunoon	18.10	18.30
Jeanie Deans	Dunoon - Gourock	19.05	19.30
Bute	Gourock - Dunoon	20.00	20.20
Talisman	Dunoon - Gourock	22.00	22.20

There is, of course, no comparison between record breaking and what we were trying to achieve in Island Hop 2000. For a start we were not trying to break any records. Secondly we were taking the luxury of four days for our trip and thirdly there are no Clyde steamers anymore (except *Waverley*, which was at this time being reassembled at Great Yarmouth - part two of her Millennium rebuild - and could not be included in our trip). Things are sadly different and we don't have the luxury and splendour of those fascinating and beautiful ships to sail on. However vessels of various shapes and sizes continue to cross the Firth of Clyde, and even in 2000 there is a daily cruise ship (albeit a 'streaker' ferry) embarking on an excursion around the various upper Clyde piers. On our trip we intended to make good use of this ship, whichever one it turned out to be. The list of ships and piers above will however set the tone for our more leisurely journey around the Clyde.

Day One - *Three's company - Five's a crowd*

The evening before the start of our trip the weather forecast isn't too good. Over the years the weather has generally been kind to us, but the two and a half weeks preceding the start of Island Hop 2000 saw the West of Scotland bathed in sunshine with not a drop of rain. It seems inevitable that it will break on the 16 May - and it does. We drive down to Gourock in a light drizzle which more or less persists for the rest of the day. For the rest of the week the wind is to change to the NW with its incumbent showers and sunny intervals. Doesn't sound promising.

At Gourock two CalMac ships are preparing to depart. The Dunoon ferry is *Saturn*. She leaves ten minutes ahead of *Juno* which, we can now see, will be the cruise vessel for the week ahead. We will be seeing a lot of her over the next few days. Both ships are heading for Dunoon and we shall meet up with them later today.

In the Gourock ticket office of Caledonian MacBrayne we encounter the first problem. The new style eight-day *Rover* Tickets no longer fit in the protective, plastic wallets that are issued with them. The chap behind the counter sees the look of disappointment on our faces and comes around from behind the counter with a pair of scissors. The tickets are trimmed to fit and the smiles are back on our faces. We assure him that we are now equipped for our journey. Then, to his amazement, we trot outside - and head for a Clyde Marine vessel - for which these tickets are not even valid! Our first destination, you see, is Helensburgh.

Our first ship looks like being *Kenilworth*, the usual Gourock-Kilcreggan ferry, from Clyde Marine's little fleet. She has just arrived from Kilcreggan and is sitting at the pier. Access is being denied because she has fuel pump problems and will have to return to her base at Prince's Pier in Greenock for repairs. I glance at my watch but the skipper reassures us. "Another ship will be here in a minute to take over."

This turns out to be *Rover* which, as she approaches Gourock pier from Greenock, has all the style and demeanor of a floating Portakabin. But she is a 'new' ship for an Island Hop and despite the problems with *Kenilworth* she does leave for Helensburgh on time.

Rover tends to pop up in various unexpected places on the Clyde - sometimes on charter, occasionally as Gourock-Kilcreggan ferry. She was built at Renfrew in 1964. The boarding of her gives us a bit of a statistical conundrum. We have never been on *Kenilworth* either but have to cross her decks to reach the *Rover* berthed on her far side. Does this mean we can tick off *Kenilworth*? I mean we have boarded her. Two vessels in one? At least we are on time, so after a dodgy start perhaps lady luck is looking down on us. Unfortunately so is the rain, so we cram into the little forward cabin as we bounce off across the river.

We are off on a triangular sail from Gourock to Helensburgh to Kilcreggan. Helensburgh Pier has deep water this morning but at low tides it can be a different picture. Sand is silting up the piling and at low tides vessels larger than the little *Rover* can have problems berthing. It is a common sight in summer to see *Waverley* tied up with a sponson hard against the south-eastern corner of the pier. Maybe if it silts up much more then one day you will be able to walk out the two miles to the exposed, wrecked hulk of the 'sugarboat' *Captayannis*. This ship foundered in January 1974 and one of the small boats who came to the crew's rescue was the very *Rover* that we are now sitting on.

At Helensburgh the strong wind and a continuous surge of water towards the wooden piles is making it difficult for the skipper to berth. A bow rope is hastily secured ashore but the stern of *Rover* is being pushed away from the pier by the surge of the sea. The crew work hard and eventually everything is under control and we sit squat against the pier.

"This isn't my usual boat, you know," says the skipper as if we were questioning his judgement.

We slip away from Helensburgh and turn west, across the entrance to the Gareloch, heading for Kilcreggan. As we pass the mouth of the loch we see a sight to behold. Emerging from the grey and overcast loch is a huge Trident submarine with its attendant flotilla of auxiliary craft and police motor-launches. She looks the epitome of menace as she gracefully turns to starboard in an arc to follow us down river. Perhaps she's coming Island Hopping with us! An officer in an orange jacket can be seen at the top of the huge conning-tower, looking like Action Man. There is nothing toy-like about his ship. This is part of our nuclear deterrent.

We arrive at the neat little pier of Kilcreggan some ten minutes behind schedule. This pier is sadly no longer a calling point for CalMac ships but at least it is in good enough condition to welcome the Gourock ferry and the occasional cruise vessel. *Waverley* still calls here in the summer. The pier was erected in 1850 and rebuilt in 1897. In that year an astonishing 39 calls were made daily by 10 different steamers. The present pier buildings are as old as today's 'steamer' Rover.

At Kilcreggan we are joined by a few more passengers. A lady with dark eye make-up, straggly greying hair and a deeply lined face joins us in the cabin and makes me startle. If she had a guitar with her I could have sworn she was Keith Richards.

We now head for Gourock and are taking a course which in about five minutes will have us beaching up on the starboard side of the Trident submarine. To our relief we steer around the stern of the black leviathan, but on doing so we are afforded an incredibly close view of her. In fact if we were not a service ferry I am sure we would have been chased away by one of the police launches. Our resident submarine expert, Gibbie, points to the flattened plateau on her back. "That's where her missiles are housed."

Back at Gourock Pier. It is a much reduced structure since our last visit several years ago (although it looks remarkably similar to the way it did an hour ago!) Bits of it seem to have been nibbled away by the sea, or sold for scrap. At this rate soon only the linkspan will remain.

We are still ten minutes behind on our schedule so it is a quick jog to the car and on to our next pier. This is the Western Ferries' jetty at McInroy's Point near Cloch.

In twelve years of Island Hopping we have never sailed on a Western Ferries vessel. Shame on us. That is about to change. We hoped to take one vessel across to Hunter's Quay, two miles from Dunoon, and then a different one back, but time will not allow this as we must be back on Gourock Pier for the 13.20 sailing to Dunoon. So we will have to make do with only one of the red-hulled ferries as it is now approaching noon.

The five vessels currently in the Western Ferries fleet are not exactly handsome, in fact Gibbie refuses to call them ships because they don't have a proper bow or a proper stern. This is unfair, however, as I could name several CalMac vessels which have the same design features! Okay, they're not pretty but they have provided a frequent and extended service across the Clyde from McInroy's Point to Hunter's Quay (near Dunoon) since 1973. This is, of course, in direct competition to CalMac's Gourock - Dunoon service.

Three ferries are in operation today but we cannot afford to be choosy. The first one to arrive at our side will have to do. This turns out to be *Sound of Sleat*, built as *De Hoorn* in the Netherlands in 1961, making her the oldest vessel we are likely to sail on during our four day trek. She has been a Western Ferries ferry since 1988.

We hope to meet a fellow steamer enthusiast, John, aboard one of these ferries, as he works for Western Ferries as an engineer. I ask the ticket collector which vessel he normally works on. "You're in luck - it's this one." So as we rumble out across the Firth we find John emerging from his engine room in his surprisingly clean white overall.

"It was only a one-in-three chance that we would find you." I claim, pointing to the other vessels.

"One-in-six," he replies, "it could have been my week off."

John describes the five vessels that make up the fleet and explains their rosters. Today *Sound of Scarba* and *Sound of Scalpay* are also in service. The other two are temporarily laid up. These are *Sound of Shuna*, which is lying tied to Kilmun Pier inside the Holy Loch, and *Sound of Sanda*, which is out of sight moored to a buoy upon the Holy Loch.

"Tell us something exciting about this vessel, John," I suggest.

He has to think for a minute, several minutes in fact. "It is the only one of the five which has been to Wemyss Bay."

As we reach Hunter's Quay, our fifth pier so far, we pass a visitor to the Clyde, anchored off Strone Point. She is *RRS Charles Darwin*, which belongs to the Natural Environment Research Council. No one seems to know what she is doing here but she apparently drifts around the world's oceans assessing climatic change through careful measurement.

Sailing back across the Firth it is now bitterly and unseasonally cold.

"We're passing over the dredging dumping ground just now," remarks John. "Remember Rhu Spit, that elongated exposed strip of sand that used to partially block the entrance to the Gareloch? We remember.

"It is lying under here now!" That must be close to the record for a projected spit! John recalls all the minor trauma that the *Sound of Sleat* has endured during her twelve years of stoic service. From snagging a submarine's Towedarray to hoovering up a gymshoe into her Kort Nossle. Sounds painful. After this he and Gibbie become immersed in technospeak about crankshafts and one-way valves.

I interrupt them to ask John which Western Ferries vessel is the best. He does not have to think long this time. "This one." He proudly returns to his engines and we return to our car.

Back to Gourock again, and we are in nice time for our next ship - *Saturn* - to Dunoon.

This is the first week of the last year of CalMac Clyde cruising. The three 'streakers' *Jupiter*, *Juno* and *Saturn* rotate around a week-long roster. This week, as already noted, *Juno* is the cruise ship. Next week it will be the turn of one of the others. On a Tuesday (like today) she operates a cruise to Largs and Rothesay which is split into morning and afternoon schedules. As we set off on *Saturn* to Dunoon *Juno* has already returned to Gourock after her morning cruise. We will catch up with her at Dunoon Pier but we are using *Saturn* just now as this will add another ship to our growing list.

Gourock to Dunoon. Boy, how many times have I sailed this route? But for how much longer? As I write, the Scottish Office has still to decide if CalMac should continue to serve this route when Western Ferries already takes most of the traffic. If CalMac do not succeed in retaining this service then the knock-on effect on other Clyde services could cause future problems which extend beyond the Clyde. All this is furthest from our minds at the moment. We are tucked up in the saloon scoffing tea and scones for lunch. There isn't much else but at least we are warm for the first time since we set out this morning.

At Dunoon we have 45 minutes to kill. Gibbie and Ian search the front for a suitable place to leave the car tomorrow. We intend positioning the car at Dunoon where we can pick it up on the last day. While they are looking into this I take a stroll along the Main Street.

At 14.20 *Juno* is tying up at Dunoon pier on the second leg of her day's cruise. We join her and discover to our amazement that the three of us have raised the passenger complement to five! I chat to the purser, who seems delighted to see us. In fact he soon knows all our first names.

"This is busy - we only had four this morning."

Three of us sit and discuss the route we are taking today. Ian feels that we should involve the other two in case they feel left out but Gibbie reacts in his typical magnanimous style, "ignore them!"

The roster *Juno* is operating today looks like this:

GOUROCK	09.30
DUNOON	10.00
ROTHESAY	10.40
LARGS	11.30
DUNOON	12.20
GOUROCK	12.40-14.00
DUNOON	14.20
LARGS	15.10
ROTHESAY	16.00
DUNOON	16.50
GOUROCK	17.20

This stretch, Dunoon to Largs, is a first for an Island Hop but had I ever sailed direct from Dunoon to Largs before? I wrack my brains for the answer. Yes: 12 September 1990 on board *Keppel* and 8 August 1991 onboard *Waverley*. Now how relevant was that?

As we approach Largs we are joined by a school of porpoises who dance around the port side of the ship. There are about ten of them - two for every passenger aboard. I've never seen porpoises so close to Largs. Perhaps they're heading for Nardini's.

Wildlife seems to be taking over. The deck crew are so bored that they are feeding sea-gulls on the car deck with what is left of yesterday's scones.

At Largs we go ashore very briefly for a photograph - we don't have one of *Juno* at Largs. We also study the movements of the two Cumbrae ferries: *Loch Alainn* is doing all the work while *Loch Linnhe* is moored to the southern edge of the pier. Later we hope to sail on both.

Two more passengers join us at Largs which makes the deck look quite crowded - when we all stand together.

We are heading for Rothesay now and as we pass Craigmore *Juno*'s sister *Jupiter* is just ahead of us on the service run from Wemyss Bay. What a nice photo that would make - the two sisters in close convoy heading for the pier, if only Ian could be persuaded to swim ashore to Craigmore with a camera. Our ship sits out for fifteen minutes to let *Jupiter* load her next cargo of cars.

After Rothesay it's back to Dunoon and we turn northwards around Toward Point and head up river past the remains of Innellan Pier. Only the stone base of the pier now remains. The timbers are long gone, although some of them were used recently in the private rebuild of Berry's Pier on the east shore of Loch Striven. Innellan Pier was last used in 1974 to take construction workers to the oil-rig fabrication yard at Ardyne, three miles away. For Ian, who has a keen interest in the old Clyde piers, it is a depressing sight. Soon we are sailing into Dunoon for the second time in three hours. It looks exactly the same.

And now Gourock again. Here we pick up the car and head down the coast to Wemyss Bay. This time the car is coming with us on a ferry as it is a integral part of the last link of today's journey, and of the first part of tomorrow's.

Jupiter takes us across to Rothesay under yet more dreich conditions. She is almost identical to *Juno*. The differences are subtle and only visible to complete ship 'anoraks', so here we go. *Jupiter* has the lower cross bars on her tripod mast painted yellow instead of black. *Juno* has a narrower band of black above the red on her funnels and also has a small bosun's cabin on the port side of her main passenger deck. The belting below the side ramps are different. *Jupiter* has a longer aerial. The ticket offices are also different, but that is not visible from half a mile away - the other things are!

Gibbie drives us off at Rothesay and heads up towards Rhubodach where we will cross back over to the mainland. We shall be staying the night at Colintraive. We pass through Port Bannatyne where the decaying pier is an even more depressing sight. At this rate Ian will soon be in tears. "I'd like to go around all the Clyde piers sometime, just to relive old memories and see what they look like now. Or perhaps I shouldn't. Let's move on." His memory must have served him well when he was a baby, for Port Bannatyne Pier was last used in 1939 by the paddle-steamer *Jupiter*.

The Rhubodach - Colintraive ferry is, surprisingly, a vessel we have never sailed on before on an Island Hop. Counting *Kenilworth* it will be our seventh vessel of the day, of which four have been 'new'. She is, of course, *Loch Dunvegan*. We have encountered her before, in 1992, in her previous life as one of the Kyle of Lochalsh - Kyleakin ferries, but never sailed on her. Previous crossings here at Rhubodach have been aboard

Loch Riddon. We don't have long to get excited by this, for five minutes later we're back on the mainland.

After a bar meal at Colintraive the rain stops and we take a walk out in the direction of Strone Point. The sun is sinking below the Argyll hills and the last of its rays are applying a gilt edge to the hills above the East Kyle. The still air is alive with the repetitive warbles of several song thrushes. I've heard that this is a declining species - not in Colintraive.

Day Two - *Up the Kyles of Bute!*

Outside the hotel at 09.05 - five minutes behind schedule. Gibbie is tense, he wants to get on the move. Off to Dunoon with Gibbie ignoring my appeals to let me drive. It is, after all, his car. At Dunoon we hope to pick up the cruise ship *Juno* again for a sail to Tighnabruaich.

The wind has strengthened and moved to the north-west, exactly as forecast on last night's BBC. Aren't they clever? When they get it right. For the time being the sun is out but some threatening, towering dark clouds are moving in to spoil it all.

Speaking of last night, Gibbie had an unnerving experience around midnight, which only now can he bring himself to relate. He had stepped outside to "take the air and go for a long stroll up the road" (Ian and I are already suspicious because Gibbie doesn't 'take the air' and any strolls he has are always short ones.) Anyway, a few steps up the road he realised he was being followed by what he thought at first looked like two grey-white ghosts, one small and one medium-sized. He quickened his pace, but the spectres were still gaining on him. He decided that the only option was to turn and confront them. He then realised that he was being followed by a ewe and her lamb. But whenever he moved off again they followed him. And whenever he stopped they stopped. Always keeping just a few metres behind him. By the time he got to Strone he thought enough was enough. But when he turned back to the hotel they did likewise, still keeping that short distance behind him. Only when he growled "mint sauce" at them did they scamper off. In the car we are not so much scampering as stopping and starting. The scenic road to Dunoon is still single-track for the majority of the twenty miles, and on every second bend we seem to meet a double-decker bus or an articulated lorry hurtling towards us.

We reach Dunoon with only ten minutes to spare - *Saturn* has just pulled away from the pier and *Juno* is advancing rapidly upon it. Now Gibbie had a trial run yesterday on where he was going to leave his car but now, at the eleventh hour, he changes his mind and drives around the streets of Dunoon clockwise three times trying to find a space that satisfies him. Eventually, as *Juno* is berthing, he decides on abandoning it on the front. He glances back at it dolefully as if he is never going to see it again. Perhaps he isn't.

"Maybe it would be better over there."

"Come on Gibbie!"

Juno's purser is there to greet us personally, again, as we lope up the gangway. This time we have all our baggage and camera gear with us. "Hallo again lads - glad you could make it."

It's nice to get a personal welcome, but then there are still so few passengers that he has the time to have a half hour conversation with each of us during the course of the cruise. He denies, however, that someone phoned CalMac at Gourock yesterday to inquire what time the cruise left and that he replied in return "Well what time can you get down here?"

From Dunoon we head across the firth to Wemyss Bay, which means that in less than 24 hours we have sailed out of Dunoon on three separate occasions: to Largs, to Gourock and to Wemyss Bay. From Wemyss Bay we head down to Largs. On this stretch none of us can ever remember sailing direct from Wemyss Bay to Largs before!

After Largs we head for Rothesay where the passenger complement reaches a peak of twenty-two - my goodness the wee lassie in charge of the catering will be run off her feet! I hope she's got twenty-two scones in.

Emerging from a door cut into the port funnel is a patient of mine, Peter, who works as an engineer on these ships. We chat about the joys of Clyde cruising but he brings the subject back to my surgery and the large poster prints of *Hebridean Isles* and *Pioneer* that adorn the ceiling above the chair. "Great!" he says. "You've just come off a twelve hour shift, go to the dentist and there's your workplace looking down at you."

We are getting a commentary today from our purser who cheerily points out anything of interest. "There's Ardmaliesh Boatyard over there." All twenty-two of us peer over to our left, apart from the chap in the grey overcoat, who has looked miserable since he got on at Largs, and doesn't appear interested in joining into the spirit of things. "To your right now is Ardyne Point where there used to be a yard that built the Brent Spar oil-rig." Let's hope we're not getting it back.

On up the East Kyle now passing the hotel, where we stayed last night, the Colintraive ferry Loch Dunvegan and a ewe with her lamb. Through the narrows - this is a lovely part of the sail to Tighnabruaich - and we are leaning over the rail of the ship almost within touching distance of the red and green buoys which guard the entrance to the narrow channel. We have all sailed through the Kyles of Bute before - indeed I can count nine different vessels which I've sailed through on - but the feeling of remoteness is always there. Ian thinks that the last time he sailed through here was on *TS Queen Mary ll*. The turn to port is more than 90 degrees, an easy manouevre on a 'streaker', and we are now on the last stretch through the West Kyle to Tighnabruaich Pier.

The pier is the only survivor of a trio of piers that were all within two miles. Auchenlochan and Kames Piers are long gone, but Tighnabruaich hangs on. It is visited in summer only by *Jupiter*, *Juno* and *Saturn*, in rotation twice a week, *Waverley* twice a week and *The Second Snark* three times a week.

Tighnabruaich means 'house on the hill' and has a wonderful sheltered location nestling below the Argyll hills in a very green, tranquil setting. Opposite is the empty north-western corner of Bute. North out of the village runs the main road to Dunoon and Glasgow. This road climbs abruptly from the village to give one of the best views in Scotland looking down the Kyles and the narrows towards the Skelmorlie coast.

We get off the ship ahead of the nineteen others and stride out to a nearby cafe where we discover, to our horror, that the contents of three coach loads of day-trippers have just beaten us to it. They sit stuffing into fruit scones, and soup of an indescribable colour and flavour. I know this, because soon we are eating the same. When the coaches and the daily steamer arrive at the same time it must be a nightmare for the staff, especially as they probably spend the rest of the day doing very little. Order numbers are being called out from the counter for the patrons to collect. It seems rather pointless for everyone seems to have ordered the same thing. Outside an elderly gentleman has spent the last five minutes trying to encourage a herring gull to take a piece of roll from his outstretched fingers. When it eventually does it nearly takes half his thumb away with it.

Suitably fed we walk on towards the next 'pier', of which only a stone structure remains. Ian films me giving an educational chat about Kames Pier. When I return home and look at the map I discover that I was standing beside the remains of Auchenlochan Pier.

Back on *Juno* and we are heading back through the narrows to Rothesay, where we will disembark. On deck Gibbie has found himself a girlfriend and is extolling the virtues of Island Hopping. She doesn't look a day under 75 but knows a good deal about the old Clyde steamers and the islands. Gibbie isn't slow at catching her out. "We'll be on Islay tomorrow night."

"Give my love to Bowmore," she replies.

"That's actually my second favourite," he returns.

"What's your favourite?"

"Glenmorrangie." He moves on to trying to plug our Island Hopping book. "Stuart's got a copy with him, if you are interested."

"Where is he?" she enquires curiously.

"Eh . . . that's him over there."

She glances over at me. "Oh. No I don't think I'll bother."

As we sail back down the East Kyle The Bay City Rollers are belting out 'Shangalang' over the PA system from the pursers own CD collection. Two minutes later it is Andy Stewart and 'Donald where's yer troosers?' These tourists must think we have wonderful, eclectic taste.

A cloud of black smoke comes billowing towards us and through its haze we see the puffer *Vic 32* steaming up the Kyle. Now a holiday boat, she looks a grand sight and gives *Juno* a phlegmatic whistle as she passes. "That was the puffer *Vic 32* ," says the purser. Then it's back to The Bay City Rollers again.

At Rothesay the temptation will be to stay aboard *Juno* for the next leg of the cruise to Largs - because that is where we are actually heading ourselves. But if we do, then we will miss out on an important Clyde ship - *Pioneer* which is due to take the next service run to Wemyss Bay. Not being his favourite ship Gibbie is all for staying aboard, but Ian and I remind him of the theme of this year's trip and he relents. In any case I have already ordered a taxi to meet us at Wemyss Bay. So we haul him off *Juno* at Rothesay, waving goodbye to his new girlfriend, and board our next ship, the intrepid *Pioneer*. This may be the last time we sail on her for there is a rumour that she is to be sold out of service later in the year. I'll be sorry - she is a fast, photogenic ship, which over the years has popped up in surprising places providing relief when other ships of the fleet have broken down. She is also the only ship I have ever felt sea-sick on, during a wild rounding of the Mull of Kintyre last year. On that day *Pioneer* 's stabilisers were out of action. It could have been Cape Horn we were rounding, such was the swell.

None of that today. We sit out on deck with the warm sunshine on our faces, drinking what must be our ninth cup of tea today. As usual, *Pioneer* 's passage to Wemyss Bay is an expeditious one.

At Wemyss Bay the forward planning has worked again - our taxi is waiting and conveys us to Largs where we dump all our gear outside the Moorings and have a debate about what we are going to do now. This part of the trip had been left open in case we had needed some flexibility. Now we don't need any flexibility, we just need somewhere to stay tonight. Unusually for an Island Hop we have no overnight accommodation booked. The choice is simple, Largs or Millport. Millport means we will have an earlier start tomorrow - but not much earlier, so we decide to be bold and head off to the Tourist Office to see if they can fix us up with accommodation on the Isle of Cumbrae. This is successful and we sit down again to discuss the next option. We obviously want to board as many Clyde vessels as we can, and two are at Largs Pier: *Loch Alainn* and *Loch Linnhe*. As the former seems to be doing all the work, and is likely to be our early morning ferry as well, we decide to hang around in Largs until the 'peak' time of five or six o' clock to see if the indolent *Loch Linnhe* comes into service and give us yet another ferry. The best way to 'hang around' is to visit a local hostelry. There we have a beer and every ten minutes I am dispatched to run out and peer round the corner at the pier, and then return and give a report on the various comings and goings. After an hour and a half of this nonsense we give up and take the 18.15 sailing by *Loch Alainn* over to Cumbrae. This not only adds another ferry to our tally but she is also a 'new' vessel for an Island Hop.

Loch Alainn appeared on the ferry scene in the summer of 1997 and after spells on the Fishnish-Lochaline and Colintraive-Rhubodach services she was cascaded to Largs. She is a bit bigger than the original Loch class of ferry, such as *Loch Linnhe*, but otherwise almost totally uninteresting.

The bus linking the ferry slipway with Millport town takes us past Keppel Pier - a bit of which still survives - which cheers Ian up.

Millport looks sadly depressing tonight. I normally see it on a summer's day when the sun is shining and the crowds of day-trippers are enlivening the old town. Tonight the sun is certainly shining but the streets are almost totally empty and we have a devil of a job trying to find anywhere to eat. It seems sadly out of character.

Over another beer and an uninspiring haddock and chips we savour the highlight of our evening on the island - the UEFA Cup final between Arsenal and Galatasaray - and even that ends goaless.

Day Three - *Hello Hello We're Back Again*

There is a degree of pace entering into the scheme of things now - which is always something we enjoy. Yes, it involves *Juno* again! We plan to catch her at Rothesay at 10.00 for a cruise to Tarbert (Loch Fyne). To catch up with her we need a bus from Millport to the ferry slipway, the ferry to Largs, a taxi to Wemyss Bay and a sailing by *Jupiter* to get us to Rothesay. All before ten o' clock. After Tarbert we will be heading for Islay, but not on *Juno*.

We have negotiated a good rate for our accommodation as we are leaving at 07.20 and breakfast doesn't start until 08.30. A packet of salt n' vinegar crisps is not my ideal way of starting the day, however.

So we're up at 07.00 and emerge onto a cool Millport which is still deserted. The bus arrives as promised and takes us the four miles to the ferry where *Loch Alainn* awaits. It looks as though the *Loch Linnhe*, firmly cemented to Largs Pier, is going to be our bogey ship.

At Largs the taxi is late, we had booked it yesterday but it keeps us on our toes for five minutes until it eventually shows. But the road to Wemyss Bay is quiet and we comfortably make the 08.45 sailing by *Jupiter*.

As we sail into Rothesay Bay we notice we are being followed by a stranger which also seems to be heading for the pier. It berths a couple of minutes after *Jupiter* and confirms our guess that she is *Poole Scene*, the latest addition to the Clyde Marine Motoring passenger fleet and now repainted in the dark blue and cream livery of the company. Two coach loads of elderly tourists (not again!) are disembarking onto the pier and forming an orderly queue to board the smart little vessel. She is chartered to take them on a sail to the 'Three Lochs' - Long, Holy and Goil. Our cruise ship *Juno* can be seen passing Toward heading our way and for a brief moment we consider a sudden change to our itinerary. But we decide that I look too young.

Poole Scene leaves the pier and we look over at *Juno* out in the Bay. To our collective horror she isn't heading for Rothesay but is off Ardyne Point and steaming towards the East Kyle. The three of us look balefully at each other. Gibbie gets out his timetable. "It says she comes into Rothesay at 10.00."

I head off to the pier office to find out what's going on. A little old lady in a purple coat, and with hair to match, is chatting to the receptionist at the window about the maternity condition of all her female relatives - daughters, grand-daughters, nieces, second cousins and all I can see is *Juno* heading into the Kyles. Eventually Mrs Violet shuffles off to the hairdressers and I get a chance to ask what is happening to our cruise ship.

The lady behind the desk is reassuring. "Oh there's an error in the timetable. She's not actually due in until 10.20. It's so the *Pioneer* can get in and out first."

Sigh of relief. All is well. *Juno* sits out in the Bay, *Pioneer* comes and goes and *Juno* berths. It appears that due to the size of the gangway on the pier only one ship can get in at a time now. The purser is there again - looking slightly bemused now by our third appearance of the week.

"You nearly gave us heart failure." I accuse him.

Today we have the grand total of fifteen passengers aboard for the sail up the Kyles of Bute into Tighnabruaich and on down the West Kyle, round Ardlamont Point and up Loch Fyne to Tarbert. We explain to the purser that we're getting off at Tarbert and not getting back on again. He looks slightly disheartened by this news. "Not getting on again"

"Don't worry, it's not your fault, we've got to get to Islay." I try to reassure him. Whether or not this has an effect on him I don't know but he doesn't give the commentary today.

So the next bit of the trip is deja vu. At Tarbert the sun is shining and we are now quite suddenly sheltered from the cool north-westerly wind. *Juno* ties up and all fifteen of us get off and head for the town leaving the crew to their boat drill.

Over an excellent lunch in a Tarbert hotel we discuss our plans. Another Clyde ferry Isle of Cumbrae is plying her trade between Tarbert and Portavadie, on the other side of Loch Fyne. We obviously have to add her to our list so after lunch we take a return crossing on her.

We board her at 14.15 by which time *Juno* can be seen heading out of the mouth of the loch on her return passage. Her purser doesn't know it yet but the chances are he'll see us again tomorrow!

I pick Gibbie and Ian's brains to see if they can remember when we previously sailed on *Isle of Cumbrae*, and on which routes. It takes them the whole crossing time to recall, and even then with a fair bit of prompting, that it was in 1993 Lochaline - Fishnish, 1996 Fishnish - Lochaline and 1998 Colintraive - Rhubodach. Trivial drivel really.

We are sitting out on deck on this crossing, for we are going with the wind and the sun is beaming warmly down on us. A chap shuffles up to

Gibbie and asks what kind of accommodation is available on Islay. On Islay? This seems a rather strange question until the penny drops and Gibbie realises the chap is on the wrong ferry and thinks he's crossing to Islay. Some people never look at a map. He could actually be forgiven if he thought he was crossing to the Isle of Cumbrae, and he will be even more confused when he does get onto the Islay ship and discovers it's called the *Isle of Arran*.

Back at Tarbert we now have some more organising to do, which means I have some organising to do. There are several links between ferry terminals to organise for what remains of today and for tomorrow, otherwise the rest of the trip will disintegrate. Get the feeling this is a 'make-it-up-as-we-go-along' Island Hop. I make my way to a telephone box.

First of all we ascertain that there is a connecting bus this afternoon between Tarbert and the Islay ferry terminal at Kennacraig, six miles away. There is and it leaves Tarbert at 16.47. But when we arrive at Port Ellen on Islay at 20.05 tonight there is no connecting bus to take us to our guesthouse in Bowmore (which we have booked in advance). We shall have to use our charm to try to procure a lift from someone on the ferry.

Tomorrow promises to be one of the most hectic and brilliant routes we have ever undertaken, or an unmitigated disaster, depending on whether we can succeed in making our overland connections at Kennacraig, Lochranza and Ardrossan. The aim tomorrow is to get back to Dunoon where Gibbie has left his car.

The first bit is fairly easy - I book seats on the bus which meets the ferry at Kennacraig to take us across Kintyre to Claonaig and hence the Lochranza ferry. Our ship from Islay is due to arrive at Kennacraig at 12.05, but we need to be at Claonaig, six miles away, at 12.35 or we will miss the boat. It is a narrow, single-track road and the bus operator informs me that his bus can wait no later than 12.10 for the Islay vessel to arrive and disembark. Great! That's going to give me a sleepless night. Having arranged all this I chicken out trying to organise the other links just now, I decide to book them from Islay tomorrow morning and hope that I don't regret that decision.

I discuss all this with the others in a Tarbert cafe, where we sip insipid tea and await the appearance of the bus. We adjourn to the bus park and watch a game of bowls being played on the green beside us while we wait. Five other passengers are sheltering from the increasing wind in the bus shelter.

The bus is as punctual as a CalMac ferry and we are soon standing at a breezy Kennacraig ferry terminal watching *Isle of Arran* arrive - punctually. In these days of planes being left on the tarmac for hours and trains not turning up at all it is refreshing to take a trip such as ours and find every single ship departing exactly on time. And I mean exactly. *Isle of Arran* has her bow visor down and recedes away from Kennacraig at exactly 18.00. Our only complaint is that the barman takes until 18.02 to lift up the shutters and allow us to drift into "Velvet Time".

Over a beer Gibbie is chosen as the Island Hopper with the most charm and is thus designated to find us a kind person who can give us a lift from Port Ellen to Bowmore. He accepts graciously but Ian and I impose two conditions. He has to comb his hair and have a shave first.

"Is there nobody on the ship that you know, Stuart ?" Asks Ian when he sees Gibbie screwing his face up at the thought of shaving.

"No."

"Well that must be a first."

This trip to Islay was planned as a pleasant diversion from the hectic business of trying to get on all the Clyde ferries. We feel we can justify this as our reward - for a visit to Islay is always rewarding.

We are now on the open waters between Gigha and Islay and the ship is pitching moderately in the swell that can be seen subtly advancing on our bow. It is cold out on deck so we retreat downstairs for a meal and, inevitably, a quick zizz (snooze) in the 'reclining chair' lounge on a lower deck. I'm first to succumb and find a seat behind a farmer and his border collie. It yelps timidly when I sit down. A couple of minutes later it yelps again when Ian arrives. When Gibbie settles down five minutes after that it growls deeply.

It is shortly after that we discover that the lounge with the reclining seats is in the same room as the children's playroom! However the gentle pitching is soporific and I'm soon dreaming about buses not showing up on time and taxis having punctures.

I wake to hear two elderly ladies somewhere behind me discussing their footwear.

"What shoes did you bring with you, Betty?"

"Just ma sandals."

"Zat all yi'v goat?"

"Aye - just ma gutties as weel."

They fall silent for a while, and the wee boy who had been playing quietly in the playroom comes over to talk to his Dad who is sitting directly behind me. Dad insists in going over every detail of his son's play, every detail of the ship and every detail of what they're going to do on holiday on Islay. It is all in such graphic detail that it is like listening to an episode of Blue Peter.

We are half an hour from Port Ellen. Time to get a lift. Gibbie looks no more like budging from his seat than combing his hair or having a shave. He says that he is not going to ask anyone for a lift because if three chaps like us asked him for a lift he'd say NO. So I take off to see what I can do.

I stand outside the purser's office and announce with barely disguised surprise that I am disappointed to just discover than there is no bus meeting the ferry that will take us to Bowmore. A gentleman standing nearby overhears me - and that is how I managed to procure us a lift.

The gentleman is Calum who leads us down Port Ellen Pier to a little jeep. He will be passing through Bowmore anyway on his way to Port Charlotte and is happy to help us out. Ian and I cram into the back seat and are fairly bounced along the 'low' road - which may be straight but certainly undulates up and down.

The remainder of the evening is spent in a Bowmore pub sampling one or two Islay malts. A burly chap sitting at the bar has been sampling more than one or two by the look of him. When he stands up to leave he finds to his astonishment that his legs won't work and he has to be carried out.

At about half past ten Gibbie finally feels the need to have that shave, but his conscience is torn between going back to the guesthouse or staying for another of his second favourite malts. His will is already weakened and he puts his ablutions off until the morning. Ian rather unkindly suggests that if he gives his beard another couple of days he'll look like Captain Pugwash.

In the cosy bar with heat radiating from our faces the malt tastes champion. Perhaps it is because it has been served to us in special 'balloon' glasses. These look like sherry glasses and helps the nose of the spirit by trapping the vapours. Trouble is I cannot get my nose into it.

Back at the B n' B I fall asleep glowing externally and internally.

Day Three - *Follow that cab*

Breakfast is at 08.10. The bus leaves for Bowmore at 08.50. The ship departs Port Ellen at 09.55. Those are the easy bits. On arriving back at Kennacraig the pace will hot up considerably.

We sit in the dining-kitchen of our very comfortable guesthouse watching our hostess scrambling our eggs and listening to her friendly chat. The only other guest is a 'dead ringer' for John Major. He is even wearing a grey suit - and he is on holiday!

The guesthouse is a credit to Scottish hospitality and our hosts as welcoming as one would expect from the very magnanimous people of Islay. On our way out Gibbie is drawn to a corner of the hall full of big toys, of the kind you can sit on and pedal along - if you are two years old. They belong to the wee lad of the house. Well I presume they do. There are tractors and bikes and ex-Caterpillar man Gibbie is in his element. He is particularly engrossed by a big plastic muck-spreader. He even gets down onto his knees and opens up the back to see what's inside!

It is a bright sunny morning out on Bowmore's Main Street. Buses of all shapes and sizes are coming and going in all directions - most of them full of schoolchildren. Our bus arrives on time and we set off speedily down the same road that we came up last night. As we pass the airport two small fire tenders are spreading foam onto the apron. Is it a drill or is Prince Charles due to fly in today? At Port Ellen Pier *Isle of Arran* is arriving but I have no time to stand and watch - I have to secure our line of advance- I need another telephone box!

A bus should be at Kennacraig to meet the ferry and take us to Claonaig for the wee ferry to Arran. But on arriving at Lochranza we will need a taxi to convey us the fifteen miles to Brodick in just 45 minutes. Likewise at Ardrossan we will only have 45 minutes to get to Largs to pick up cruise ship *Juno* to Dunoon. I have three taxi numbers for Arran. The first two companies cannot help us and the third won't answer. Wonderful! This is all we need. If this link in our travels fails then it will certainly take the gloss off the day.

Isle of Arran is now starting to load so I return to the phone to try the third number again. But now I cannot find the piece of paper with the taxi numbers on it. As I frantically search the countless pockets of my new leather jacket a lady comes up and gestures that she wants to use the phone. Outside Gibbie and Ian are ready to board the ship and are also gesticulating at me. Then I see the bit of paper on the floor at my feet. I quickly dial and a groggy voice reluctantly answers. I pleadingly make my request. "I'm already picking someone up at Lochranza and taking them to Brodick. I'll get the three of you as well."

We've struck lucky yet again. I now phone an Ardrossan taxi company and book a cab to meet us at Ardrossan Pier at 14.45. When I go outside the others are waiting at the foot of the gangway for me.

The ship is up and away exactly on 09.55 as timetabled. This is good for we cannot allow the ship to arrive late at Kennacraig. It's time for a second breakfast. All our land links are now secured and if all goes well we should have a fascinating day trying to get to Dunoon.

Out on deck the starboard side of the ship is a sun trap and as a consequence a dozen or so passengers are sitting or standing there with their faces held up to the sun - pretty silly, isn't it? We're amongst them. The ship is rolling gently due to the slight swell as we turn in a gentle curve around the south coast of Islay. The distilleries of Laphroig, Lagavulin and Ardbeg on the port side look like the white superstructure of ships marooned on the rocks.

Gibbie desperately wants, and may I say needs, to shave, but is eyeing the sea cautiously, fearfully, even. "I can't shave in these sea conditions." After ten minutes conditions have moderated and he peers over the side again. "I'm away for a shave. If you hear the tannoy asking if there is a doctor aboard you'll know I've cut my throat." He says dryly.

The sail across to the entrance to West Loch Tarbert and on up the loch is simply glorious. We pass the hill guarding the eastern entrance to the loch, Dun Skeig, which Gibbie one day hopes to climb for a aerial photograph of a passing ferry. I'll believe it when I see it!

The tension is tightening now. We have to be off the ship fast as our bus won't wait past 12.10 and the ship isn't due to dock until 12.05. So we descend a deck and form the head of a queue, quietly praying that the gangway isn't hoisted onto the deck above. Normally we slag off people who queue to get off a ship, but this is desperate stuff.

We reach the pier at exactly 12.05 but it takes an agonising five minutes to get the ship secure and the gangway aboard. I stand and try not to look as anxious as I feel, barely able to resist the temptation of just jumping over the side onto the pier. At 12.11 we are released and run down the gangway. To our relief the bus is still there. The driver doesn't hang about. It may be six miles of single-track road but he treats it like the M6 and we can see that if the bus holds together we will make Claonaig on time. It does - minus a millimetre or two of brake lining.

There are now two more Clyde ferries to sail on to complete our tally, and one of them, *Loch Tarbert*, arrives at the slipway at Claonaig just two minutes after we do. As we cross over to Arran the wind is going with us again and consequently it is delightfully warm.

The yellow minibus can be seen waiting on the slip at Lochranza, as promised, and ourselves plus two other passengers and are bundled in unceremoniously. Unfortunately a little old lady in an old Toyota pulls away in front of us, and for the next fifteen miles in front of us she remains. We just cannot get past her. I look at my watch as we reach the summit of the hill out of Lochranza, where we have 12 miles still to go, and see that it is 13.20. My brain then does something very silly. I get it into my head that the ferry from Brodick leaves at 13.35 instead of 13.50 and the effect of this is that everyone on the bus except me is quite cool about our progress. I am, however, in a blind panic, looking constantly at my watch and counting down the miles. I promise myself never to plan a day like this again. It's added years to me - I'm now nearly as old as Gibbie! I also vow never to buy a Toyota.

When we arrive at Brodick Pier I believe that there is only one minute to go before the ship leaves. And, as you know, these ships never sail late.

"Hurray up Gibbie, there isn't a second to lose!"

Gibbie and Ian look at me nonchalantly and point casually at the line of cars still waiting to board Caledonian Isles.

On board the last of our Clyde ships, number thirteen counting *Kenilworth*. She is the biggest of them all and her time-keeping is as flawless as the rest. We are happier now for there is only one link to go and there is an air of confidence that the taxi will be there waiting for us.

I am actually the first passenger down the gangway at Ardrossan and see a cab waiting among the throngs of people hanging around the ferry terminal. We get in and tell the driver that we only have 40 minutes to get to Largs.

"No problem." The car is hemmed in on all sides but with some deft work at the wheel we are through the masses and on the road again.

Our target now is *Juno* which should be returning from her Tighnabruiach cruise and be berthing at Largs at 15.30. She will convey us direct to Dunoon, and hopefully Gibbie's car. It will then be a simple job to cross on the next service vessel to Gourock - and home.

Our driver seems to have overestimated our impetuosity. On leaving Seamill we are idling along at 95 mph and eventually reach Largs just 15 minutes after getting into the car. Whew!

We are now standing at the head of the pier with 25 minutes to kill - not a situation we expected to be in at 09.45 this morning. Out on the Firth, sailing over from Rothesay, is the reassuring and unmistakable sight of *Juno* (unless it's *Jupiter*, of course) heading for Largs. We've done it! All our connections have fallen into place immaculately. The only Clyde CalMac ship that we have failed to get aboard is Loch Linnhe. And we are standing looking at her right now! She is berthed at the same spot at Largs Pier as she was two days ago. But what's this? She's moving! Unbelievably she moves away from the edge of the pier. I look at my watch and Ian looks at me.

"Don't even think about it," he warns, "We don't have time."

"We do!"

"WE DON'T! My pals shout in unison.

They're right of course. In any case for some unexplained reason she moves back onto her place at the pier again. I know why now. She is tantalising me, teasing me, proving that she hasn't become a fixture of Largs Pier but can move in her own right, and not give us a chance to sail on her in the process.

The purser of *Juno* looks at us in tacit, open-mouthed astonishment as the three of us head up the gangway for the fourth time in as many days. He doesn't say anything, but I sense that he is mystified as to how on earth we got to Largs. He last saw us in Tarbert about 24 hours ago when we had told him that we were heading for Islay. Now he clearly cannot fathom how we got here, to Largs. And we don't tell him. I'm sure he'll be delighted to be back on the Gourock - Dunoon roster next week.

On passage between Largs and Dunoon we perform the ritual of the Annual Toast. As we film the ceremony and put the glasses to our lips a gust of wind blows neat Grouse over our faces to the bemusement of half a dozen passengers watching us.

On our arrival at Dunoon an announcement is made to the effect that as the Gourock vessel, *Saturn*, is running late (having got a lorry stuck on her deck earlier in the afternoon) *Juno* will be taking the next service run to Gourock. This means a fifteen minute delay at Dunoon. It also means that *Juno* is the last ship of our trip - fortunately we have already sailed on *Saturn*, and hadn't left her 'til last.

We all go ashore to look for Gibbie's car. It is exactly where he had left it and none the worse for being abandoned for two days. Gibbie drives it aboard *Juno* and the cruise vessel thus becomes the 16.50 Dunoon-Gourock service vessel.

From her decks, as we sail off on the last leg of this year's Island Hop, we watch a dozen gannets plummet fifteen metres into the rich pickings off the starboard side of the ship. Has the wee girl in charge of catering been jettisoning the last of the pancakes and scones again? The gannets seem very close to us. Further away to starboard a Royal Navy frigate, *HMS Sheffield*, is heading very slowly down river. She pauses and turns to port. From our position her bow is pointing directly at Inverkip Power Station. We stare in silent hope that she will fire her big guns and blow its towering, ugly chimney to smithereens. Wouldn't that be great? But sadly no.

We are in happy mood as we drive off at Gourock, our starting-point and finishing-line. We have had considerably success in our 'ferry-bagging'. We knew we would not get aboard all the Western Ferries ships and have been unlucky with *Loch Linnhe* but the rest have been attained. On the way around our complex route we have sailed into, or onto, twenty-one piers or slipways and seen the remains, intact or otherwise, of about ten more. Half of these are no longer used and as we look back at Dunoon Pier we can only hope that this one will not be added to the list.

Our minds now look ahead to next year when we will have three new ships to sail on - *Lochnevis*, *Clansman* and *Hebrides*.

Here is the list of sailings for Island Hop 2000

Kenilworth	Gourock	T 1000
Rover	Gourock - Helensburgh - Kilcreggan - Gourock	T 1005-1130
Sound of Sleat	McInroy's Point - Hunter's Quay - McInroy's Point	T 1200-1245
Saturn	Gourock - Dunoon	T 1320-1340
Juno	Dunoon - Largs - Rothesay - Dunoon - Gourock	T 1420-1720
Jupiter	Wemyss Bay - Rothesay	T 1815-1850
Loch Dunvegan	Rhubodach - Colintraive	T 1930-1940
Juno	Dunoon - WemyssBay - Largs - Rothesay - Tighnabruaich - Rothesay	W 1000-1445
Pioneer	Rothesay - Wemyss Bay	W 1515-1545
Loch Alainn	Largs - Cumbrae Slip	W 1800-1810
Loch Alainn	Cumbrae Slip - Largs	Th 0800-0810
Jupiter	Wemyss Bay - Rothesay	Th 0845-1915
Juno	Rothesay - Tighnabruaich - Tarbert	Th 1020-1230
Isle of Cumbrae	Tarbert - Portavadie - Tarbert	Th 1415-1505
Isle of Arran	Kennacraig - Port Ellen	Th 1800-2010
Isle of Arran	Port Ellen - Kennacraig	F 0955-1205
Loch Tarbert	Claonaig - Lochranza	F 1235-1305
Caledonian Isles	Brodick - Ardrossan	F 1350-1445
Juno	Largs - Dunoon - Gourock	F 1530-1710

Postscript - *Pioneer* was not sold this year but sailed on for a few more seasons, as you shall see if you read on.

And as I write this, in April 2008, the Gourock - Dunoon route is still under a fug of uncertainty. However CalMac are still serving the route, still with a 'streaker'.

2001 New Ships for a New Age

The Plan

OUR THEME THIS YEAR IS VERY SIMPLE, and made the choice of route fairly straightforward. Since last year not one but two new ships are now plying the hallowed waters. Even better, Hebrides and Lochnevis were both born in Clyde shipyards.

Hebrides is a product of the efficient Fergusons of Port Glasgow. A twin of *Clansman*, she has now become the regular ferry serving Uig (Skye) to Lochmaddy (North Uist) and Tarbert (Harris). Thus displacing our favourite *Hebridean Isles*.

Lochnevis, on the other hand, is the last build from Ailsa Shipyard at Troon and is about to bring a vehicle service, for the first time, to the Small Isles - Rum, Canna, Eigg and Muck. When she took up service in early 2001 she displaced CalMac's last passenger-only vessel, *Lochmor*, which was sold.

Apart from those two, we have still to sail on *Clansman*. We have also still to sail on the new Jura ferry *Eilean Dhuira*. However, we are not likely to manage all of these ships.

Apart from the new ships there is another bonus, however. The knock-on effect of the arrival of Hebrides on the 'Uig triangle' is that *Hebridean Isles* has been displaced to the Islay route. This means that as well as sailing aboard 'new' ships, *Hebrides* and *Lochnevis*, we can incorporate into our journey the Wednesday afternoon sailing to Colonsay and Islay from Oban by the *Hebridean Isles*. A favourite route, but now on a different, and favourite ship.

The previous Islay ship, *Isle of Arran*, has become spare vessel, giving CalMac their first spare ship since the sale of *Claymore* four years ago. As usual there are other goodies on the way: a decent visit to Raasay and Gigha, stepping ashore - hopefully - onto Muck and Eigg for the first time, and a 'new' vessel for us on the Kilchoan - Tobermory route. We also have some new places to stay overnight - Kyleakin and Isleoransay on Skye, and a couple of old favourites to stay in - Tobermory and Port Askaig.

Day One - *All Quiet Beneath the Bridge*

On the surface there would appear to be a considerable change to the beginning of this year's Island Hop (the 13th - but I'm not superstitious). The mode of transport would appear to have undergone a significant metamorphosis. Gibbie and I are standing in a lay-by adjacent to Glasgow Airport taking pictures of planes landing. Surely we haven't swapped a steamer for a Boeing? The answer is much simpler, we are waiting for the third member of our Island Hopping team, Ian, to arrive and fancy we can now spot his aircraft as it approaches terra firma. I had hoped he could persuade the pilot to abort the landing in order to add excitement to our Island Hop video (or perhaps get onto the Ten o' clock News). However this request seems to have fallen on deaf ears, or possibly not been conveyed to the flight deck at all. All the planes we observe touch down uneventfully. The problem is that we are not sure which one Ian is on, and when we move around to our rendezvous point we find he has been standing waiting on us for half an hour. It turns out he was on the Airbus which passed over before we had the camera out of the 'Gibbie Bag'.

Ian has been flying a lot recently. His eagerly awaited holiday in Japan had only come to its conclusion a week ago and is the reason for us moving our Island Hop to the end of May. The reality that our usual week, the third week in May, brought continuous sunshine and soaring temperatures is immediately made clear to Ian. Any breakdown in the weather (which is indeed forecast) will be entirely blamed on him, and as we step out from the airport concourse, under a gradually greying sky he makes his first unfortunate comment.

"Weather was nice in Japan!"

This May western Scotland has witnessed only two showers of rain. But we as head north, in Gibbie's car, the indications are that a fair bit of precipitation is about to be condensed into these last few days. Nevermind.

"Nice to see you, Ian. Good flight?"

"Yes, but where have you guys been? I've been here for ages. Bet you've been down at Gourock on a ferry already."

He's half correct. We have been down to Gourock, but not to sail, just to collect our Island *Rover* tickets. We were tempted - *Pioneer* was departing for Dunoon, and The Second Snark for Kilcreggan. But we had some plane-spotting to do.

These tickets are our passport to the isles. They give eight days of unlimited travel on the CalMac network, and that includes a bike. Even though we only need four days, and don't have a bike, this is still good value for us.

Our journey north to Kyleakin on Skye for our first overnight stop is uneventful except for an episode of acute embarrassment to myself. At the toilets at Crianlarich Station Ian had held the door open for me to enter following his own visit, and I had closed it behind me without realising that I should lock it as it was a single toilet. I need say no more....Sorry Missus!

I am already feeling slightly disadvantaged by my two cohorts. Gibbie is sprouting a beard which is still in its infancy but gives him an uncanny likeness to Captain Pugwash. While Ian is already sporting the full works of facial hair. I am made to feel the odd one out as I do not have facial hair - in fact I am now at that age where I hardly have any hair left at all.

We reach a gloomy Kyleakin at 18.15 and at our accommodation I am shown to a faded little room, with a wash-hand basin that must have been designed with the notion that some African pygmies would one day be staying at the hotel.

After a dinner which looked as though it had been prepared and plated two days ago, I take a little stroll, leaving the 'hairy-faces' behind, around the quiet little village. Now by-passed by the Skye Bridge the place look deserted, until I happen upon Saucy Mary's, a small pub crammed with young backpacking types intent on having a good time. By contrast our hotel is full of Wallace Arnolds, most of whom seem to be slipping terminally into post-prandial comas.

Outside the misty, damp gloamin' stretches across to Kyleakin's former twin, Kyle of Lochalsh, and out under the Skye Bridge to a distant, pale horizon. Only the numerous mustard coloured clumps of gorse on either side of the sound add any degree of colour to the scene. It is so still. Even the cars and box vans are silent as they slide over the thin arched span of the bridge on their way north.

In our bar Gibbie and I find a large barmaid, on her platform behind the counter, intimidating Ian as he tries to buy a drink. Intimidation gives way to awe when she steps out from behind the bar and we discover that she has not been on a platform after all. I hope her wash-hand basin is perched higher up the wall than mine.

One last look around outside before retiring. It has started to drizzle and a small fishing boat is purring down the sound towards Kyle of Lochalsh. Its green starboard light alerts Ian and I to a previously undisclosed problem that Gibbie has been having with colours. He knows it is a green light because it is on the starboard side of the vessel, but he admits he cannot make out the colour of it. His granddaughter Hazell has found this visual disability amusing. She has recently been teasing him with various objects and demanding to know what colour they are. In that typically astute, feminine approach she has even resorted to bribery in order to extract the correct response.

"I'll give you this jelly-baby, Grandpa, if you can tell me what colour it is." The reality for Gibbie is more serious, he now realises that he can never be an airline pilot.

Day Two - *Raasay and Roddy*

Outside before breakfast; it is a calm, dry morning. A large grey heron is flapping labouriously overhead, while on the Skye Bridge a white tanker is struggling up the slope. We intend to start the day at a gentler pace as we linger over breakfast. Despite the large number of Wallace Arnolds this is served speedily by the waiting staff, who all seem to be German.

We head for the car while Saucy Mary's backpackers are being loaded into a fleet of yellow minibuses emblazoned with various energetic adjectives: 'Fantastic', 'Passionate', 'Stunning'....One minibus is astride a ramp with its bonnet gaping. I cannot make out the expletive of its side. 'Broke' perhaps?

We are heading for the small ferry terminal at Sconser, where our Island Hop will begin in earnest with a visit to Raasay. We are taking the car across in order to get at least a taste of an island which we have previously only stepped on and off, back in 1993. Our timing has to be precise. Due to repairs at Raasay Pier the ferry service is to be suspended at the middle of the day, but this will not affect our planned sailing.

The ferry is *Loch Striven*, a former Cumbrae ferry, and we slip over to the other side with two very black, African clergymen. What I mean is that the two clergymen,and their wives, join us on the ferry to Raasay. They were accompanied by a pretty white Scottish Presbyterian guide. I mean she was white - not necessarily pretty!

Raasay has a fairly enviable position. It is tucked tightly against the sheltered eastern side of Skye, whose huge mountains help to protect it from the south-westerly extremes of weather, like a big sister protecting her little brother. If Mull is a cycling paradise, in my own humble opinion, then Raasay is a walkers' nirvana. Various routes of varying length spread out from the ferry landing site in the south and give a choice of terrain. From lush, deciduous woodland to heritage trails to rocky moorland and hillside track. Having the car we are going to stick to the good old tarmac.

The island is about a dozen miles long by about three across with the only village, Inverarish, in the south-west corner. We head off eastwards to visit the site of the disused iron ore mine. Here First World War German prisoners-of-war were made to toil - digging ore. According to Gibbie their employment in such a manner was counter to the Hague Convention. He would know - he helped write it. An outbreak of influenza then struck the island, from which many of them succumbed. And that was basically the end of mining on Raasay.

We stroll among the ruined mine buildings - no sign of any diggings, but plenty of midges. The remains of the rail track, which leads in a straight line from the mines down to the pier, can still be seen.

We head off to the end of the road where a stunning view southwards towards the Kyle narrows makes us pause long enough to get eaten alive by midges - the little darlings. We then continue our whistle stop tour in a northerly direction, through some lovely deciduous woodland and then out onto moorland where we re-join the lower road near the tidal Holoman Island. On the road ahead the walkers are already out. And so is the sun.

Although it looks wild and isolated Raasay is actually easy to get to and we all agree that our brief visit was worth the cost of taking the car over.

Sailing back across, with our African contingent carefully holding onto their hats, the view across to the giant cones of the Red Cuillins is stupendous.

We drive straight to Uig in the north of Skye, in bags of time for our sailing on the brand new Hebrides. But there is an uncertainty. This will be the first time that we have sailed on a crossing which requires the implementation of 'passenger registration'. A European Union edict has stipulated that sailings of a certain duration will require all passengers to register with the port of departure "no later than thirty minutes before sailing time". This piece of legislation came about after the tragic Estonia disaster in the Baltic, when the ferry company did not know exactly how many passengers were aboard. We are not quite sure what this registration will entail, but we want to photograph the arrival of Hebrides from the hill above Uig, and this will encroach on the thirty minute check-in time. So we reckon on registering first before returning uphill to film our ship.

As it turns out the CalMac staff at Uig are treating the new regulations in their usual quietly efficient, unfazed Hebridean manner. So we decide we have time for a lingering lunch as well.

Up the hill to film the arrival of Hebrides from North Uist. The sky is now overcast but at least it is dry and we are keenly looking forward to this nice long return sailing on a new ship.

Hebrides is a younger sister of *Clansman*, which was introduced on the Oban routes three years ago. She is not quite identical to her older sibling - some of the differences can even be spotted from a distance. The lack of the two large lifeboats either side of Hebrides' funnel (which *Clansman* possesses) is immediately noticeable. There is also more deck space on Hebrides, albeit enclosed, on either side at the rear deck. Generally speaking (at the time of writing - for these things change) if the funnel appears partially hidden, it is *Clansman* you are looking at, if the funnel appears to be in full view it is *Hebrides*.

This will be the first time any of us have sailed on *Hebrides*, but then she has only been in service three months. The irony is that we have still to sail on *Clansman*! (In fact both Gibbie and I have sailed on *Clansman*, but not on an Island Hop).

Launched by the Queen in August 2000 *Hebrides* is the third Western Isles passenger ship to bear that name, and at 99 metres the longest of the three. She has a capacity for 108 cars and 612 passengers, a gross tonnage of 5506 and a top speed of 16.8 knots. From the enthusiasts' point of view a chance to improve on some design features of the *Clansman* has been lost - notably the lack of deck space. Nowadays it seems that naval architects want their passengers, sorry customers, to forget that they are at sea at all. I have always thought that sitting out on deck, when the weather is favourable, is one of life's luxuries and enjoyed by most people who sail on a ship - not just enthusiasts. So, as you may now have gathered, I think that *Hebrides*, like her sister, has insufficient deck space - and no open view over the bow.

From our lofty position, up the hill overlooking Uig, we have a great view of her speeding into Uig Bay in a large curve. Our vantage point offers a splendid photo opportunity. Like her sister she looks bow heavy and is pushing a relatively large surge of water ahead of her bulbous bow.

As *Hebrides* is only spending thirty minutes at Uig Pier we'd better get on our way. In that time we have to get back to Uig, park the car and march Gibbie up the longest pier in the Hebrides onto the ship.

Gibbie is hoping that the skipper will be Roddy Morrison who has had an unbilled starring role in previous Island Hops - not that he is aware of it. Gibbie's wishes are fulfilled for not only is Roddy today's skipper but he is at the foot of the gangway to greet us personally. Or so we think. He is actually taking a photograph of his ship. Aren't we supposed to do that? Roddy promises to give us a tour of the bridge during our crossing, and we intend to hold him to that.

We are late in leaving the pier due to a delay in a single car reaching Uig on time. Now that we are in the age of the mobile phone I suppose it is possible to phone ahead to the ferry office. "Can you hold the ferry for us for five minutes - we're late." In this case he could have added: "....and by the way we're just leaving Portree!"

After seven minutes of waiting, with the deck crew shaking their watches, a VW Golf comes flying down the road, up the pier and straight onto the rear end of *Hebrides*. The red-faced occupant is clutching a mobile phone, but then so is his wife and so are his three children.

Off we sail across the Little Minch on a return crossing to Tarbert on *Harris*. This being a new ship we take a tour of her. She is certainly very plush inside, with an interesting centre-piece in the reception area - a simplified three dimensional CalMac flag set on a wooden surround with a message of welcome.

The Observation Lounge on the upper deck is huge and has an uninterrupted view over the bow. Tan-coloured, upholstered, bay seating at either side is complimented by a central bank of purple coloured reclining seats. We'll have a shot on them later.

Other differences from *Clansman* include a repositioning of the Purser's Office, a more open plan restaurant and some attractive bucket seating in the bar - which we shall also try out later. One other pleasing feature of the ship is the numerous pictures positioned on the walls. One of these is causing acute confusion to a middle-aged couple. They are looking intently at a stunning colour photograph of the previous *Hebrides* and pointing at her open rear deck.

"There," says the lady pointing at it, "that's where we want to be."

Off they wander to find their own little corner of the ship. Five minutes later I spot them confronting the Purser. "We can't find the rear deck - you know the one with the nice wooden seating."

"Which deck madam?"

"The open deck with the old fashioned railings and wooden seats that float off when the ship sinks."

This is one spot of confusion that looks as though may take a while to resolve and I wander off - even though I alone hold the key to its resolution. We leave the heady smell of new carpets and find our own little corner of deck space up on top. *Hebrides* may be a very comfortable ship but I am more impressed with her internal comforts than her external design features.

It is a smooth passage across a featureless sea to Harris, but soon the start of the day's prolonged rain forces us to try out the internal comforts.

The reappearance of Captain Morrison brings us back to life; the promised visit to the bridge is forthcoming and we join half a dozen other chaps on a 'follow-the-leader' to the hallowed deck above. The skipper leads the way through the officers' mess, and his own cabin where he pauses briefly to put on a cassette of Gaelic folk music. Humming merrily he then leads as onto the bridge where the mate, Alistair Ross, is keeping an eye on the helmsman. The 'helmsman' is the satellite navigation system which is in firm control of the ship. Alistair gives us an interesting overview of the controls of the ship frequently interrupted by a tirade of quips from Captain Roddy.

"You see those glass wings to the bridge," Roddy points, "that's so that when it's foggy you can see which side the pier appears out of."

Much guffawing from all around us - even from the satellite navigation system! We eventually descend back to the Observation Lounge just as the rocky islets at the entrance to Loch Tarbert are indeed appearing out of the mist. As we tie up at Tarbert I catch the attention of the crewman at the gangway.

"I'm just running ashore for five minutes to take a couple of photographs."

He looks at his watch "make it two minutes." I do as I'm told.

There is a delay again at Tarbert as we prepare to leave. Some poor elderly lady almost takes an unintentional cruise across to Skye. Down on the car deck she is a bit dilatory in kissing her daughter goodbye. The gangway has to be raised again to let her off. This in itself is quite an involved process nowadays. It involves the pierhand grappling with grapple-hooks and jumping from bar to gate, on the large metal gangway, like a demented monkey. The lady had a close shave - her cruise would not just have involved a trip to Skye, but would have included a return trip to North Uist as well, before she could have sailed back to her native island.

On the return sailing we decide to have a bucket. A bucket seat, that is. The only ones we can find are in the bar, but we have a reasonable excuse - it is raining outside again.

As we near Uig a pale sun spot is illuminating a large patch of sea ahead of the ship but we never seem to sail into its glory. A fair head wind is throwing up a hefty bow wave. The delays, the wind and the tide are acting symbiotically to make us fifteen minutes late in arriving back at Uig ferry terminal. We are in no rush, our sailing is over for the day and all that remains to be done is find our guesthouse. This may not be as easy as it sounds, for it is with surprise that my two colleagues discover that I don't know exactly where it is. I know roughly where it is, but not exactly.

With me at the wheel we set off to see if I can find it. It's somewhere at the other end of Skye. The others are no use - by the time we are up the hill out of Uig they are sound asleep with their beards almost touching.

Skye is a land of rainbows as we head south to the Sleat peninsula. One particularly dazzling kaleidoscope seems to be chasing the car up the side of Loch Sligachan. Little rain is falling on our side of the loch but the peaks of the hills are alternatively disappearing behind low cloud and then making unexpected reappearances out of the mist.

After a few false starts we find our excellent little guesthouse. We should have recognised it - it is the one with the friendly collie waiting for us half way up the driveway.

A sublime evening in a local inn puts the nightcap on the day for us. I am the only one brave enough to try the Gaelic whiskey, which has the effect of sending me to bed at half past ten. It is still daylight outside but a ferocious gale has suddenly erupted from the south and given us just a little cause for concern regarding tomorrow's sailings.

Day Three - *Gremlins*

The barometer is rising and the wind dropping, but both very slowly - far too slowly for our liking. At least *Lord of the Isles* is sailing for she is backing onto the linkspan at Armadale in front of us. She seems a waste of a good ship, on this short twenty-five minute crossing to Mallaig. But she is one of our favourites and always a pleasure to sail on. At Mallaig we will change ships on to *Lochnevis*.

The sun is trying hard to break through a gauze of low cloud as we head across the Sound of Sleat.

Lord of the Isles has been refurbished since our last sail on her two years ago. Rich magenta tones dominate in the Observation Lounge, where we plonk ourselves down. The strong wind is rocking the ship gently from side to side but we are confident that our next sailing - the highlight of the whole trip we feel - will not be affected by the weather as the sea state looks pretty calm. But out to our left a fishing boat returning to its Mallaig base suggests otherwise as a huge plume is thrown up from its modest bow as it plunges into a wave. We can take it as long as *Lochnevis* can. It isn't just a new ship that beckons, 'new' islands - Muck and Eigg, are waiting for us too.

As we turn into the shelter of the harbour, which has recently been extended, *Lochnevis* is sitting waiting for us. Built at Ailsa Shipyard in Troon on the Clyde (their last ship before closure) she seems a sturdy and interesting looking vessel. When the piers and slipways of the four Small Isles that she serves (Canna, Rum, Eigg and Muck) are completed she will provide the first car ferry service to those islands. Is this a good thing? Her predecessor Lochmor has been sold by Caledonian MacBrayne to new owners in Campbeltown. Her future role is uncertain.

On disembarking from *Lord of the Isles* we have 45 minutes before *Lochnevis* sails from Mallaig, and so Gibbie and Ian zoom off to find a convenient place to leave the car, while I pop into the CalMac office to see if passenger registration is required for our sailing. To my horror the chap behind the desk is the bearer of ill tidyings. "*Lochnevis* has broken down - she will not be sailing today. Emergency passenger arrangements are being made but that does not include day-trippers. I'm sorry."

It is one of those disappointing moments where, for a brief moment, I think he is joking. But he isn't. There is no arguing. The weather hasn't snookered us - the ship has! And this is not the first time a new ship has scuppered our well laid plans by breaking down. The reason for *Lochnevis*' immobility today is, apparently, a computer hitch. That just seems to make matters worse. I mean, if one of her propellers had fallen off or her gear box exlpoded we would fully understand!

Ian and Gibbie now think that it is me who is joking when I break the news to them. There is no way we are going to get to Muck and Eigg today. Just what will we do? Our deliberations over the consequences of this great disappointment are interrupted by the sudden arrival of the Island class ferry *Raasay*. We quickly realise that a unique photo opportunity is about to present itself, and so we quickly dump our gloom and jump back into Island Hopping mode.

We photograph *Lord of the Isles*, *Lochnevis* and *Rassay* at Mallaig harbour, and then stroll round to the linkspan to watch the small ferry load. She has sailed up from Tobermory to take supplies to Eigg. These seem to consist mainly of cans of beer; it would seem that the people of Eigg consider that they are in for a siege.

A small passenger vessel has been speedily chartered to take foot passengers to Eigg, but *Rover* Ticket nutters like us will not be included as numbers are limited. So we stand around and watch, and debate what we are going to do. Our destination after Eigg was to sail to Tobermory on Mull via the Kilchoan (Ardnamurchan) ferry, so it would seem prudent just to head straight for this next link, a few hours earlier than intended. One thought occurs to me - as *Raasay* has just sailed up from Tobermory perhaps she is going back there later this afternoon. Could she take us and the car with her?

"I don't think I want to spend three hours on Raasay sailing to Tobermory," says Gibbie out of the blue. He has a point, but I have the audacity to put this idea to the chap behind the desk in the office. He gives me a look which says "you cannot be serious?"

As we drive away from Mallaig, with at least a few interesting photographs as compensation for missing out on one of the highlights of the trip, we cannot quite take in the irony of the situation. We had feared the weather - but it is modern technology that has failed us. Over coffee in Arisaig, ten miles south of Mallaig, we mull over our plans. Various ideas are aired, including going to Iona, but Gibbie's plan comes up trump.

If we make the 13.45 sailing from Kilchoan (easy) to Tobermory we can then race to Craignure, dump the car and just make the 15.00 sailing to Oban (not so easy). This in turn will give us a good chance of photographing *Clansman* from close range as she passes our ship off Duart castle about 15.15. We will also have time for a stroll around Oban before returning back to Mull on the last sailing of the day at 18.00. Excellent plan - that's why we bring Gibbie! His plan is at least better than his beard which is looking less endearing with each day that passes.

Gibbie drives the fifty miles of single-track road to nearly the tip of Ardnamurchan which is the most westerly point on the British mainland.

The section from Lochailort to Salen we have done before, but the last twenty miles is new territory for all of us. Along the northern shore of Loch Sunart - empty but for the tiny islands of Carna and Oronsay - the car winds up and down and left and right through the woods until at last, beyond Glenborrodale, we turn inland. A fascinating stretch of road leads around Ben Hiant. At the top of the climb at the beautiful little Loch Mudie. We stop to admire the view over to the island of Eigg. We are being teased for we should be on Eigg just now instead of standing here on Ardnamurchan looking at it.

There is no traffic whatsoever as I step to the side of the road to answer an urgent, indeed pressing, call of nature. Listening out for cars I am mortified when a young lady on a bicycle comes silently round the corner on my side of the road. Ian and Gibbie are much amused, and she is positively laughing.

"That's the second time in three days, Craig!" Ian calls.

Kilchoan, just a few miles further on, is cosily situated on a tidy little bay adjacent to Mingary Castle. The sun is now out and as the ferry is still about twenty minutes away from the slipway I wander off along the shoreline. The rocks are being playfully splashed by the shallow waves of what is now the Sound of Mull. The bright sunlight is highlighting the numerous clumps of thrift, which are dotted all over the shore. The clumps are very big and the plants look in fine health despite some of them being perilously close to the sea. Their deep purple flowers add welcome dashes of colour to the grey rock strata around me.

Loch Linnhe fills up with a fair number of day-trippers heading over to the Mull capital, Tobermory. She is also a former Cumbrae ferry, indeed she and *Loch Striven* were built to partner each other on the Largs -

Cumbrae route. We sit out on the top deck and enjoy the warmth of the sun on our faces for the first time on this trip. The ferry waddles from side to side all the way across and brings smiles to our faces. We're like children on a funfair ride.

At the other side the smiles vanish. We're in a hurry now and have to get down to the business of getting ourselves the twenty-one miles to Craignure as fast as legally possible. The road out of Tobermory has been improved since our last visit here, but not enough of it. Too few miles south of the colourful capital we are back to the drama of a single-track road. However we make it to the ferry terminal at Craignure on time.

Ian and I stride up the gangway onto the *Isle of Mull* while Gibbie strategically dumps the car. He is trailing behind us as we pause at the top of the gangway where three crewmen are trying to hurry-up the stragglers. Ian gesticulates behind them at Gibbie. "Better hold on a minute, there's a guy with one leg coming behind us."

We cast off Craignure Pier at 15.00 precisely, and strain over the port side to get the best camera shots of *Clansman* coming out of Oban on her way to Tiree. As we will not be able to sail on her, yet again, this is the closest we are going to get to her.

There she is - the sun emphasising that familiar contrast of black and white that makes MacBrayne steamers instantly recognisable in these waters. Ultimately we are disappointed as *Clansman* takes a route north of Lady Isle, while our ship passes to the south of it. This results in a broad channel of water between us, and thus a more distant and less imposing set of photographs.

At Oban we have just over two hours ashore and decide to search for our Holy Grail - a pub that sells real ale, a distinctly rare species in the West Highlands. We cut up a back street and in the Lorne Bar find a shining, golden example of one. It is a smart looking pub as well. A large oval bar in the centre of the room has its polished brass bar secured with a series of brass elephant trucks. Pity we've only got the two hours.

The next leg or two of our journey seems vague somehow. We do manage to catch the 18.00 sailing back to Mull, we do postpone dinner until later in the evening and I definitely don't drive back up to Tobermory.

Our guesthouse has had the dubious pleasure of our collective company on a few occasions now, but this time there is a surprise in store. It transpires that the owner, Lorna MacLeod, was brought up as a child in the same house that I currently live in with my family in Glasgow. We discover this when I am signing the register. She is beside herself with joy at this and rushes off to her Mum's to get the family photograph album. Her family lived in the house from 1960-1971. Listening to Lorna describing my own house to me is a strange experience.

We adjourn from the nostalgia to find a restaurant with a spare table. It is not easy. There are now half a dozen excellent restaurants in

58

Tobermory, but tonight all seem full. There must be an empty table somewhere. There is and eventually we find it.

Ian and Gibbie are in a fishy mood but I settle for kleftiko, which is a long shank bone of lamb which has been slowly cooking since a week ago last Thursday. If I had a dog it would appreciate the leftovers. Gibbie is wolfing down a lemon sole with an accompaniment of asparagus.

"Do you know that asparagus does strange things to your urine?" I chip in as he is about to shovel down another mouthful.

Gibbie pauses, fork in mid air, a frown appearing. "No, does what?"

Seeing the look on his and Ian's face, and not wanting to spoil their meal I back down. "Eh...I'll tell you later."

"Tell us now."

"No I'll tell you later when your not eating."

Between mouthfuls we agonise over our missed *Lochnevis* sailing. It should have been the highlight and given us two new islands. By the time I'm licking the last of the strawberry pavlova from the corners of my mouth we are beginning to look at the positive side. The photographs of Raasay and *Lord of the Isles* should be interesting and from the anorak point of view would not have been possible had we managed to sail on *Lochnevis*. She will just have to wait for a future year.

Tobermory, like ourselves, has a serene glow about it tonight - perhaps it the luminous orange flush from the floodlit church. The air is calm and the main street colourfully populated with replete diners.

Loch Linnhe is moored at the pier, but there is no sign of Raasay, which is presumably still at Mallaig. We head off to the Mishnish to augment our glow considerably.

An hour later we're cramming into a not so big family room. Whenever we have to share a room I am always the last to fall asleep. It's no wonder, really, with Gibbie and Ian snoring the room sounds like Heathrow.

Never mind, tomorrow we have a train journey to take.

Day Four - *Taking An Old Friend To Islay*

This morning we have collectively decided that Tobermory is not the best place to spend the night on an Island Hop. We always seem to be fuzzy headed in the morning. It must be the air.

I take a pre-breakfast stroll around the new car park at the southern end of the village. There is a very vocal wood warbler trilling his lungs out in the trees above. This has me standing in the middle of the car park with my head cocked to one side. Ian wanders up to me and informs me that I am looking rather odd.

One of the main targets of the day is the 13.00 sailing by *Isle of Mull* from Craignure to Oban (yes -again!) But that's hours away - we have a train to catch first and a sea crossing to take even before that.

'Sea crossing' is a bit of a euphemism. We are actually just taking a return journey on *Loch Fyne* from Fishnish, just north of Craignure, to Lochaline on the mainland. Why? Because it's there, it's our reason for doing all of this, isn't it? At Lochaline that popular culinary outlet of ours, Jean's Tea Bar, beckons but after the huge breakfast we had none of us feels like a 'Barge Special'.

To our surprise *Loch Fyne* is almost full on the way back over to Mull. A stream of lorries and cars are loaded aboard. The introduction of this larger ferry a few years ago seems to have paid off on this back door route to Mull. Or perhaps it is the friendliness of the crew. The young skipper addles up to us and asks how we are today and where we are heading. This is always a dangerous question to ask us. Ian gives him the abridged version. The ticket collector is also welcoming; a pretty young lassie with golden locks and a wide, refreshing smile.

One minor fright on the way back across, however. I drop my pencil-of-the-day (which happens to be the yellow one) over the side of the ship. It floats off up the Sound of Mull. I am lucky, but for a quick flick of the wrist it would have been my precious notebook instead. Both danced from finger tip to finger tip for a few agonising milliseconds before the pencil finally went. Had it been the notebook you would now be looking at a blank page. The pencil colour is not important but belies a minor idiosyncrasy of mine- others may consider this a euphemism for an obsessional psychopathy! Let me explain. As I hate writing my notes with a blunt pencil I always bring four with me on our trips, red, blue, green and yellow. One for each day. So I start each day with a new colour. Now I have only three pencils left - but thankfully still the notebook.

Gibbie thinks all this is nuts, and the look on my face as the pencil goes over the side hilarious. "Why don't you just bring a pencil sharpener!"

The train we have to catch operates, of course, on the miniature steam Mull Railway, which runs a mile from Craignure to Torosay Castle. We double check that we can take a return journey to Torosay and be back in time for our all important 13.00 sailing. We can, but Ian makes me check for a third time - he's a bit like that when the itinerary is tight.

We set off along the bumpy, narrow gauge track behind much wheezing and spluttering. It's not Gibbie this time, it's from the locomotive. The three of us are comically crammed into one tiny carriage, like the proverbial sardines. It is all good fun and at least we can say at least one part of this year's trip is by steam power. Just a pity it isn't a ship. The loco is called *Lord of the Isles*, which is, I suppose, at least relevant.

At Torosay, just forty-five minutes before our sailing, all three of us have subclinical heart failure when the loco uncouples, reverses around the carriages, with us still sitting inside them, but instead of re-coupling whizzes away down the track and out of sight. Ian is the first to speak.

"Eh don't you think he's forgotten something?" But it is only bunkering coal and it is back with us in a couple of minutes. At Craignure the stationmaster is all smiles. "Did you enjoy that?" I half expect him to add "sonny".

Isle of Mull is berthing when we arrive back at the pier and soon we are passing beneath her gnathic portal. And so for the second time in twenty-two hours we are sailing on *Isle of Mull* over to Oban.

We will be busy when we get there. The interest this time will be the comings and goings of vessels at Oban over the next hour and a half. Aboard the ship we sit down over lunch to work out which ships will be doing what. Gibbie aids his digestion with a Kilmarnock Pie (which actually looks, and apparently tastes, rather good). By studying the timetables we come up with the following schedule, ending with our own sailing out of Oban aboard *Hebridean Isles*.

13.40 *Isle of Mull* arr Oban from Mull (with us)
14.00 *Isle of Mull* dep Oban for Mull
14.10 *Clansman* arr Oban from Tiree
14.25 *Hebridean* Isles arr Oban from Colonsay
14.45 *Eigg* dep Oban for Lismore
14.50 *Clansman* dep Oban for South Uist & Barra
15.15 *Hebridean Isles* dep Oban for Colonsay & Islay

From *Isle of Mull*'s upper deck we spot one of those ships, *Clansman*, following in our wake, about thirty minutes behind us. Closer to us, on the boat deck of *Isle of Mull*, there is a dummy dressed up like a crewman, with survival suit, boots, gloves and lifejacket. It is draped, as if it's had too much to drink, over a rail beside one of the lifeboats.

"He looks in bad shape," remarks Gibbie.

"Yeah, I saw him having a Kilmarnock Pie earlier on," returns Ian.

We chat about what each of us wants to do on arriving at Oban. I am taking my cameras up to my favourite spot on Pulpit Hill overlooking the pier. Gibbie is heading down the Sound of Kerrera to photograph the passage of *Hebridean Isles* coming up towards Oban. Ian is heading for - Boots, the chemist! Neither of us dares asks him why.

Gibbie has to register us as passengers for the next leg of our journey, to Port Askaig on Islay via Colonsay. He must also position the car in the correct queue. My concern, however, is the big black cloud which menacingly threatens my photographic ego trip. Sure enough, just as *Hebridean Isles* enters Oban Bay from the south, and squares up to *Clansman* which is already at the pier, the heavens open, and I have to dive for cover under an overhanging rock. Fortunately the shower doesn't last long and I get my pictures.

After *Clansman* departs for the Western Isles, *Hebridean Isles* docks at the linkspan to off load her vehicles; her foot passengers have already disembarked from further up the pier. She begins to load for Colonsay and Islay, and, if anyone is daft enough, Kennacraig as well.

We have taken this route a few times before, of course; the last time aboard *Isle of Arran*. Since the arrival of the new *Hebrides* at Uig the displaced *Hebridean Isles* is now an Islay vessel and this Wednesday trip is her only scheduled appearance at Oban during the course of a week. She is a great favourite of ours, and we are fair chuffed, not only to be sailing on her again, but sailing to somewhere different on her. Thus the need for the photography. It is moments like this, when the eye is screwed up against the viewfinder, that the absurdity of a hobby like this is most apparent. The photos and video clips will soon be catalogued, edited, filed away to join the thousands of similar snippets. What is it all for? Don't ask me, I haven't a clue, I just tag along with the others.

Far below me Ian has reappeared clutching a bag and Gibbie is nonchalantly watching the hustle and bustle on Oban's Railway Pier - which is particularly animated on a Wednesday afternoon.

Once aboard *Hebridean Isles* there seems a delay in departing. No one seems to be in any particular hurry but eventually we are off down the Sound of Kerrera - next stop Colonsay. We proceed very slowly at first. A group of multicoloured, cagoule-clad children in canoes are waving up to us frenetically from their position on the edge of a little rocky islet far below us. The ship must seem huge as it creeps past them.

Once past the ferry slipway on Kerrera we speed up. Those huge dark clouds are still above us but away to the south there is clear blue sky - and that, of course, is where we are heading. I head downstairs to the 'quiet' lounge for forty winks and when I emerge forty winks later we are in a different world. The cloud has been left behind in Oban and the warm rays of the sun are bathing the deck. Ian is leaning against the rail on the upper deck soaking up the sunshine, so I join him. The two of us bask there for what seems like ages as the ship gently pushes through the light waves. There is no sign of Gibbie - we believe he is still comatose downstairs. In fact by the time we are swinging to starboard towards Colonsay's Scalasaig Pier there is still no sign of him. Did he definitely come aboard? Ian and I toss a coin to decide who should seek him and wake him. Ian wins so off I go.

"Must have been the Caol Ila last night," he mutters when I find him in the lounge. "Where are we?"

"Kennacraig."

The ship is fifteen minutes late in arriving at Scalasaig and I dare to step ashore for a very quick photograph. Immediately I move off down the pier I am hailed back and thoroughly admonished by an elderly chap in a peaked cap for not having dunked my feet in a bucket of disinfectant; foot and mouth disease has still not burned itself out.

The next leg is to Port Askaig on Islay and the ship, still running late, is busy with day-trippers returning to Islay or the mainland. Colonsay is still only attainable as a destination for a day-trip on Wednesdays. In fact the island is now served three times a week by three different ships: *Hebridean Isles* on Wednesdays, *Isle of Mull* on Fridays and *Clansman* on Sundays. We have dinner on board watching the chiseled, grey coast of Jura slipping slowly past on the port side as we head into the Sound of

Islay - that narrow strait of water that separates Islay from Jura.

Ian now chooses the moment to inform us that we will be greeted at Port Askaig by his sister-in-law, Shirley, and her husband, Louis. They are on a whisky-tasting holiday on Islay. Ian assures us they always spit it out.

We steam down the narrow turbulent channel, past the wreck of Wyre Majestic, whose hull is gradually being reclaimed by nature. Anyone waiting to disembark or embark at Port Askaig is in for a fright: *Hebridean Isles* breezes right past. The tidal flow going with the ship makes manoeuvring at the pier tricky, so the skipper takes the ship well down the channel before turning hard around to starboard and then pushing slowly back up to the pier. We have seen all this before, but this is the furthest we have seen a ship sail down the Sound. For anyone on the pier the ship sails clean out of sight. On board there are a few puzzled expressions, until it becomes apparent what is happening.

We creep up to the pier, and sure enough there are Shirley and Louis waiting for us. Shirley is waving a copy of "Away with the Ferries".

A pleasant evening follows around a table in the busy dining room of the Port Askaig Hotel. Shirley and Louis have booked a table for dinner, for all five of us! Over our second dinner of the day (our culinary advisor Ian got it wrong!) Gibbie is accused, not for the first time, of not eating his greens. He is quick to respond, "I do eat my greens - I had asparagus last night."

Louis' response is quicker. "Do you know that asparagus makes your wee-wee smell strange?"

Ian and Gibbie look at me - and silence falls over the table.

Shirley and Louis have picked a good week to come to Islay for another reason. The distillery at Bruichladdich has just re-opened. Closed since 1994 the new manager is in our dining room with his extended family. Shirley passes up her copy of "Away with the Ferries" for him to sign. He looks underwhelmed! She and Louis had been at the opening ceremony at the distillery today and had - I'll be polite here - thoroughly enjoyed the hospitality.

We have a fine old blether with the owner of the hotel in the 'snug' after our meal. The tourist season has been slow due to the restrictions from Foot and Mouth Disease, but is now picking up (especially since Shirley and Louis arrived). The malt whisky industry is also looking prosperous - the island's distilleries are now firing on all cylinders - just like Shirley and Louis!

Day Five - *Gigha Fright*

I wake wondering whether we have ever had a 'Day Five' before. A subdued breakfast. The swathes of mist that are rolling over the rounded tops of the Paps of Jura sum up our mood. Suddenly our waitress bursts forth into the dining room and everything changes. She is bright and breezy, and intent on telling us about her sore finger.

The middle finger of her left hand is sporting a fresh bandage. She cut it badly on a saw yesterday while pruning a tree in her garden and describes the injury and subsequent treatment in glorious technicolour detail. All this while depositing my full breakfast in front of me. I look at the sausage and now cannot face it.

I drive to Port Ellen along the quieter road and we are in time to film *Hebridean Isles* arriving. She had returned to the mainland last night and was now putting in an appearance at Islay's other pier.

There is much deliberation by the crew and we cannot figure out why. Our car, and most of the others, are loaded but there seems to be much hanging around. Then an oil tanker appears and much shuffling has to take place in order to accommodate it at the open end of the car deck. Then we are off to Kennacraig, West Loch Tarbert, two and a half hours away, our fifth port of call aboard *Hebridean Isles*.

Out on deck, under a sky which cannot quite make up its mind on what to do next. We discover a potential problem with the ship. Steam is issuing forth from a U- shaped pipe. Something looks as though it is boiling over. Two of the crew are looking at it.

"BING BONG!" The tannoy crackles into life.

"Here we go," says Gibbie in his knowledgeable engineer's voice. "Problems with the pipes - abandon ship."

"BING BONG - this is the last call for breakfast!" So that's it - the boiled eggs are ready.

We now have to discuss exactly what we are going to do when we get to the other side - in other words how are we going to kill time before we go home. I have had an idea (for once). We could spend some time on Gigha and also film *Hebridean Isles* sailing back down West Loch Tarbert, on her way back to Islay, from a favourite spot of ours half way down the loch. The timing would have to be accurate, for *Heb Isles* is still running 20 minutes late, and the timing of the ferry to Gigha is fairly tight.

Gibbie and I filmed *Lord of the Isles* from this 'favourite spot' a couple of years ago and we are hoping to add another set of photographs to our collections. Having disembarked at Kennacraig we immediately set off south. But we cannot find the road leading to our 'favourite spot'. Three times we drive around the little village of Clachaig trying to find the correct turn-off down to the little bay. We pass the same villager carrying her basket of shopping on all three occasions. Each time she gives us the same suspicious look as if she is trying to memorise our descriptions for 'Crimewatch'.

Eventually we find our road, but there is another problem. The spectre of Foot and Mouth Disease is present again - the road down to the shore is blocked. We are being firmly asked not to proceed - so we don't. However just a hundred metres back up the approach road we have a reasonably lofty view over the loch, and to our surprise there is *Hebridean Isles* sailing down within good range of our lenses. She has made up time and we still have time to make that Gigha ferry connection.

The number of cars parked at Tayinloan suggests that a lot of day-trippers are on the island. It is a breezy crossing on *Loch Ranza*, the third of the original Loch class ferries of the trip. At the Gigha side a fire-engine and half a dozen other vehicles are waiting to cross back to the mainland. We are in our car, as we intend driving the length of the island in the short time available to us - all five miles of it. But lunch is first.

At the hotel over a very fine bowl of broth we enquire about the visit of the fire-engine.

"Shed fire." The barman is economical with words.

"Wouldn't it have burned down by the time the fire-engine got over from the mainland?" I felt it was an obvious question.

"It did."

It transpires that Gigha's very own fire station will open in a few days. It will save the ferry being called out in emergency. Gigha's sheds are now safe.

We drive down to the south of the island, where the fairly substantial pier is located. Not much activity here, which prompts Gibbie to break with Island Hopping tradition and phone his wife Janette from the phone-box. As this may be a long and intimate call Ian and I decide to move as far away as possible. We take a stroll along the beach. When we return ten minutes later Gibbie looks perturbed. The first question Janette asked him was "I hope you have shaved?" It looks as though the Pugwash look may not have much longer to go.

We now drive up to the north of the island - there is only one road. The island looks very green and grassy, with the farms, gardens, fields and the golf course fashioned around the low vegetation, leaving neat untouched patches of it. The fields are full of Friesians - good to see after the weeks of dark days for farmers.

As we pass the road which leads down to the ferry slip Ian looks at his watch. "Shouldn't we just head down, our ferry leaves in fifteen minutes?"

"No rush," I confidently assure him. "Ferry won't be busy, we can drive on a couple of miles more." So we carry on. At Tarbert Farm there seems little else to see so turn the car back and drive down to the slipway with just four minutes to spare. "Boy you cut it fine sometimes," says Ian without the slightest indication of admiration.

"Oh I'm just confident with the planning," I add. "The ferry will be half empty . . ."

The ferry comes into view and it is full. It is positively brimming with cars. "Where did they all come from?" I'm in big trouble. If we miss this ferry the rest of the day will fall into disarray.

When we count the cars crammed onto *Loch Ranza* there are eleven. I know she holds twelve. Fortunately so do the crew (well they should). The left-hand row is moved up a little at a time and there is just enough room for us to squeeze on at the end. On the way back across I keep my distance from the others. Our next destination is the Tarbert-Portavadie ferry.

Gibbie drives off onto mainland Kintyre. "Now Stuart, we're going to drive straight to Tarbert for our next sailing - no detours."

"Quite right, Gibbie, exactly my thoughts."

We sail out from Tarbert at 17.15 aboard Isle of Cumbrae - our first time aboard her on this route. It is incredibly gloomy around us - almost like a fog. Perhaps the elements realise that our trip is nearly over for another year. A handful of yachts are silently heading for Tarbert, their sails limp. The wind has certainly been acting strangely today. Leaving Islay this morning it was from the north, on Gigha from the west and now what breeze there is is issuing from the south.

We drive onto the Cowal peninsula at Portavadie at 17.39 and head immediately for Dunoon. There we find we have missed the extra peak hour sailing by five minutes. Shame as it was performed by *Pioneer*. Instead we board a practically empty *Juno*. I for one am glad it is empty for Gibbie insists in filming the Annual Toast is the upper saloon and I feel a touch conspicuous. In front of a camera there is the usual analysis. Shame about missing out on *Lochnevis*.

Ian remarks that the ferries seem busier this year, but we are sailing a week later than usual. Perhaps this is why we almost never got off Gigha. Ian has noticed another interesting statistic. Prior to this year's trip he claims we could count the number of times we have had dinner with wine in a proper restaurant on the fingers of one hand. After this trip we might have to use our toes as well. Especially if we continue to have two dinners each night.

Ideas are aired for next year. Two CalMac ships have still not been sailed upon - *Lochnevis* and *Clansman*. Both of these have been missed out due to breakdowns. None of us have broken down yet - although if we hadn't got that ferry out of Gigha!

WAVERELY, Mallaig

Aboard WAVERELY, off Ardnamurchan

HEBRIDEAN ISLES, LORD OF THE ISLES, Oban

Ian and Stuart Lochboisdale, 2008
Photographing on Eriskay, 2008

2002 Paddling in Hebridean Waters

The Plan

AT THE END OF ISLAND HOP 2001 there was only one micro seed of a suggestion from which to nurture any kind of plan for the 2002 trip, apart from the fact that we had still never sailed on *Clansman*. I don't know who it came from but one of us said something like: "Isn't it time we used *Waverley* in Hebridean waters?"

When several months later *Waverley* Excursions announced that the paddler would have an extended Hebridean season in May 2002 then that seed grew into a wonderfully portentous moment of inspiration.

For months rumour and uncertainty surrounded exactly what *Waverley* would be doing, but eventually a sailing timetable was published, and the tactician buried his head in it for a full week to extrapolate the best cruises to suit our extravagant and fastidious needs.

"It isn't all about the *Waverley* you know," Gibbie warned with pointing finger.

Indeed not. There are still two CalMac ships which we have not sailed on, *Clansman* and Lochnevis. This apparent omission is not due to any fault on our part, as you will know if you have been paying attention to the previous pages. This year we surely must go for them, and what better vehicle for linking their respective territories than *Waverley*. In short we would use the paddle-steamer as a link between sailings out of Mallaig (by *Lochnevis*) and out of Oban (by *Clansman*).

No scheduled sailings now exist between these ports. But with *Waverley* sailing between them - once in a northerly direction, and a few days later in a southerly direction - we could abandon the overland route, choose one of her cruises and in true Island Hopping spirit sail all the way from Skye to Oban.

Everyone was delighted - well the three of us were delighted! Another unique Island Hop had truly sprouted from that initial seed.

The plan was very simple. We would catch the train from Glasgow to Mallaig, and the following day sail to the 'Small Isles' aboard Lochnevis. The next day again would be *Waverley* Day, and we would take a whole day excursion on her, that would eventually see us arrive in Tobermory on Mull. Down to Oban on *Waverley* the next day and hence a trip on *Clansman* out to one of our favourite islands - Barra. If none of the aforementioned vessels broke down then it could be a wonderful Island Hop.

Day One - *Positioning Day*

Uniquely, Island Hop 2002 begins in my surgery. Drills are poised in mid air on several occasions this morning as the deadline for my departure at 11.30 nears. By 10.30 the queue is enlarging - my practice manager Diane is cramming them in with gay abandon. The tension is building. Not in my patients, you understand - they are their usual calm selves, but in me. The whole concept of this year's trip has had me on tenterhooks for days. Two new ships, *Waverley*, trains instead of cars. Surely this was the year when something would go wrong and ruin our plans before we get started? Thirteen previous Island Hops has bred a degree of paranoia into me, and I suspect the others as well.

The queue does not seem to be diminishing and my dental nurse, Lauryn, is not helping my nerves. "Don't think you're going to make it in time!"

But as departure time nears everything seems fine yet again. Mrs. Smith gets her new dentures fitted in record time and I'm out the door and into a taxi at 11.30 before she can figure out which is her upper and which her lower. I had promised Gibbie and Ian a pick up at Gibbie's house at 11.40, and at 11.40 on the dot the taxi and me are there. They don't turn a hair! With a casual nonchalance, which borders on foolhardy trust, they accept my time keeping and we're off to Queen Street Station.

Talking of hair, Gibbie's beard, cultivated during last year's trip, is surprisingly still there. Strangely it is a two-tone mix of dark brown and white, as if he has a badger stuck to the lower half of his face.

Once on the train it emerges that I was not the only one suffering from pre-Minch tension about our trip (PMT to experienced Island Hoppers). Gibbie has had a bit of a fright. As his hand was upon the door handle on his way out of the house the telephone rang. On answering his heart sank as his elderly aunt reported her latest catastrophe, which demanded his instant attention. Gibbie retorted with considerable angst, "What! You've *knocked* yourself out?" Panic is quickly followed by relief and an escape route. "Oh you've *locked* yourself out. Here's my brother's phone number, I'm not in."

Our train pulls away up out of Queen Street Station at the start of a five hour train ride to Mallaig. Today is a 'positioning day' for us. We will not actually see a ship until tomorrow morning but need to be up in Mallaig tonight. My wife tried to argue that we were sneaking away for an extra day, but I tried hard to persuade her that this was a vital day.

Ian, our nutritional advisor and part-time archivist - although he can never remember one year's trip from the next - informs us that we have not taken a train on an Island Hop since 1995, seven trips ago. He seems so certain that he must be correct.

We've not reached Springburn when an argument breaks out between Ian and Gibbie. It starts with gauge sizes and progresses to the allegiance

70

of the long gone St. Enoch's Station in Glasgow. Ian firmly believes it was affiliated with the LMS Railway. Gibbie, seemingly assured, says it was the North British Railway. Being much younger I can only referee on this one and after a yellow card Ian seems to be losing every argument.

Climbing above Loch Long the weak sunshine casts a gloomy glow and the grey naval boats silhouetted on its still waters combine to give an achromatic wash to the whole scene. The loch divides into the twin fingers of Loch Long and Loch Goil, and just beyond a black and white police launch sits motionless in the middle of the water guarding the naval base of Coulport from straying fishermen and hippie protesters. Coming over the head of Loch Long we feel like we are on an aircraft instead of a train due to the height of the track here. Soon the railway swings over to the Loch Lomond side, winding high above the water. The refreshment cart comes around. Tea is being rationed. There's plenty of it, but at £1.35 a cup it is worth considering whether we should invest in one each.

Gibbie and Ian have calmed down and are now onto the annual review of their pensions. As this doesn't affect me I just sit and tacitly look out of the window. Meanwhile, the middle-aged couple across the centre aisle from us exchange a few words. It's the first time they've spoken to each other since we left Glasgow, an hour and a half ago. The diesel engine drones on. At Crianlarich Station we do the splits - the train that is. The front half sets off for Oban, and then our half revs up ready for the next stretch towards Mallaig. Wouldn't it be funny if Gibbie, who is off the train having a puff, got back on at the wrong end!

On again. The further north we go the better the weather and the rails are singing in optimism. Either that or it's the same old problem with the wheel flanges again. I close my eyes to the world outside of the speeding train and turn my mind inwards to what we are actually doing, sitting here speeding northwards and westwards yet again. Yes it really is Island Hopping time again. By now, as we embark on the start of another adventure, we feel increasingly that we are the characters of the whole Island Hopping story, playing out our respective roles in yet another chapter, in the same arena. The script is merely pencilled in and the plot will unravel over the next four days. What we encounter will dictate the script for us, and the ships and islands we encounter will turn from ideas and plans into the next episode of Island Hopping tales. I look up and the reality is that Gibbie has his face stuck in the *Daily Telegraph* and Ian is trying for the sixth time to open his enormous map of Scotland at the correct bit.

Around us trees are having a serious think about bursting into foliage despite several pockets of snow lying isolated on the highest mountain gullies. Away to our left the peaks of Glen Coe look as moody as ever, but to our right Schiehallion is highlighted by the sun. Visibility is slowly improving and an ever more confident sun is changing the moorland around us into harmonising shades of sepia and ochre.

71

At Corrour Station, on Rannoch Moor, the sign reads 1347 feet above sea level. But as it's lying on its side on the ground we take that to mean 1345 feet above sea level.

At Spean Bridge Station an elderly gran is the only disembarking passenger. She has been queuing by herself to be first off for ten minutes. She alights at the front and her grandchildren are there to meet her at the rear. There is a happy reunion somewhere in the middle of the platform.

Just a few miles further on, at Fort William, we get off to stretch our legs. We have about fifteen minutes here before we reverse back out on the last leg to Mallaig. A sleeper train sits at the other platform, a huge class 37 diesel locomotive, in EWS colours, growls unattended at the front.

Along the glittering shores of Loch Eil the train's horn is giving a virtuoso performance to the sheep that stray too close to the line - as they do. The wheels are playing along with a rattling that is reminiscent of a Cozy Powell record.

Before the really glorious scenery begins I settle down to read the instruction manual of my new Sony camcorder - all 215 pages of it. I'm lost by page five and that's only the 'Table of Contents'. In fact it's the 'Table of Contents' for the 'Table of Contents'. Then I discover it's the section written in Russian that I'm trying to decipher. So, that means there's only 107 pages to go.

The rail noises have changed from Cozy Powell to a kettledrum as we race down the coastal plain into Mallaig. The guard makes a rare announcement, but it is incomprehensible. We cannot make out if he is using English or Gaelic, or perhaps Russian for that matter.

Exactly five hours after leaving Queen Street Station we step onto the platform at Mallaig. After checking in to our hotel, which has the letters of its name board missing or rearranged in Fawlty Towers style, we head for the harbour to look for signs that tomorrow's ship Lochnevis is not sick or broken down. Last year's disappointment with her has left Ian, in particular, in a mildly neurotic state.

A few fishing boats are sitting in the basin of the harbour but of greater interest is the presence of the very healthy looking *Lord of the Isles* and Lochnevis. They look as though they are fully functional and looking forward to our company tomorrow. Ian is not so sure and steps closer for a better look. But what's this? What has he spotted? He gestures at one of the bridge windows.

"There you are, look! That window is broken and has been temporarily repaired with a bin bag. She can't sail in that state!"

"No Ian, the window is fine, there is a blind on the inside of the glass fluttering with the air stream from the air-conditioning unit. It's you that's got a pane loose." I have to be blunt sometimes.

Over excellent scallops and lemon sole we make nice comforting fishy noises about tomorrow's weather forecast and the exciting prospect of a visit to Muck.

Day Two - *Thunderbirds Are Go!*

Down at the harbour early, *Lochnevis* is definitely sailing. We will take her on a non-landing cruise to Eigg, Muck and back to Eigg again. When I say 'non-landing' what I mean is that everyone else will be landing on one of those islands except the three of us and the crew. I've never set a foot on Muck but maybe we will be able to step ashore briefly. The harbour is busy. Two seals are snorting disrespectfully at us out in the middle of the basin as they watch the morning ablutions of several fishing boats preparing for a day's work.

Lochnevis is also being made ready. A small radio controlled, hydraulic crane on her starboard side is hoisting various sacks and bags onto the car deck. A crewman beckons us aboard. It was built by the Ailsa yard at Troon in 2000 to replace the smaller *Lochmor*, on which we have sailed in 1990 and 1996. When the older ship left, CalMac waved goodbye to their last passenger-only vessel, for *Lochnevis* can take up to fourteen cars.

Looking around *Lochnevis* we are all suitably impressed. There are two large, and nicely upholstered lounges, on two different decks, one also serving as a cafeteria. There is a decent area of deck seating, and a view over the bow from a small area of forward deck - much to Gibbie's joy. Having said all that she is a rather strange looking ship. The lofty glass capsule that serves as her bridge looks like an airport control tower. Her rear ramp is enormous and one gets an excellent view of it from the Observation Lounge where all the windows face aft. And there is a single funnel, which is positioned on the starboard side. She certainly leaves an impression on Gibbie, and him on her, for within a minute of stepping aboard his hands have managed to find a patch of wet red paint. Now he is walking about the deck like Lady Macbeth.

We sail out of Mallaig on time with the grand total of fifteen passengers aboard. Out past the breakwater we are heading firstly for Eigg, which can be seen slumbering on the horizon like some kind of strange, dorsal-finned sea creature. The morning is bright with patchy sunshine and excellent visibility. A slight breeze from the south-west is rippling the surface of an ultramarine sea. Following a trail of red paint I find Gibbie standing at the front, overlooking the bow and already in deep conversation with a chap who is returning to his home on the island of Muck. He tells us about the lack of readiness of the slipway construction on the two islands. This will mean that tenders will be used today to bring passengers between ship and shore. Had the slipways been ready we could have at least stepped ashore. (We could of course get off at Eigg and pick the ship up again on her return but had unanimously agreed that the cruise on a 'new' vessel was more desirable).

As Eigg nears the 'dorsal fin' transforms into the famous Sgurr, the giant plug of volcanic rock which dominates the southern end of the island.

The tender can be seen leaving the jetty and making its way towards us. We stop, without anchoring, well out in the bay. The tender is *Laig Bay* and she comes along our starboard side. Everything from a crate of lager to a mattress is loaded onto her via a door level with the car deck. The passengers then follow. It is all performed safely, efficiently and without fuss, and soon our engines are revving again as we turn south towards Eigg's wee sister, Muck.

Several rafts of manx shearwaters, fifty at a time, are fluttering around on either side of the ship. Muck looks low and rocky ahead of us. We approach its southern shore. About twenty-five people live here, mostly living off the land. The chap Gibbie was talking to tells us there are seven children at the school . . . but there is another family arriving he adds with more than a hint of optimism.

A concrete pier suddenly materialises from behind a rocky bluff. Perhaps we are going to tie up after all? But no, there is the tender sending up a sizeable bow wave, as she scoots across towards us. On her bow is her name - *Wave* - so we do!

Through binoculars I get a disappointingly distant view of the buildings around the jetty. That is as close as we are going to get. Muck, and its looming neighbour Rum, will remain for the time being the only two inhabited Hebridean islands that I have never set foot on.

Back towards Eigg, we seem to have plenty of time on our hands and the ship has noticeably cut speed. But rather than sit back and relax there is a bustle of activity among the crew. I ask Alistair, the young second officer, what is happening.

"We're going to have a 'man-overboard' drill - any volunteers?" Strangely enough both Ian and I look simultaneously at Gibbie.

Alistair and two of his colleagues head off to change into survival suits and emerge a few minutes later like the Tracy Brothers from Thunderbirds. Wearing bright orange suits, huge boots and large white motorcycle helmets (well they look like motorcycle helmets) they climb up onto the gantry that supports the inflatable fast-rescue craft (FRC). Once aboard the craft is lowered into the sea by a series of cables. 'Supermarionation' Calmac style. Once on the water the anchoring line is relaxed, the engine started and the five metre long, bright orange craft races across the sea like a speedboat that's just been 'Tangoed'. It looks great fun and it's quite a spectacle.

For the next half hour, as we gaze lazily over the ship's rail, the FRC speeds this way and that, sometimes vanishing behind a rocky island and then suddenly reappearing again, its crew hanging on tightly and obviously thoroughly enjoying their energetic lunch break. Perhaps they spend every lunchtime doing this!

Eventually, because they've presumably found their 'man overboard', or because they are running low on fuel, the FRC is brought back alongside *Lochnevis* in a series of gradual stages, as if it is reluctant to come home. It is hooked up and hoisted back onto its cradle. "Come in Thunderbird Four your time is up."

Afterwards, following our second visit from *Laig Bay*, and as we head back to Mallaig, I chat to Alistair. He has been with CalMac for only two weeks and thoroughly enjoys his new position - especially the lunch breaks. I ask if he can organise a visit to the bridge. After checking he returns apologetically; the New York terrorist attack of 11 September 2001 has had a knock-on effect which will change access for ever.

Back at Mallaig *Lord of the Isles* is sweeping out majestically from the harbour, giving us a superb photo opportunity. She will return soon to take us over to Skye. Once back ashore we hang around the harbour having a final look at Lochnevis which is tied up now for the rest of the day. Seems a bit of a waste to have her day over by half past three. Also seems a bit of a waste having such a fine ship as *Lord of the Isles* spending her summer shuttling back and forth on the twenty minute crossing between Mallaig and Armadale. I'm sure she misses her Western Isles jaunts. Things may be about to change, however. A new vessel is being constructed for the Mallaig-Armadale route and *Lord of the Isles* may be heading back to her rightful home at Oban. Let's hope so.

As we stand around, taking a few video shots for the annual cinematic epic, Ian looks up and with a commendably casual aside mutters, "Here comes the *Waverley*."

This is a complete surprise to us; we hadn't realised she was due to pop in to Mallaig this afternoon. She is on a cruise from Skye to Kyle, Mallaig and Loch Nevis, and this is her calling in on her return before heading back up the Sound of Sleat. According to the timetable she is now heading for Broadford, which is exactly where we are heading. We look at each other for the tell-tale eye-wink which means "let's take her instead of *Lord of the Isles*". But it is not there. We sensibly decide to stick to the game plan even though we don't know how we're going to get from Armadale to Broadford. Why take the easy route when there is a more difficult and complex alternative?

Waverley's unexpected arrival sends all three of us into a frenzy of activity and we depart to different points of the harbour from which to photograph and watch the paddler's arrival and subsequent departure. We had not expected to get our first sight of her until tomorrow, so an unexpected photo opportunity, such as this, is exciting and not an event to be missed. Every year there is always some surprise in store for us, usually an overlooked shipping movement which takes us by surprise and adds to the theatre of the occasion.

A good sized crowd gets off *Waverley*. There are smiles and cameras and red, black and white woolly hats all around. Mallaig harbour is buzzing in the warm afternoon sunshine as passengers wander around, swapping stories of where they've been, where they're going and where to get the best photograph. It is all very bewildering and disorientating to find ourselves caught up in the melee and surrounded by so many people who, unsettlingly, are exactly like us.

With three phlegmatic blasts on her whistle, which sends plumes of snow white steam billowing skywards, the steamer backs out of Mallaig and well out into the open waters before turning her bow northwards up the Sound of Sleat towards Kyle of Lochalsh. Shortly after *Lord of the Isles* appears at the breakwater entrance and Mallaig has seen the arrival of three ships within an hour.

We board *Lord of the Isles* for what is likely to be the last sailing for us aboard her on this route. Today she fairly races across the sound to Armadale on Skye and we relax in the bar to discuss the next leg of the trip. "So when does the bus leave from Armadale to Broadford?" enquires Ian innocently enough.

"Eh, there is no bus, it's a lift or a taxi," I mumble.

Ian and Gibbie give me that 'here we go again' look that has been honed over the years from well practised expressions of dismay from the numerous occasions when things don't seem to have been thought out in advance. "No bus?"

"No bus"

Armadale arrives and we find ourselves queuing on the wrong deck, waiting to disembark. When we eventually realise Ian finally flips. "There's no gangway, we're on the wrong deck, there's no bus, we didn't even know the *Waverley* was coming in to Mallaig." With an air of despair, "the whole trip's falling apart!" A quick turn of the head and a wink reassure me that his anguish is pretence.

Ashore at Armadale it is Ian who manages to procure a lift from a *Waverley* enthusiast on the pier who is heading up to Broadford to photograph her arrival. And then a bus appears. So we have the choice - now that's what I call planning!

Jack speedily conveys us the fifteen miles to Broadford, and we arrive in nice time for another photo of *Waverley*. We will be joining her here in the morning, but for now we head back down the road a few hundred metres to our hotel, where Gibbie deals with the necessary paperwork at the reception desk.

"We have a triple room reserved for you sir," says the receptionist without expression.

"Oh - so it's three-in-a-bed tonight chaps!" bellows Gibbie to the astonishment of the elderly couple sitting within earshot. (He is joking, you realise!) Tonight we have a special meeting, over dinner, arranged by Gibbie. Two of his German friends are also in Broadford and he has arranged a get-together for all of us in the hotel lounge, commencing at 19.30, and with a finishing time dependent on how keen they are on whisky. Let's hope they speak English. My German is confined to the names of Bundesliga football teams.

Hans senior and Hans junior are father and son. Their reason for visiting Scotland is explained by the younger. He is a ship and steam enthusiast and with *Waverley* he can indulge in both passions. But he cannot come on our trip tomorrow. He and his Dad are off on a fifteen mile walk. "We like walking also."

With their good English, and a fair bit of head nodding and shaking, we manage to pass a pleasant evening. They both order 'haggis, neeps and tatties' from the supper menu and when it arrives Hans senior is clearly puzzled by the unfamiliar orange mash on his plate. "Gibbie, what is this please?"

"Swede," says Gibbie. "Turnip," says Ian. "Neeps," says I. All simultaneously. It takes a good few minutes to unscramble the confusion on that one.

Both Hans like their malts, with a dash of water. Much head nodding at the end of a pleasant evening when we part company. In fact in every sense of the expression it has been 'Hans across the water'.

Up in our room Gibbie sets about trying to set an alarm clock. God help him if it goes off at 4 am. Ian has fallen silent.

"Is that you sleeping already, Ian?" I ask, hardly expecting an answer.

"No I'm just closing my eyes before Gibbie takes his trousers off."

Day Three - *Waverley Day*

Wake to pitter-pattering rain on the outside of the window. I throw back the curtains a touch despondently, and find the tentacles of a monkey-puzzle tree trying to reach inside. We descend to a vacuous dining-room where the staff are conspicuous by their absence. We quickly gather that we have not been expected, but after dividing our forces one of us finds a couple of pale-faced waiters lurking in a corner. It transpires that at 07.15 a bus party cleaned the kitchen out of all provisions, and the staff out of all their energy. And we've been overlooked. I hope the bus party was actually staying at the hotel. Perhaps they were just driving past and fancied a breakfast! Our excuse of a breakfast is hastily assembled - bacon, egg and sausage served on a saucer, and orange juice in an eyeglass. It all just goes towards reinforcing my opinion of some of the hotels on Skye.

Broadford has a sleepy, only half awake look about it this morning. A bit like us. The pier is a pleasant stroll down from the hotel and already people are beginning to gather for the arrival of today's one and only ship, *Waverley*. This will be our first sail aboard her on Hebridean waters, and a long sail it will be.

Our route will take us from Broadford up to Portree, and then on a cruise up to the north-eastern corner of Skye towards Staffin. Retracing our route will bring us back to Broadford, and then across to the mainland pier of Kyle of Lochalsh, and on down the Sound of Sleat. Around

Ardnamurchan into the Sound of Mull and finally into Tobermory. All this will take about twelve hours, covering some 140 miles (land miles), and will provide us with a valuable and unique link between Skye and Mull. It is a wonderful route, but unfortunately nobody has told the weather, which in contrast to our mood, is dull, grey and bored looking.

Waverley can be seen making her way across from Kyle. A crowd of almost 100 has gathered on the stone jetty and there is a general air of anticipation. Cameras click and enthusiasts swap notes on 'f' numbers, exposure settings and vantage points.

"No not there - go round the other side where the light's better."

"I'm 250 at f 8, what are you?"

"Mine's 128 mm, are you wide-angled?"

"No, it's just the way I walk."

As the ship approaches and ropes are hurled across to eagerly waiting hands I suddenly get a strange disorientating feeling of being usurped. This is our Island Hop - we normally say these kind of things to each other. These people are intruding on our private trip. Has the sanctity of our annual sojourn to the isles been desecrated? But no. These people around us are even bigger shipping enthusiasts than we are. It is us who are intruding on their cruise. Gibbie's words from the planning stage return to me. "Remember what Island Hopping is all about, it's about travelling, not just about the *Waverley* sail". Of course he is correct and today's cruise is just another link in our route.

We leave Broadford at 10.45 and onto an uninteresting sea. We sprint anticlockwise around the circular island of Scalpay. Its eastern coast is low and lumpy and great swathes of mist are rising from its slopes, like steam. Then on into the Sound of *Raasay* with the Red Cuillins away to our left looking distinctly extraterrestrial, as if out of place. The *Raasay* ferry *Loch Striven* is just departing Sconser on the Skye side as we hug close in to Raasay Pier, which, of course, we visited last year.

Downstairs for a heat, and a roll and sausage - a must on every *Waverley* trip.

Ian is intrigued by the improvements made to the ship since his last trip aboard her, three years ago. She was partly rebuilt at Great Yarmouth in the winter of 1999-2000 with the assistance of Lottery cash, and has just been awarded another £3m to complete her reincarnation as a 1940s steamer. She now looks pretty close to what she must have looked like when first built in 1947. The white of her hull has been toned down and her deckhouses scumbled in a teak finish. To me the only negative aspect of her partial rebuild is the mandatory construction of an escape hatch which rather spoils the spaciousness of the rear deck and of the restaurant one deck below.

Soon we are turning into Portree. The scenery around us is becoming more dramatic and is closing in about us as we paddle into this most sheltered of harbours. This is another pier we have never sailed to before.

On the pier to meet us are the bubbling, energetic contents of Portree Primary School. They, their lunch-boxes and their teachers come aboard for the two hour sail up to Staffin and swell the number aboard the ship to a healthy 540. A school lesson with a difference, they are going to get a view of their island from the decks of a paddle-steamer for the first time. So are we, but we are more subdued and making less noise about it.

We round the northern point of Portree Loch and the bow turns northwards into a gentle swell which sends a ripple of delight through the crowded decks. Everyone seems to be up on the top deck as we sail past the precipitous cliffs which run almost the entire length of the north-eastern coast of Skye. Yet another "Prince Charles' Cave" is pointed out to us - what a prodigious troglodyte he was. A bit further on the "Old Man of Storr" comes into view, standing erect like a giant - well like a giant bit of rock!

It is still overcast and dull and the sea is the colour of pencil lead but everyone aboard is having the time of their lives. Apart from the steamer enthusiasts, Island Hoppers and schoolchildren, there are a good number of Skye people aboard, watching the passing rock scenery in fascination at seeing familiar landmarks from the sea instead of the road. The old boy beside me is so engrossed he is completely unaware of the enormous dreep at the end of his nose.

Around us the well behaved children are chattering away in English with their teacher giving them the odd word of chastisement in Gaelic.

Gibbie is behaving himself also - at least we hope he is. Ian and I haven't actually seen him for the last hour. That's the thing about *Waverley*, so many bits are worth visiting that one can vanish amongst the crowd for ages enjoying one's own bit of the ship. After a quick search we find him at the blunt end and drag him unceremoniously up to the sharp end where the view is even better. At Kilt Rock the waterfall issues vertically 130 metres from a small stream above and provides the most dramatic climax to a scene already studded with stupendous highlights. Atop the cliff a crowd of people are watching our passing in astonishment. They look like LS Lowry creations from our perspective. Imagine their surprise - if they had not known of *Waverley*'s cruise in advance - to see a paddle-steamer splash her way past so far below them. The gulls and guillemots are certainly surprised. From sitting indolently on the surface of the water ahead of the ship they are suddenly flung into near panic as our bow nears. They clearly haven't seen a paddle-steamer for years either.

Staffin Island is ahead of us, and we turn anticlockwise off its northern tip in an arc around Staffin Bay. We cannot completely circumnavigate the island as the narrows between it and the mainland of Skye are too narrow!

Waverley is running half an hour late back to Portree - giving the locals a good run for their money. I descend to the toilets with my video camera - there is an excellent forward view of the bow breaking the water from the portholes there. A brief explanation to the occupants of the gent's toilets as to why I am waving a camera around is met with preoccupied approval. When I am finished two chaps arrive to use the facilities. One is short the other tall.

"Nice toilets eh Jim?" The short one says.

"Aye, if you were any taller Andy you'd be able to see out of the porthole."

"If I was any taller Jim I'd be able to pee out the porthole!"

Back upstairs a couple of hundred school kids are preparing to disembark - most of them red-lipped from oversized *Waverley* lollipops. I ask one lad if the entire school is aboard. "No, some are going to Glasgow for the day instead," he replies.

"Which is best?" I probe. "*Waverley* or Glasgow?"

"Glasgow," he replies without hesitation, "in Glasgow you could get to go on the *Waverley* every day."

By the time we take a rather squinty reverse out of Portree, which requires a five-point-turn to put right, we are an hour late, but those of us still aboard are not complaining. Disappointingly, however, we are being enveloped in misty rain. For the school party their day is over but we still have five hours paddling to go and it would be nice if the sun were to shine. It doesn't look promising.

Back at Broadford Pier the bow heaving-line is deftly caught by an enthusiastic border collie - it's difficult getting pier hands these days! The ship practically empties here and consequently, for those that remain, takes on the aura of a private yacht. It is very wet up on top now and so we descend to the "launderette".

This is the name we have given to the lower bar where the portholes are on the waterline and are washed by the wake from the paddles. The engine rhythm seems faster as the engineer slides the throttle lever forward a few more notches in an attempt to make up some time. It is obviously working for we have passed under the Skye Bridge before we realise it and soon pulling into Kyle of Lochalsh. And lo and behold there is the same border collie battling with his owner to be first to catch the heaving line again. It must have fairly ran across the bridge! All its efforts are not in vain, however, as a bottle of whisky is seen to change paws.

We have our dinner in *Waverley*'s restaurant as we sail down the Sound of Sleat for the first time since 1990 aboard *Lochmor*. Unlike that trip the mist and rain are blocking out the wonderful landscape which we know lies on either side of us.

When we eventually emerge from the Sound of Sleat, the horizon to the south and west is slowly clearing and I venture out on deck. Eigg and Muck lie away to our right and out on the open sea *Waverley* suddenly seems very lonely. With only about fifty passengers still aboard and only two others out on the top deck I stand and survey an empty ship upon an empty sea. She cuts magnificently, and yet purposefully through the water, heading now for Ardnamurchan Point.

As the clouds close in again I have that wonderful, wild experience of being at sea with no land visible in any direction. We could be anywhere. The sea is calm but the evening air is now chilly. I cannot drag myself indoors, however, as this is such a unique experience that I have to savour every moment. Away to the west the sun is again trying to fight its way through a gap in the clouds. Suddenly a beam of sunlight drops like a shaft of gold onto tiny Muck. The spotlight moves off the island and makes its way across the water towards the ship. Within a couple of minutes the red, white and black funnels are illuminated as if in celebration of her achievements today and I am briefly warmed by the rays. All around is battleship grey but *Waverley* seems aglow, and I appear to be the only person witnessing it. Then, as quick as it arrived, the spotlight passes across and heads off towards the mainland in search of another subject.

The tall lighthouse at Ardnamurchan appears to the left and we sail close in to the shore, cutting the corner into the Sound of Mull tightly. The ship seems to be going faster than ever as she and her crew anticipate a good rest at Tobermory.

We arrive at Tobermory fifteen minutes early, having left Kyle 30 minutes late. It has taken just three and a quarter hours between the two piers. Tobermory is very calm, with no wind, and the crew are disembarking from the ship almost as fast as we are. It has been a long day for them and there is the promise of a ceilidh in a local pub.

"Find out which pub," says Gibbie, "so we can choose another."

He's not in sociable mood - two hundred school children have exhausted him.

We check in to our usual Tobermory hotel, where we are now treated as regulars, and find solace in the Mishnish Bar, where I think we are also becoming regulars! Relaxing over a couple of beers we exchange views on a fascinating day of cruising, and watch out of the windows at various members of *Waverley*'s crew wandering about looking for a ceilidh.

We are sharing a room again tonight and soon Gibbie is making similar noises to *Waverley*'s great engines; but then I've not started myself yet.

Day Four - *Clansman at Last!*

Out early to capture a unique photograph. *Waverley* is moored at the pier with relief ferry *Raasay* alongside her. The sun is peeking through teasingly, and with patience I get my picture.

Raasay is not the usual Kilchoan-Tobermory ferry. That honour is normally given to *Loch Linnhe*, but she has been called away to the Clyde to help cover the breakdown of another ferry. *Raasay* is left to deputise for the *Linnhe*. She moves off for her first crossing of the day, leaving *Waverley* free for her 1000 sailing from Tobermory to Oban. We will be joining her for that, but not before a hearty breakfast.

The weather is definitely brightening this morning and there is a hint of excitement as we pull gently away from Tobermory Pier. This is our last leg on the route from Skye to Oban. The ship is fairly quiet - the big crowds of the day will be awaiting her arrival at Oban.

The ship slowly comes alive as we paddle southwards right down the centre of the Sound of Mull. Officers are straightening their ties and adjusting their jackets. Stores are being shifted about. Ropes coiled or uncoiled. The engines are gradually being warmed up to full speed. And the catering staff are shoving square-sliced sausage into pre-sliced morning rolls. Soon we are shoving the same rolls into our faces for our second breakfast. Island Hopping is hungry work.

An offer is made to us to visit bits of the engine room never visited before. We eagerly accept. Ken, the chief engineer, keeps a watchful eye on us as we descend in single file into the forbidden and exciting depths below the rotating cranks, oscillating valve gear and dancing big-ends. Two retired engineers, Gibbie and Ian, are literally in their element and point out condensers, feed-pumps and steam-pipes like excited schoolboys showing off their favourite football cards.

"There's the Weir's feed pump," points Gibbie.

"Yes, and there's the spanner you need to hit it with when it sticks," replies Ian.

These guys really know their stuff!

For me, I am just happy to wander about underneath, filming *Waverley*'s engines from an angle I've never seen before. Strangely enough all the moving bits seem smaller than they do from above but the crankshaft is being spun with such awesome power and harmony by the three pistons that I can only stand and gape, and inhale the hot vapours that ooze from all around. And in addition to the sights and smells there are the sounds. Swishes from escaping steam, thumps from the crank, oohs and aahs from the feed pumps and the rhythmic rumbling from the perpetual motion of the connecting rods. It's enough to make you want to be an engineer. Then I look at Ian and Gibbie and think - well maybe not.

The control levers are pointed out to us. Gibbie and Ian nod in complete understanding. I just nod. Above our heads a simple clock counter records each revolution, by means of an angled steel rod, with a metronomic click.

"How do you know how many revs per minute?" asks Gibbie.

"Count them with a stopwatch!"

Back upstairs to cool down and we spot a ship coming down the sound towards us. It turns out to be the new lighthouse tender *Pole Star* heading outwards to....well to a lighthouse we presume.

I meet a lady at the stern of *Waverley* who is trying to photograph the Lochaline - Fishnish ferry *Loch Fyne*, which is passing across our wake on her way to Mull. She asks me which ferry it is, so I tell her. I also tell her that if she wants to photograph a bigger and better ferry she should look over the port side in ten minutes as we are due to pass *Isle of Mull* also heading for Mull. As we pass the impressive Duart Castle a maverick *Isle of Mull* slips stealthily past on our starboard side, heading in to Craignure. As we sail past Lismore Light my wee lady is still leaning over the port rail and I don't have to courage to tell her that sometimes ships don't behave the way you expect them to.

We are heading in to the North Pier at Oban, another first for us, and there is a very large crowd waiting. Waiting for *Waverley*, not us. The paddle-steamer will be taking an afternoon cruise up Loch Linnhe to Loch Eil and it looks as though a few hundred will be partaking. We won't be among them, we don't have time as our ship to Barra, *Clansman*, leaves in about three hours. We hold a committee meeting on the decks of *Waverley* before she docks to discuss what we will do for three hours.

"Eat oysters," suggests Gibbie rather unhelpfully.

The wee lady peels herself off the port rail and comes up to me. "Your big ferry cannot be sailing today."

I make an instant decision just as the ship ties up. I'm going to try for a taxi and dash two miles to Dunollie Castle to film *Waverley* passing this well known photographic vantage point as she heads into Loch Linnhe. I won't have much time to get there as the ship will be loading up as soon as we disembark. Hopefully there might be a taxi lurking on the pier. Gibbie and Ian choose not to join me so we agree to meet up on the Railway Pier in about an hour.

There is indeed a prospecting cab on the North Pier and in a flash I am in it with bags and cameras flailing. As the car speeds off I realise with regret that I have not given *Waverley* a decent goodbye. What a wonderful day and a half of cruising she has given us. As far as the Island Hop is concerned she's got us from Skye to Oban as promised. Full marks.

I arrive breathless at the top of the hill, wishing I had left my bag with Gibbie. As I set up cameras as fast as I can on this lofty vantage point I can hear *Waverley*'s whistle echoing around the bay. I cannot yet see her, but she is there, around the bend, reversing outwards from the pier. Then she comes into view, her decks crowded with a new set of eager passengers. She passes, the beat of her paddles reverberating and almost filling the narrow band of water between Dunollie and Kerrera. Soon she passes from view but not earshot, then she has gone.

Two more vessels arriving into Oban keep me at this exclusive viewpoint longer. The little *Eigg*, with her ridiculous raised wheelhouse, is coming in from Lismore, and just behind her *Isle of Mull*. After all this activity I head into Oban, on foot. Half an hour later I find Gibbie surrounded by a bunch of seafood groupies at the oyster bar on the Railway Pier. His oyster slurping antics have attracted his usual audience, much to his delight.

"So how many have you had, Gibbie?"

"Seven," he replies, and then turning to an onlooker, "now I'll show you that just one more time." As he is obviously quite happy I leave him to it and head off to rendezvous with Ian in a favourite Oban watering house where we can enjoy a pint of real ale. I find him lurking about outside - great minds think alike.

The *Clansman* is a 'new' ship for us. This is remarkable considering she has been sailing out of Oban to Coll, Tiree, South Uist, Colonsay and Barra for four years now. But as you will have read, we should have been aboard her in 1999 out to Castlebay. She was out of service on that occasion and we sailed on *Lord of the Isles* instead. Today she is here, in the flesh, operating normally, and at 14.50 we depart Oban aboard her.

We follow Eigg out into the bay, and then turn at the narrows at the north end of Kerrera to head back up the same stretch of water we sailed down just three hours ago. That's Island Hopping for you. We explore our 'new' ship.

Comparing *Clansman* to *Waverley* is like comparing an elephant with a swan. Where the paddler has style, grace and aesthetic lines, *Clansman* has beam, bulk and block coefficients. We should not compare, however, for they are two very different ships from two very different ages. One now a working pleasure museum, the other a modern ferry, taking passengers to their destination in comfort.

Clansman is a sister of *Hebrides* and is consequently very similar, but by no means identical. Our previous criticism of *Hebrides* was that she has very little open deck space. Unfortunately *Clansman* has even less. Rather disappointing, but it seems that passengers want less contact with the natural elements now and prefer to be kidded into thinking that they are really in a floating hotel, which is conveying them to their destination with the minimum of fuss. Or do they? The passenger lounges of the ship are very nice and it is actually possible to sit down and see out of the windows. *Clansman* is obviously a fine member of the now very modern CalMac fleet.

We join the fresh-air seeking passengers on the cramped rear deck, just glad to have finally made it aboard. Looking around us it is clear that apart from *Clansman* and *Waverley* being totally different kind of ships, their respective passengers are also different - apart from us. The anoraks have gone, only to be replaced by cagoules as a different kind of outdoors-type heads for Barra.

Out into the open sea and the bulbous bow of *Clansman* is chucking up an impressive wave, although the sea is not by any means rough. I hang over the side to get a better view and get hit by spray despite being a hundred metres from the bow and ten metres above the sea. The sun is out, and by a trick of the light the sea on the port side looks deep blue, while on the starboard side it looks grey. A group of birdwatchers on the starboard side are getting excited by the sudden appearance of a single manx shearwater. Also on the deck are a couple of crew members who are touching up the paintwork on the port side.

"Look Gibbie - some fresh paint to get your hands into." Further along the port side the windows of the lounge are being washed by means of a very long brush held by a crewman from way above. They obviously take pride in their ship.

After five hours, sailing in weather which is improving the further west we go, the string of islands that form the southern end of the Western Isles chain are closing towards us and changing perspective as Barra nears. We turn into Castle Bay and due to repairs to the pier stroll ashore by means of the rear ramp on the car deck. What now? It is not yet eight o'clock and we had our dinner aboard the ship. Apparently there is the promise of a ceilidh tonight in the bar of our hotel. But then we've heard that before. Let's hope this one materialises.

I have an idea which I will have to hard sell to my colleagues. Why don't we take a taxi to the other hotel on the western side of the island to film the sun setting into the sea? Gibbie and Ian look at me incredulously, but are soon as enthusiastic as me once they realise they can sit in a panoramic lounge right up to the last minute before venturing outside with their cameras. Twenty minutes later we are sitting in this lounge. A group of naturalists (not naturists) sit behind us swapping zoological observations. They are mostly geriatric (which makes us glad they are not naturists) and the group leader has to frequently repeat his questions with the volume turned up a notch.

"Anyone heard a corncrake today?"

"Did anyone have cornflakes today?" An elderly lady repeats with a puzzled look on her face.

"NO. Did anyone hear a CORNCRAKE today?"

Before his group can answer a local chap sitting at the bar shoots his hand into the air.

"There was one calling in my garden last night - I've not cut my grass since last summer."

The group fall silent and stare at him as if he has just proffered a profanity.

Out of the panoramic window the sun is sliding gently towards oblivion.

"Anyone see a rabbit today?"

Our local is on a roll. "There's one at the end of my driveway - squashed - been there three days now." The group leader looks as though he is about to cry.

I drag Gibbie and Ian outside to find a veritable crowd, of Albion Rovers proportions, at the side of the hotel with their cameras also at the ready. This gives my idea a degree of credibility, and consequently my colleagues stop slagging me. We perch on some large rocks just above the water level. "I shouldn't sit on this," offers Gibbie, "I don't want my piles back."

Just as the sun is within a couple of minutes of dipping into a sea that stretches from here to North America a bank of cloud materialises on the horizon and the final climax is not what was anticipated. Our taxi driver has returned for us. "How was your sunset?" He asks.

"Not up to our usual standard, but we've seen a squashed rabbit."

The sun may have gone but the night is still young. Back at the hotel we try to convince our hostess that we have at least tried to make something of our ephemeral visit. Now where is this ceilidh?

"Do we really have to go, I'm feeling a bit tired?" complains Gibbie. Ian and I twist his arm and at ten o'clock we meet in the bar, which has the general layout, size and demeanour of a small barn. The ceilidh band tune up discordantly.

"To think I sailed five hours to listen to this," mutters Ian.

Not much later the band and ourselves are in full swing. The drummer, piper and two accordion players have us foot-tapping, singing and getting into Celtic spirit (literally) for the next three and a half hours. The hundred other punters in the bar are lapping it all up as much as we are. And while they play and we foot-tap the TV above the heads of the band is showing a re-run of the 1961 European Cup Final between Eintracht Frankfurt and Real Madrid.

Gibbie seizes an opportunity during the band's 'tea' break to make a request. "Can you play the Rowan Tree?"

The piper is quick on the return, "How does that grow?"

Gibbie doesn't get his request but does manage to take to the floor with a middle-aged blonde who reportedly hails from a fishing village on the Clyde. "Girvan?" asks Gibbie.

"No - Cambuslang!" And a bit later she voices her fears, "I hope I'm going to make the ship in the morning."

"Don't worry," replies the ever resourceful Gibbie, "it won't go without me - I'm the captain."

The music continues. On the TV screen Real Madrid win 7 - 3 and the band go into extra-time until 1.30 am.

Day Five - *Sleepy Heads*

Wake with a heavy heart, and an even heavier head. Down at breakfast there is no sign of Gibbie.

"Where's you pal?" Asks our hostess as she sits down a large teapot with a thump and a generous rack of toast with a noisy rattle.

"Here he comes now, "I gesture towards the door as Gibbie wanders gingerly in and sits slowly down onto his seat with a leaden sigh.

"Too much Barra air?" She asks.

"Too much of your band."

"Did you sleep well?" Our hostess persists.

"It took me so long to get the foil top of the sachet of milk for my tea that by the time I managed it was time to get up."

It is the most beautiful of mornings and it is an easy job rolling Gibbie down the hill onto the pier. *Clansman* is creaming across the bay and is an impressive sight. Several cameras are out, not just ours, as she seems to attract a fair bit of interest. One of the intending passengers is Gibbie's dancing partner from last night. She slides over to him.

"Where's your uniform, Captain?"

We sail out of Castle Bay onto a picture postcard sea. Away to our right the peripatetic *Hebridean Princess* is slipping quietly southwards down towards Mingulay. Cocktails on the beach?

If yesterday afternoon's sail to Barra was smashing, the return trip today is stupendous. Calm sea, unremitting sunshine, distant islands punctuating the horizon. All this induces a serenity aboard the ship. Within an hour of leaving Castlebay half the passengers are asleep, and half gazing out at the view. The first half just happens to be the ones who were at the ceilidh last night. Not Ian nor I - we sit out at the stern open deck and sip tea. Gibbie is in the lounge with the rest of the ceilidh passengers.

"Almost as good as the sheltered afterdeck of the *Hebridean Isles*," remarks Ian.

Around the ship, and across her wake, stream groups of seabirds. Shearwaters, kittiwakes, guilemots and gulls. Shame for the birdwatchers left behind on Barra - counting rabbits.

Looking around the small deck, so small for such a large ship, I realise there are passenger information signs everywhere. One just accepts their presence nowadays but if you actually step back and look you realise there are internationally approved symbols all around. Blue information signs, green emergency signs, red fire signs. God help you if you are colour-blind, in the event of an emergency you may end up congregating in the disabled toilet clutching tourist information leaflets.

Up in the observation lounge (just follow the signs) the atmosphere is comparable to a country hotel. Passengers sit around with their shoes off, reading newspapers and occasionally giving a glance out of the panoramic windows. Outside the hills of the north end of Mull edge ever closer, and the entrance to the Sound of Mull gradually wider. The general effect is of being aboard some kind of broad low-flying aircraft rather than a ship. To starboard the island of Coll, lying blue-grey on the horizon, is going to have *Waverley* as a guest in a couple of hours. It will be the paddler's first ever visit to the island and unfortunately for us she is sailing via the south end of Mull rather than via the Sound of Mull and we are therefore denied a glorious photo-call of her passing at full steam. I rather regret that. Her passenger complement is likely to be several times the population of Coll.

We arrive back at a sunny Oban on schedule and out trip is all but over for another year. Not quite, however, as our train back to Queen Street Station is not due to leave until 18.00. We realise that we have time for a quick return sail to Craignure aboard *Isle of Mull*. It will fill the time and give us a chance to indulge in our Annual Toast. So we watch *Clansman* load up and sail down the Sound of Kerrera to Colonsay. She is as hard working and well travelled as her predecessor *Lord of the Isles*.

How many times have we sailed over and back to Mull upon *Isle of Mull*? As we depart on the 16.00 sailing we gather on the spacious upper deck and set up cameras to record the toast to Island Hop 2002. Ian is sent to the bar to procure three malts, only to find it is shut. Sunday opening, or should I say Sunday closing! What a load of nonsense. So we have an imaginary toast and smack our lips as authentically as we can. Well we can remember the taste.

Turning around at Craignure we sail down the Sound of Mull again, the third time in thirty-six hours, and on the third ship. The deck is busy with passengers returning from Mull and Iona. Above them a gull is being hand-fed the leftovers of a loaf. It hangs motionless above the deck, as if on strings, swooping gleefully down to take bread from its benefactor. By the time it has swallowed half a loaf of bread it is noticeably a different shape.

Next to us a couple stand together talking with considerable animation on their respective mobile phones. Perhaps they're talking to each other?

On the train home. It is a pleasant enough journey despite the carriage being densely populated by an assortment of tourists. A "West Highland Way" walker sits across from us with his boots off and slowly drains a bottle of red wine, his eyes gently getting heavier with each mouthful. He looks as though he's earned it.

We swap opinions on our Hop. We agree it has been as successful as any other. Ideas are considered for next year. Amid our chat an elderly gentleman swaggers down from the leading coach to use the toilet at the head of ours. When finished he takes a wrong turning and wanders confused through the train, searching for his wife. The train stops at Ardlui for ten minutes, waiting for a northbound train to pass through. Most of us get out for some fresh air. By the time the wee man gets his pipe lit it's time to get back aboard again. He now takes the same wrong turning and wanders back down through our carriage for a second time. By the time he returns to his wife over forty-five minutes have past. Who knows, after a few more years of Island Hopping the three of us will probably be like that - wandering blissfully happy around a ship looking for each other. In fact just as we did aboard *Waverley* this year come to think!

We now look forward to next year. Our respective roles now cast in stone: Gibbie the strategist, Stuart the tactician and Ian the one who says "don't do that it's bad for you."

2003 Testing New Routes

The Plan

THIS WAS A CHALLENGING ITINERARY TO DEVISE. There were no shortage of ideas, as there were quite a few new, exciting changes to CalMac's timetables. The challenge was trying to utilise as many of them as possible, and link them together.

A new ship was due at Mallaig, serving Armadale on Skye. However at the time of our trip *Coruisk*, as she was called, had not entered service. With *Lord of the Isles* having already been moved back to Oban, to reinstate a three big ship presence there, an interesting substitute was sent to Mallaig. *Pioneer* moved from spare vessel on the Clyde to become temporary Mallaig-Armadale ferry. We just had to have a sail on her.

The Wednesday sailing from Oban to Colonsay had changed and the ship was different as well. Now back at her old haunt, Oban, *Lord of the Isles* would take the sailing instead of *Isle of Arran* or *Hebridean Isles*. Instead of starting at Kennacraig and making her way to Oban via Islay and Colonsay, she would start at Oban, sail to Colonsay, then as far as Port Askaig, and then return north to Oban.

Even more interesting was the start of a new direct route from Tiree to Barra. That was a must as the ship, either *Clansman* or *Lord of the Isles*, would presumably sail through the Gunna Sound, between Tiree and Coll. And once on Barra why not try the brand new route from Ardmhor, on Barra, to Eriskay? This route completed the chain of ferries and causeways linking the Western Isles, and was new for 2003.

There were a few other goodies with which to embellish our Island Hop. Why not stay overnight on Iona, as we had never done that before. There was also the chance of a 'new' island for us, the first since 1999.

This was a trip with particularly long sailings. Out to Islay, via Colonsay; and out to Barra, via Tiree. We could add a third, by taking an extended sailing aboard *Hebrides* on the Uig Triangle.

Much to do - but to achieve it all we would require a car.

Day One - *Female Company*

We're standing on the spot that we have stood on so many times before. You've guessed it - the hallowed spot is Oban Pier and the ship sailing slowly across the bay towards us is *Isle of Mull*. We have sailed on her so often that I fully expect one of her lounges to be named after us one day.

Looking around the windy pier we count three other CalMac ships tied up. There is Eigg, with her elevated wheel-house. She lies beside Bruernish which is up here acting as spare vessel. The third idle ship is *Clansman* - but she won't be idle for long; she is loading traffic for the island of Barra.

As well as being the twelfth time I've boarded *Isle of Mull* at Oban on an Island Hop it is also the third time I've started an Island Hop with this particular vessel. But for various reasons it is actually the first time all three of us have inaugurated our annual sojourn to the Isles in this way. That seems surprising but the statistics don't lie - so at least we have something to get excited about this early on.

The drive to Oban at the start of Day One is also something new and poor Andre (Gibbie's long suffering Citroen Xsara) is again being dumped on a street and being reassured that we will be back - in a day or two.

As you may have gathered we are sailing to Mull but are really bound for Iona. Such is the strength of the wind whistling outside the CalMac terminal building, sending the flower baskets above my head gyrating in the strong breeze, that I ask at the reception desk if the Iona sailings are still functioning. Despite my mild concerns all seems well and we sail off at 16.00 across a bumpy Oban Bay on our first ship of Island Hop 2003.

Downstairs out of the wind for some tea. The steward behind the cafeteria counter spots me eyeing the various culinary options laid out before him. "Do you fancy a meal, sir?"

"No - I'm just admiring your steak pie." As I sit down with my mug of brew I realise that the steward must think I'm a bit daft.

"I see that Island Hopper is back again!"

At Craignure I find myself first in the queue to disembark. Why I cannot fathom. Gibbie and Ian are nowhere to be seen. Around me are Americans, each identifiable by a dog-tag on their suitcases and shoulder bags. I fear that Mary Lou, from South Dakota and the rest of her travelling companions are also going to Iona. In which case space on the connecting bus at Craignure will be at a premium.

Sure enough, when we pour down the gangway onto an even windier Craignure Pier we all seem to have the same goal in our sights - a Bowman's coach. Someone has done their sums and there is just enough room for all - Gibbie, Ian, me, the white haired lady who will get off at Bunessan and the Americans - all of them female. Ian and I sit on opposite sides across from each other and raise simultaneous eyebrows at each other as they all pile aboard. We feel very conspicuous, for being male.

I find myself reminiscing again as the bus struggles up the first hill. Yes, if my memory serves me correctly the last time we took a bus to Fionnphort was when Gibbie and I took it on our very first Island Hop back in 1989. A lot of water has passed under our bows since then.

Fionnphort is at the western extremity of the large and lush island of Mull, and is the ferry point for the neighbouring island of Iona. The bus drivers must hate this road. Thirty-seven miles with thirty-six of them single-track. For us it is an interesting ride and it's good to let someone else do the driving. For the Americans it is the next leg of their journey to Iona. They 'ooh-ahh' at sheep scurrying across the road kamikaze style. They 'ooh-ahh' at the numerous small churches we pass on the way. And they 'aaah-ooh' each time the bus shudders to an unscheduled stop as an approaching car fails to pull up at a passing place. Realising that we are not one of them they glance nervously at us and seem reassured when we return relaxed, knowing smiles.

At Fionnphort we complete the ferry-bus-ferry transfer and climbing up to the top deck of Loch Buie I look across to Iona, a mile away across the Sound, and feel a twang of anticipation as our own adventure begins in earnest. As the small car ferry lurches over to that haven of peace and tranquility smiles appear on our faces with the realisation that yes - we are at sea. Looking across the lounge the window on the far side displays only sky, and then a few seconds later only sea., as the strong north-westerly wind sends the ship off on a perpetual roll. We like this. Some of those around us clearly don't, but then we are old sea-dogs.

Iona is bathed in sunlight as we step onto island number two at about 18.30. Everyone steps out in the same direction - uphill towards the hotel or, if they are really in a hurry, the abbey. The trees swish in the breeze, twite twitter from field to field and the rooks in the rookery crow in heraldic fashion as we encourage Gibbie to stride out like the rest of us - uphill like a conquering army of tourists.

Our hotel is quiet and peacefully serene. It is also full of women.

"There are lady ministers here," whispers Gibbie as he surreptitiously clutches his pre-dinner malt closer to his chest.

"That's a relief," returns Ian," at least we won't get molested in our rooms at night."

Over a delicious dinner in a crowded yet spacious dining room I glance around between forkfuls of venison and discover that Gibbie's *lady ministers* are two elderly ladies with knitted polo-necks under their blouses - and a bottle of Rioja at their elbows.

It is altogether a very comfortable start to our trip and we feel suitably sated in the cosseted environment which we find ourselves in. We retire to the lounge which overlooks a lush corner of the island. Around us our fellow, female guests sit and read or contemplate. They seem to be so relaxed that I decide to try some of their therapy myself. I reach for the "book of thoughts" that sits on the sideboard next to me and before opening it ponder on whether our Island Hop could be classed as a spiritual journey of the kind that these ladies are embarking on. I convince myself it could and open the book at the last page. (I do this with newspapers as well - old habits die hard). The page contains penned thoughts and the very last one reads "Don't believe everything you think." Oh well, it was worth a try. Snapping the book shut I look around the room.

The room is a paradigm of tranquility. Everyone is now reading; mostly magazines or books on Christianity or feminist theology. Ian is thumbing quietly through a gardening magazine. Gibbie is positively drooling as he flicks through the pages of a his own magazine - which is about guided-missile destroyers! I feel like escaping for, I am beginning to feel guilty for being male.

"Anyone fancy going to the pub?"

"Yes!" Declare Ian and Gibbie simultaneously.

Even the thought of a mile walk there and a mile walk back doesn't deter Gibbie. They're not the only keen ones. To our surprise the eyes of two young ladies sitting near us positively light up on hearing my suggestion. "Gee!" Yes they're American. "Can we come with you?"

This has never happened to us on an Island Hop before - being invited to the pub by young women - or even any women! We can hardly say 'no'. So the five of us head downhill to Iona's main conurbation, where we spend a very convivial hour, discussing island-hopping and feminist theology.

The girls, Wendy and Sandy, are from Vermont and are spending a month's vacation touring Scotland. So far they are suitable impressed.

It is Ian who makes the embarrassing slip. I can see it coming. He innocently asks, "So, are you girls friends or work colleagues?"

Wendy and Sandy glance at each other. "We're sisters of a kind." Unfortunately Ian fails to see the subtle inference here. "You don't look like sisters." I kick him under the table.

Walking back uphill an hour later. My friends have gone on ahead while I stop to phone home. The moon emerges briefly as I stride happily past the ruins of the nunnery and around the bend past the Celtic cross. In the ghostly gloom a bench materialises ahead of me at the side of the road and as I skip past it quite unexpectedly talks to me. "Are you not speaking?"

I jump out of my skin, having not seen Gibbie sitting there, having a breather. He nearly scared the wits out me.

Day Two - *Welcome Back LOTI*

Up at 07.30. Over breakfast our imminent departure on the next ferry seems rather pointless. We are the only ones checking out of the hotel. The pace of life here is definitely relaxed and unhurried. Although we have only just got here - it is time to move on. Such is island-hopping. We should really spend the week here and just think about all those ferries.

Iona has grown on me over the years. I have had two family holidays here, and of course this is the fourth time we have included it on an Island Hop itinerary. Add a handful of other visits over the years and I feel I now know its soft contours and hidden bays quite well. It is the atmosphere of the island which draws people here. Being one of the cradles of Christianity it is often a certain type of visitor who comes here. But despite the number of visitors to the island there is no overt commercialism. Despite the Christian importance there is no piety. Despite there being a car ferry on the service now there is no traffic. It is as if the mile of sea separating Iona from Mull were ten miles or fifty miles.

I take a stroll outside and scan the fields in front of the hotel with binoculars. The wind has dropped slightly and the sun is breaking through with more confidence.

A familiar rasping call from the field immediately below me gives away the presence of an elusive corncrake. This rare summer visitor to the *Hebrides* breeds in long grass and has declined dramatically since the 1970s. Many are inadvertently killed by the farmers' grass-cutting machinery at harvest time as the birds are reluctant to fly away from danger. As the birds run to the centre of the field they are vulnerable to being killed by the final cut. But thankfully the corncrake is slowly making a recovery on the islands due to a more enlightened approach to grass harvesting. By commencing grass cutting in the middle of the field, and by leaving an uncut margin at the field perimeter, the birds can run to safety and are spared. The vast majority of farmers are happy to make these simple changes to their field working, and the birds are returning. In fact there are three birds in the field in front of me, but despite the close presence of one in particular, and frenetic searching with my bins, it remains invisible.

A courtesy bus delivers our bags to the pier head, an act which causes Gibbie great annoyance. Had he known a courtesy bus existed he would have ridden up to the hotel yesterday when we arrived. Apparently he walked right past it when he disembarked from the ferry. I can confirm that - I watched him!

Loch Buie is rotating out at sea just in front of us, to align the correct ramp with the concrete slip. Around us thirty woollen clad visitors have strung themselves across the head of the slipway and are holding hands in what looks like an impending act of collective worship, or perhaps suicide.

We hurry aboard the ferry and ascend to our usual lofty position. Ian is bemused by the human chain on the pier, which looks as though is about to break into song.

"Oh God, not here!" He exclaims.

In fact they have amassed to bid farewell to one of their number, who must apparently be on the ferry. As the little ship pulls away, with a noisy beat of diesel and a grating of the ramp, the crowd on the slipway starts imitating a "Mexican Wave". If we were vain we could consider that the enthusiastic, if somewhat over-the-top, farewell is being directed at us.

So we leave Iona with style and are soon on the other side and loading our bags into the back of a bus. Ian buys tickets and we set off back along the narrow road again. Ten miles along the road Gibbie remembers he has an OAP bus pass. He is annoyed with himself for forgetting this.

"It gives me free travel all the way up to Tobermory. That includes Craignure as well. I will take this up with the driver, and get a refund."

So the unfortunate driver has now to contend with a single-track road, hairpin bends, sheep on the road and a disgruntled pensioner.

I, on the other hand, am quite content. We are under no pressure on this leg of our trip and I sit back to watch the unfolding scenery and count the buzzards on the miles of open road to Craignure Ferry Terminal.

Our schedule is quite a relaxed one, actually, for an Island Hop. The 11.00 sailing from Craignure will take us back to Oban, and at 15.00 we will sail out of Oban on a cruise to Colonsay and Islay aboard *Lord of the Isles*. In the four hours between sailings we have scheduled a visit to the island of Seil, but more of that later.

By the time we rumble up to join a collection of buses at Craignure we've counted four buzzards, three golden eagles, a white-tailed eagle and five peregrines. Actually I exaggerate - it was just the four buzzards.

Gibbie enters into deep conversation with our bus driver (once we are stopped) about the important part OAPs play in today's modern society and Ian and I join the reasonable crowd waiting to board *Isle of Mull*. The bus driver suggests he take his ticket to the company office, in Oban.

Craignure has changed since our first Island Hop. Today we are queued in an orderly fashion within a long plastic tube which runs most of the length of the pier. A huge gantry serves as a gangway and this is electrically positioned to take stock of the tides etc. Men in hard hats and life jackets tend the ropes. One step over the line onto the actual pier results in public humiliation. Back in 1989 we could wander up to any point on the pier to watch the ship arrive or depart. In fact on one of our first sailings from Craignure I actually unslipped the stern hawser from the bollard and stood on the edge of the pier as *Isle of Mull*'s bulk slid gently past, a metre from my nose. Could you imagine me doing that now?. I would be lined up against the electronic gangway and shot. Either that or I would be banished to South Uist in disgrace.

To be fair I rather like the plastic tube on the pier. Keeps the wind and rain off and it even has seats in it. There is no rain and little wind today but the seats prove useful as we wait for about four hundred people to disembark from the ship. Of course - this is the busy 10.00 sailing from Oban. All aboard, the ship sails a couple of minutes early and we make straight for the cafeteria for our second breakfast (I've noticed that I now put on weight when I go Island Hopping). At Oban Gibbie takes his bus ticket to the company office, as advised. "That's no use here, you should have taken it to the head office."

"Where's that?"

"Craignure."

"Craignure! I've just come from there. That's a letter of complaint I'm going to have to write."

We retrieve the car and, with me driving, head south from the town towards Seil, which as you know, is linked by hump-backed bridge to the mainland. Why Seil? Well it adds another island to our list for the year, it's easy to get to in the time we have available and we've not been there for a few years. Anyway we might bump into Princess Diana's Mum, who apparently lives there. We drive the length of Seil - it doesn't take long - and watch the ferry struggle across the Cuan Sound from the neighboring island of Luing. A brief look at each other to see if we will bother to make that journey as well. No. No point in getting carried away, is there?

We settle for lunch at the inn adjacent to the Bridge Over The Atlantic. It is warm enough to sit outside and we watch in amusement as coach after coach pulls up at the mainland side of the bridge and discharges passengers. These poor souls then have to walk over the bridge while the bus gingerly advances across, without running them all down. Once on Seil they get back aboard again. Why? Well they can now claim to have walked over the Atlantic. So that's twice they've crossed 'The Pond' in the space of a week. The coaches seem to have synchronised their arrival perfectly. As one completes the task and heads off to Easdsale the next coach pulls up opposite us and the whole process begins again. Perhaps they are timed to leave Oban at ten minute intervals.

Back at Oban just forty minutes before *Lord of the Isles* is due to leave for Colonsay. Needless to say she has arrived at the pier and we are all very pleased to see her back at Oban - she has been on duty at Mallaig for four years. With the arrival of the new ship imminent on the Mallaig-Armadale run *LOTI* has returned to her rightful home. Here she will join *Clansman* and *Isle of Mull* in a triumphirate of large ferries sailing daily out of Oban - for the first time since 1989.

We all have duties to perform now. Ian heads off to the office to complete the necessary passenger registration forms, Gibbie finds a cosy spot to abandon (park) his car and I check all our bags into the hotel where we will be spending the night. Why do I always get the strenuous jobs?

To my dismay the hotel I've chosen has a depressing air to it. It becomes clear when the receptionist opens the door of my room, and screws up her nose at the sights and smells that greet her, that I have chosen badly. Oh well, at least it will be dark when we arrive back into town tonight.

That's the bad news, the good news is that the upper deck of our next ship, *Lord of the Isles*, has been opened up to passengers and extra seating provided. This will give us much better views on the long sea journey that lies ahead of us now. We head up top as the ship pulls away from the pier and find that many of our fellow passengers have also discovered the new deck.

The route we are taking now is from Oban to Colonsay and Port Askaig on Islay. This is the first time we have sailed on this route aboard

Lord of the Isles, although she is a ship we have spent many a happy hour on. We are, understandably, rather fond of her. The route is actually a new one for this year. Previously the Colonsay/Port Askaig sailings on summer Wednesdays commenced at Kennacraig early in the morning, called at both islands and then sailed up to Oban. The ship then retraced her wake back to Kennacraig via both islands again. This year the ship starts at Oban, calls at Colonsay and Islay and then returns to Oban in the evening - which is just as well as our hotel is there! This represents the first major change to the Wednesday Oban-Islay schedule since 1989. Our cruise today will last about eight hours.

So the route has been tweaked, and the ship is new to this route, but it doesn't stop us reminiscing about similar sails over the years, up or down the Sound of Kerrera, aboard Glen Sannox, *Claymore*, *Isle of Arran*, *Isle of Mull* and *Hebridean Isles*.

I've written about this sail so many times, so I will not repeat myself here. Suffice to say the sun is out, the sea is calm and the various islands sink slowly past us as we sit on the top deck drinking tea and wondering just how much longer Gibbie's snooze in the 'quiet lounge' is going to last. Eventually, as Colonsay approaches, I am dispatched to find out if he is still alive. And of course this also happened a couple of years ago aboard *Hebridean Isles*. Maybe he finds this sail boring.

Getting ashore to take the mandatory photograph of the ship at Scalasaig Pier is becoming less of a joke with each passing year. The price of a great picture is being left stranded for a couple of days. But today it would only mean being stranded for three hours as the ship is due to call back again after visiting Islay. The poor chap at the head of the gangway looks confused as he doesn't know whether to hand me a boarding card or take one away from me. I am back aboard within five minutes. Ironically the lorries that are reversing on are making such a dog's breakfast of it that I would have had time to take a decent photograph and a stroll around the island for good measure.

We head south-east now towards Islay, and there is an astonishing sight in the bar. No, it's not Gibbie buying a round of drinks, it is ten German tourists with thirty plastic beakers, each quarter-full with a different malt whisky. But nobody seems to be drinking any of them. They are simply sitting around looking at them. Do they want any help? Is it a free whisky drinking session? The answer remains obscure.

Watching the ship berth at Port Askaig, against a strong tide such as is running today, is always a spectacle, whether you are on the ship or observing from the pier. Last time we were here (2001) we were aboard *Hebridean Isles* and she steamed down the Sound right past the pier before turning. Today the skipper does it differently. He spins the ship around just off the pier and reverses gently against the tide. The net result is that we slowly appear to drift sideways towards our berth and in five minutes we are neatly alongside. It looks easy but I bet it isn't. As cool a piece of parallel parking as ever I saw.

A vaguely disappointing dinner aboard the ship as she heads back to Colonsay - still with our Germans aboard, who still haven't touched a drop. Back at Scalasaig again there are three great northern divers in full breeding plumage right alongside the ship. The closest view of these birds that I have ever had. The sail back to Oban seems long and we pass the time watching Celtic playing Dundee in a league game on a television set in the bar. "This will be close, Dundee are good," I inform Ian who, living down South, may not be aware of such facts. By the time Celtic score their sixth goal I'm outside watching the sun dip into the Atlantic on one side of the ship and the moon rise above Jura on the other.

We leave the celebrating Celtic fans in the bar and trot up to the observation lounge to monitor our progress. It is silent and peaceful - until the southern approaches of the Sound of Kerrera when a mobile phone signal is reached. It's arrival through the ether is heralded by half a dozen simultaneous electronic tunes; everything from Dad's Army to Laurel and Hardy.

"Hello, yes I'm on the ship . . ." As darkness gathers the hills and islands around us fold into the sea and sky. We are tired and looking forward to our beds. Hope mine has been made up.

Day Three - *Three Ians and a Minke in the Gunna Sound*

There isn't a problem wakening - the repositioning of the gangway on the pier does the job perfectly. My arousal is speeded along when I open my eyes and spot a 'bogie' on my duvet which certainly does not belong to me, so I am out of bed fairly quickly.

I'm up and out at 07.30 before breakfast in order to get a photograph. Five CalMac ships are in Oban Bay. Eigg and Bruernish are tied up together on the left. At the pier *Clansman* sits idle, just as she had last night. At the linkspan *Isle of Mull* is loading up for Mull, and lying off from the pier *Lord of the Isles* sits patiently waiting for a berth.

Isle of Mull had berthed at Craignure last night and sailed over at 07.15 this morning on her first run of the day. Another interesting ship is due in soon. We passed Hebridean Princess moored at the southern end of Kerrera last night and she will appear at Oban soon. With so much traffic it should be an interesting hour and a half.

Heading back to the hotel for breakfast I spot Ian - always an early riser - strolling along on the other side of the road, coming towards me. I wave and gesture to him and wait for him to catch me up. It is only when he gets nearer that I realise it isn't him at all but a similarly hirsute doppelganger trying to confuse me. The chap must think I'm a complete idiot. I am obviously in desperate need of my bacon and eggs.

This morning we will be sailing at 09.00 on either *Clansman* or *Lord of the Isles* out to Tiree and then Barra. It promises to be a terrific sail and the weather looks promising as well.

The car, Andre, is coming with us, so we are at the pier in good time. It appears that *Lord of the Isles* will be taking the honours and we're not unhappy about that. *Isle of Mull* has already left and *Clansman* will be heading out to Colonsay after our departure. No sign of Hebridean Princess yet.

As we take our places once again upon the lofty upper deck of *LOTI* Eigg scuttles out from her own jetty and heads off for Lismore. Up on deck we meet two friends, both called Ian. They are heading out to Barra, but then returning with the ship (a 'boomerang' trip) whereas we shall be heading forever onwards. So we are now a party of five - three of us called Ian! This is bound to cause confusion for the rest of the morning.

This reminds me of one of my favourite Gibbie stories. Many years ago, in the 1950s, when Gibbie was just a lad and everything was in black and white, he and four pals were stopped by a policeman in the general environs of Govan Cross, in Glasgow, for singing too loudly in the street. The policeman took umbrage at their truculence and demanded that they give him their names. He started with Gibbie's pals, but by a curious turn of fate all four of his co-accused were called 'Jim'. How about that for a coincidence! So when the policeman turned to Gibbie he asked,

"So I suppose you're called Jim as well?"

"No," replied Gibbie, "but my middle name's Jim!"

Poor Gibbie got reported to his parents for giving cheek. His pals were admonished.

Lord of the Isles sails promptly at 09.00 and her place at the linkspan is immediately taken by *Clansman*. As we turn to starboard *Hebridean Princess*, showing impeccable timing, comes into the bay and passes us so closely we can see into all the state cabins. She takes *Clansman*'s place at the pier and will lie there for the bulk of the day exchanging one ingot of passengers for another.

With all the hustle and bustle over we can relax in the morning sunshine and let *LOTI* take us to our destination. After today's cruise we will have spent almost fifteen hours of the last twenty-five aboard her - we should just have stayed the night on her. (The reason we didn't is because her overnight cabins are no longer in use). Even the crew are giving us looks of familiarity - if you see what I mean.

The sail up the Sound of Mull has got to be one of the best sails anywhere on the west coast. It takes two hours from Oban to clear the top and pass out into the Sea of the *Hebrides*. On our left the hills and mountains of Mull. On our right the moors and woodlands of Morven, with the odd cottage dotting the landscape. Half way up we pass the ferry *Loch Fyne* heading for Fishnish. Further on *Raasay* is cutting diagonally across towards Tobermory.

Out on the open deck after lunch, with the Ians. The wind has dropped, the sea is calm and the sky near perfection. Kittiwakes, fulmars, razorbills and guillemots pass by in flurries, going about their business in a variety of directions and with great purpose.

Coll looms ahead but the ship is ignoring her and sailing direct to Tiree. The number of sea birds increases as we near land and a pair of common terns flap past. As we get close to the linkspan at Scaranish it becomes apparent that the tide is low - very low.

Away to port lie the Treshnish Isles. Gibbie fancifully thinks that one of them looks like an aircraft carrier. But I think he's been too heavily influenced by his 'guided-missile destroyers' book.

Then one of the Ians tries to spoil our day: "You chaps hoping to cross to Eriskay from Barra later, aren't you?"

"Yes," replies Gibbie,"but I don't like the 'hoping' bit."

"Little chance. Ferry was off yesterday at the time you plan to cross. Tide was too low. It's even lower today."

"Thanks Ian, that really cheers us up."

We have missed sailings in the past due to mechanical breakdown, bad weather, misreading the timetable (me - who else!) but never due to a low tide. This could cause serious problems as we need that last sailing of the day to get us on our way up the causeway from Eriskay to the Uists. Our hotel for the night is at Lochmaddy on North Uist. We will just have to keep our fingers crossed, and wait and see.

Despite the tide *Lord of the Isles* has no problems unloading and loading at Tiree and we are soon on our way again.

The exciting bit now lies just up ahead. Because the ship is now sailing direct from Tiree to Barra (the first time we have ever done this) she is saving time by cutting through the rather treacherous strait of water between Tiree and Coll known as the Gunna Sound. This infamous strip of water is less than a mile wide between the north-eastern point on Tiree and the island of Gunna, which lies between Tiree and Coll. Just ahead, through binoculars but soon visible without them, I can see a flurry of activity which represents a battery of rocks barely concealed by the sea. A green buoy to the west of these shows the safe passage through the Sound. In fact these rocks are normally invisible but today's low tide has brought their razor edges to just below the surface of the sea.

They were completely invisible to all aboard the MacBrayne steamer *Loch Seaforth* in March 1973 when she passed through here in darkness. She ran onto them and was holed. Fortunately all were able to escape the sinking ship, which was towed to Scaranish Pier, Tiree, where she eventually sank.

So thirty years on we scan the obstacles on either side of the ship as she slips steadily but comfortable through the gap. She takes a 45 degree turn to the north once past the buoy and we are safely out onto the open sea again. Arctic, common, and little terns fly over to screech at us, and then return to their business.

The colour of the buoy causes Gibbie great consternation as he feels it should be red. He, and all three Ians, participate in a debate up on the top deck. Ironically Gibbie is colour blind, so we tell him that really it is red!

I peer over the starboard rail and watch the sea swish past. Suddenly, about thirty metres from the side of the ship, the grey mottled flanks of a minke whale break the surface and then slide back below again. It doesn't re-surface. I look around for someone to collaborate my observation but Gibbie and the Ians are still arguing about the colour of buoys. No one on deck seems to have seen it except me - so you'll just have to take my word for it. I saw a minke whale.

Away ahead now an island chain is becoming more defined on the horizon. Berneray, Mingulay, Pabbay, Barra and South Uist lie to the north-west of us. I am having one of my happy moments; it is induced by that feeling of being on the open sea with land a mere smudge in the distance. I feel that I haven't got a care in the world - apart from whether the Eriskay ferry will be running. I look over at the others to see if they have a care in the world.

".....I tell you, it shouldn't be green it should be red...."

We approach Barra and for the first time we see puffins fluttering past. A pair of them fly out from the shores of Vatersay. Turning into Castle Bay we can see that the tide has risen a bit. Hopefully that means that our Eriskay sailing, two hours away, should be okay.

The pier at Castlebay looks busy. Very busy. It is only when we drive off that it becomes apparent why. In less than a week's time Celtic play FC Porto in the final of the UEFA Cup in the Spanish city of Seville. The mass exodus of Celtic fans is not confined to the central belt of Scotland. A rather battered looking bus, painted green and white, is preparing to board the ferry on the second leg of its journey to Seville. The first leg was getting it from its home on Vatersay to Barra. Aboard are a ebullient group of Celtic fans, and probably a few hundred cans of lager. Well-wishers from all over the island are here to cheer them on their way. It is a happy atmosphere as wives, girlfriends, schoolchildren, shopkeepers and even the nice lady from the Tourist Office are gathered on the pier to wave scarfs and blow kisses. And we thought it was a welcoming party for us!

We stop in the village for me to film *Lord of the Isles* leaving for Oban, with the Celtic fans, lager and two of the Ians aboard. We have also stopped to let Gibbie pump some air into an ailing tyre. This malady is attended to by means of a foot pump. The garage is closed because the owner is on the pier. The sight of Gibbie and Ian taking turns at the pump causes great fascination to a small schoolboy, who muscles in between them in order to get a closer look. He must think we mainland folk are primitive.

Tyre fixed, we peruse on whether we should visit Vatersay, which is linked to Barra by causeway. But time is ticking by. Instead we drive up the east side of the island to the new ferry terminal. This is one end of the new route from Barra to Eriskay. This now means that it is possible to drive from Vatersay to Lewis. The last link in the chain of ferry services across the Western Isles is complete. The mainland links are all still in place, of course, Ullapool, Uig, Oban, but tourist pressure and the demand for alternative routes off the islands have resulted in ferry points crossing the Sound of Barra and the Sound of *Harris* being developed.

This new ferry route will take about forty minutes to get us over to Eriskay and is being inaugurated by *Loch Linnhe*. From Eriskay we can take the causeway to South Uist. Eriskay is, of course, an island on its own right but the causeway, from the north end of the island to Ludag on Uist, has been built since our last visit. It was opened in July 2001. Loch Linnhe is only keeping the route warm for *Loch Bhrusda* which will be the designated ship for this route. At the moment she is on the Sound of *Harris* service and will continue there until the new *Loch Portain* arrives to replace her.

A sturdy breakwater guards the entrance to the new slipway and *Loch Linnhe* can be seen making her way over. I set up stall with my camera at the end of the breakwater, jockeying for position with a pair of irate oystercatchers. Looking at the amount of sea lapping the slipway there appears to be no problem with the tide: one of the Ians was exaggerating!

The car is booked on this sailing, which judging from the queue of cars, looks to have been a sound bit of planning. I can see this being a popular route. *Loch Linnhe* takes a few turns en route past the island of Fuday on her way to Eriskay. Gibbie keeps a sharp lookout for treacherous rocks - his nerves haven't yet recovered from his passage through the Gunna Sound. "That Voith-Schneider unit down there is making a funny rumbling noise."

"It's probably just clipping the tops of the rocks," Ian suggests, rather unhelpfully.

We arrive at Eriskay at 17.40, at the southern end of Coilleag a Phrionnsa - the Prince's Strand. This beautiful stretch of sand is so named because it was the first landing on Scottish soil by Bonnie Prince Charlie, from a French ship in 1745. From here to the village, or more importantly the Am Politician pub, is about a mile and I decide to walk it. Gibbie and Ian drive on with strict instructions on how to get there and what to order once there.

The road, recently constructed to serve the ferry terminal, curves gently uphill. I stride out and quickly heat up in the strong late afternoon sunshine. The view from the top of the hill is stunning. Barra and its attending islands shimmer in the haze away to the south. Looking north is South Uist, a couple of miles away. Nearer still, in the Am Politician car park, lies Andre. They've found it!

In a rocky hole, just beside the freshly landscaped road, a starling attends its squawking young. Just above, on a telephone wire, the daddy starling whistles and sings its mimetic outburst of song. Its song contains an incredibly accurate rendition of a curlew. Back home it is song thrushes and mobile phones that starlings imitate, but up here they have to copy what is available. So the beautiful plaintive call of the curlew has found its way into the repertoire of this bird and is being enthusiastically, and accurately, delivered from a telephone wire.

I take a short cut across a grassy field and arrive at the Am Politician just as the head on my beer is settling. The lounge has been improved since our last visit and a conservatory has been added. On the glass roof, half hidden in a corner, a pair of blackbirds have built their nest and three sturdy looking chicks lie in it, pouting and gaping. Within a minute of us watching from down below the adult male arrives and thrusts a worm down the gullet of the lucky youngster. Okay, I'll stop sounding like Bill Oddie now, but suffice to say that the bird life on Eriskay seems to be thriving.

Perhaps it is because of the glorious sunshine, but we are reluctant to leave. However there is a drive of over forty miles over four causeways and four islands in front of us now. Our base for the night is North Uist.

The causeway between Eriskay and South Uist looks a solid piece of engineering and blends in well with the landscape. It is about a mile long with a slight dog-leg in the middle. Since its completion the population of Eriskay has apparently risen - so the human life seems to be thriving also.

Once on South Uist the drive up the spine of the Uists is fairly uninteresting and punctuated by frequent pull-ups at passing places. We cross onto Benbecula, onto Grimsay and finally on to North Uist proper. Away to our left lies the low lying fertile tidal island of Baleshare which we hope to visit tomorrow.

North Uist is unique among the Western Isles as it has more water on it than land - a look at a map will illustrate what I mean. It is no wonder fishing is so popular here. We're soon eating some at our hotel, shoveling in forkfuls of salmon and reminiscing on a fine day of Island Hopping. Today the weather made it for us. Had it poured with rain our day would have taken on a different complexion.

Fall asleep trying to work out where the Celtic Bus will be now.

Day Four - *Lots of Hebrides*

"The best scrambled eggs I've ever had," say Ian and Gibbie in unison. It certainly looked it. My order for breakfast was, "The full works, please." The waitress returns moments later with a quizzical look on her face.

"Do you want *everything*?"

We stagger out to the car at 09.30 convinced that we won't eat again till tomorrow. Andre's flat tyre is bearing up well - which is fortunate for none of us feels like bending over to pump it up.

We are off across to the west side of the island this morning. There is an opportunity to add a *new* island to our Island Hopping tally - a difficult thing to achieve nowadays. Baleshare is linked by causeway to North Uist. It is a very low lying, sandy-shored island measuring three miles long by one and a half miles across. It is so flat that there isn't a single contour crossing it on my OS map.

"So why go?" Asks Gibbie. He is prone to a touch of under-whelmment after a full breakfast.

"It's full of waders," I reply, keeping to the wildlife theme of this year's trip. Gibbie frowns as he struggles with a mental picture of a sandy island covered in discarded over-sized welly-boots.

"Curlews, redshank, dunlin...those kind of waders." I enlighten him.

The Western Isles are rich in these particular birds and a much publicised programme is underway at the moment to eradicate the hedgehog from the Uists as these have a taste for young wader chicks. So on Baleshare we hope to see some waders, and heaven help any hedgehogs we spot crossing the road on the way there.

The beach on the west side of Baleshare is wild and empty. We are almost as far west in Europe now as it is possible to go - and it looks it. Ten miles out to sea from us lie the Monach Islands, their white beaches glinting in the sun. A bar of sand once extended from North Uist to the Monachs, but this was breached in the sixteenth century when a giant tidal wave crashed through and rendered the Monachs islands. The human population eventually deserted the islands in the 1930s.

We leave the windswept beach to the gulls and drive slowly along the empty road towards the causeway. There are redshank and lapwing fluttering around us and we stop to watch. When Gibbie spots a lapwing chick in long grass near the car he is beside himself with gooey, paternal comments and decides that he now likes Baleshare after all. "But I wouldn't like to spend a week here."

"How about a day?" asks Ian.

Back to Lochmaddy now and we take up different positions to photograph the arrival of our next ship, *Hebrides*. Gibbie chooses the pier. This turns out to be an unfortunate choice for he gets a bellowing from a pierhand. He is quite miffed by this. "If he'd only asked me nicely. I think I shall write a letter of complaint."

He's got a lot of letter writing to do when he gets back home. Perhaps he can do it on the ship as we are having a nice long cruise today on *Hebrides*. But first of all we have to get the car onto the ship. We are issued with passenger registration slips for this leg of the journey, which is from Lochmaddy to Uig.

This is the first time we have sailed out of Lochmaddy on *Hebrides*. She shows incredible manoeuvrability in the close confines of the bay, and she is no doubt as stable a ship as her sister, *Clansman*. Thankfully, this is not put to the test as the Little Minch is calm.

Over lunch we have a chat about the next leg of today's trip. Timing will be of the essence as we have a potential problem, of the kind that only Island Hoppers like us could devise for ourselves. When we dock at Uig on Skye we have to get the car off and park it somewhere at the ferry terminal as we only have a car ticket for this leg of the journey. Whoever drives the car off then has to obtain three new passenger registration vouchers for the next leg, from Uig to Tarbert on *Harris* and back again. He will then have to get smartly back up the quarter mile of pier and back onto the ship again. All this in about fifteen minutes. Assuming only one of us has to do this, what happens to the counting system back on the ship when two passengers fail to disembark at Uig? And who is going to be the mug who gets to do all this? Well it's blatantly obvious it's going to be me of course. Who else? I can run back up the pier faster than the other two. We discuss our complicated sailing schedule with Melanie, the dark-haired, bright-eyed girl behind the reception counter aboard *Hebrides*.

"I would speak to the purser if I were you. I'll just get him for you." We know good advice when we hear it. If all that sounds complicated you can imagine what it was like trying to explain it to the purser. He scratches his head and tries his best at giving us his advice.

"Nobody has wanted to do this before." What he doesn't add, out of politeness is, "why can't you just go from A to B like all the other ordinary passengers," or better still, "why didn't you take the Sound of *Harris* ferry from North Uist to *Harris* like any other normal person?"

In fact he radios ahead to the office at Uig, and returns with the advice that in order to keep his numbers right we must all drive off in the car at Uig. And then drive back on again at Uig!

It all adds a bit of pressure to what has so far been a very laid-back Island Hop. The ship arrives at Uig. The turnaround time here is thirty minutes, but as we assemble in the foyer waiting to go down to the car deck there is, for some unknown reason, a hold up. Furthermore Andre is on the mezzanine deck and that means we will be among the last to be unloaded. By the time we are allowed to return to the car fifteen minutes have elapsed.

I drive off with the others, deposit them on the pier near the ferry and drive down to the CalMac office. The car is parked and I run inside to collect our passenger registration slips. Despite the pre-warning there is still confusion and I'm all a-fluster. "Hi. The purser phoned ahead. We've just come from Lochmaddy and need new passenger registration slips for our non-landing cruise to Tarbert."

"Sign here. Just the one car?"

"Yes, I've parked it. We're not taking it"

"So you're going over to Lochmaddy and back?"

"No, we've just come from there - we're going to Tarbert."

"Right, non-landing to Tarbert, sorry I thought you had just got off the ship."

"I have, but I've got to get back on it again."

He takes the registration slip from my hand, thinks for a few seconds and then pushes it back to me. "Have a nice trip."

"Thanks. Errr there are three of us."

"Where are the other two?"

"On the pier."

By now the poor chap is totally confused. He writes out three new slips. "Your taxi awaits," he gestures outside.

"Taxi?"

Now this is what I call service. My own personal courtesy bus takes me back up the pier, and the CalMac office returns to normality. As the bus nears the ship I spot Ian and Gibbie standing at the foot of the gangway. Their faces are a picture of confusion and concern. The ship is about to sail and they cannot see me anywhere on the pier. Not knowing that I am on the bus, they are expecting to see me in full flight, clutching three pieces of paper and racing quarter of a mile to get aboard on time. It is wonderful to see the anxiety on their faces.

I can see Gibbie mouth "Where the hell is he?" When I step off the bus after a few seconds of enjoying this spectacle their expressions change to surprise, relief and then hilarity. *Hebrides* can now sail.

The route from Uig to Tarbert and Lochmaddy used to be triangular, in that the ship would sail between North Uist and *Harris*, as well crossing to Uig. Nowadays it plies back and forth from Uig to each island in turn.

Over the many years of sailing in these parts we've often had some splendid weather, and today is no exception. Sailing with the wind the limited deck space on *Hebrides* is a sun trap.

Later we are in the bar choosing a bottled beer each. There is a selection of ales from Skye and the choice is a difficult one to make. Melanie is now the barmaid and surprised to see that we are still aboard. So makes up our minds for us and we each end up with a bottle of Red Cuillin. We stretch out, sipping our beer and eaves-dropping on the conversations of our fellow passengers; always a laugh. Two very elderly ladies are speaking loudly, but in refined, well rounded tones. "I mean, sex, politics and religion were never discussed around the table. Come on, what's wrong with discussing politics or religion?"

Back out on the open deck. An officer comes around and appears to be counting us. Perhaps there is confusion as to how many passengers are aboard. Perhaps I could tell him why. A little further on two crewmen holding paint brushes join us on deck and open a little gate to gain access to a bollard on the starboard side, which is in need of a coat or two.

"Wish they'd shut that door there's a terrible draft coming in." Ian is in witty mood. Quite a gale is being funneled up narrow Loch Tarbert as the ship makes a cautious approach to the pier. With such powerful bow thrusters the skipper makes his handling of the ship look easy - even more so when we pull away on the return sail to Skye. The ship is swung around in her own length and then pointed back in the direction of Uig. We didn't bother to get off at Tarbert - too complicated. So that makes Port Askaig, Tiree and now Tarbert that we have sailed into without stepping ashore.

Downstairs to the cafeteria discussing whether we have an early tea or just a quick snack. Melanie is now behind the counter here. She is even more amazed to see we are still aboard; she also spots our indecision on what to order. "You chaps are a bit unsure of yourself today, aren't you?"

Up in the roomy observation lounge, overlooking the bow of the ship, I stand for a full ten minutes and watch the lumpy mass of Skye approach. Standing still for ten minutes aboard a ship is unusual for me. A television screen above my head demonstrates the satellite position of *Hebrides*.

The sea looks very sombre now, under an advancing blanket of cloud. We heard the weather forecast earlier, apparently a front is advancing towards us from the south, meaning that the weather is going to break. It will be a slow process however, and none of us are complaining about the weather that has been dished up to us so far.

Ahead of the ship now is a large *flotilla* of manx shearwaters, sitting on the surface right in line with the passage of the ship. At the last second they scatter in different directions and then amass again in a wheeling low flock away to our right.

In the lounge passengers sit quietly flicking through newspapers or magazines, or simply resting. It is like a private cruise with twenty invited guests. To say the lounge is comfortable would not do it justice. Gibbie is in as near a supine position as it is possible to get without actually lying on the carpet. Ian is studying his newspaper with mathematical precision and I am off for my fourth cup of tea of the cruise.

To Gibbie's disappointment there is no courtesy bus awaiting us on arrival back at Uig, the absence of which causes him to moan that I always get preferential treatment. The purser and Melanie wave us off the ship - no doubt both delighted to see the back of us. There is time to collect the car and drive up the hill out of Uig to the viewpoint at the southern edge of the bay. Cameras click to record the departure of *Hebrides*; she is heading to Lochmaddy this time.

Our base for the night is at an 'establishment' in Broadford, I cannot bring myself to be any more specific than that, in fear of upsetting someone at Visit Scotland. Our hearts sink when we are greeted by a grey-faced receptionist, who has almost every flabby bit of face pierced with some kind of ironmongery. She looks like the victim of some kind of horrible angling accident. In her opening gambit to us she has called each of us *sweetheart*, *luvvy* and *precious* in turn. Gibbie looks as though he is going to be sick. Later, when my food order is placed in front of me, it looks as though he has been.

It has started to rain outside and we look like a captive audience for the Country & Western Night that is about to begin around us. Various other guests appear. Now I wouldn't like to be called ageist, but judging from the maturity of the other guests, there is a fair chance that the number of place settings for breakfast, which is only twelve hours away, will need rounded down. Even Gibbie agrees that having a walk in the rain will be more fun. So we do.

Day Five - *Farewell to an Old Pioneer*

Ian and I are down early before the bus party makes it to the dining-room. This takes a fair bit of jostling, queue jumping and pushing of elderly people aside, but we manage to be the first to be seated - and thus served. Gibbie is late. When he appears he looks uncharacteristically agitated, and totally unconcerned that his scrambled eggs are getting cold. It appears that last night, just like the final evening of last year's Hop, he was at a ceilidh. Well maybe not so much at the ceilidh, more above it. At 1am he was downstairs in his pyjamas remonstrating with raucous revellers, with the aim of persuading them that their music was a touch too loud. I would have thought that his very manifestation in his pyjamas would have been enough in itself to stop the music! This morning he is not a happy man and is off to see the manager.

"I would prefer to write a letter of complaint - but as I'm still here I might as well meet the man in person."

"Just be careful, it might be that bird behind the reception, you know, bangle face." Ian warns.

But Gibbie is undeterred. "If it is she's going to get a plateful of cold scrambled eggs all over her nose rings." While Ian and I wait in the car Gibbie makes his point and emerges with a discounted bill.

We are off now to see a ferry we have never seen before. The privately run Glenaculish plies across the turbulent Sound of Sleat, at its narrowest point, at the remote and ancient crossing point at Kylerhea. It is amazing that we have never been down here before. I drive over the beautiful but mind-boggling rollercoaster single-track road to the ferrypoint.

Ferries have crossed from this place to the mainland for centuries, although even into the twentieth century cattle had to swim it. Judging by the rapids today I wouldn't fancy that if I were a coo.

The ferry is at the Skye side. It can take three or four cars, which are positioned on a turntable. This is swung around by hand. The ferry sets off sideways across the Sound to Glenelg, half a mile away. We consider crossing as foot passengers but time is against us as we have a bigger goal to head for now.

At Armadale the car is booked on the 11.45 sailing, the last sailing of Island Hop 2003. But this will be no ordinary sailing. Despite crossing here before, aboard Iona and *Lord of the Isles*, this crossing will be more auspicious. Today it is a real veteran that is providing the service. *Pioneer* is at last about to be retired from the CalMac fleet after almost thirty years of service. Today she is operating her last sailings for the company, from

Armadale to Mallaig. We arrive in bags of time to film her arrival at the Skye pier.

Pioneer has served this route before, of course. In the 1980s she was, for a while, the regular Armadale ferry. In those days she had a hoist, which was needed in the days before Mallaig and Armadale required linkspans. Today her hoist is long gone and she is at the very end of her long CalMac career. I'll be sad to see her go.

Pioneer was designed for the West Loch Tarbert - Islay route, launched on 1 April 1974 and entered service on the Islay route in August that year, replacing *Arran*. My first ever sail on her was in July 1978 when I sailed to Port Ellen aboard her. After five years as Islay ferry she was replaced by *Iona* and became Mallaig - Armadale vessel, a role she performed for ten years. As this was seasonal work she relieved on many different routes during the winter, including routes on the Clyde. In 1989 she was substituted on Mallaig - Armadale service by, yet again, *Iona*, and became CalMac's spare vessel. In this role she sailed over the entire network, with the exception of Ullapool and Stornoway.

In 1993 the Wemyss Bay - Rothesay service was expanded and Clyde cruising was re-introduced by CalMac. *Pioneer* thus became secondary Rothesay ship, and occasional cruise ship (see AWTF 1994). In her final years her duties were largely reduced, but she still acted as relief vessel, and it is in that role that we find her here today at Skye.

The old ship is having a busy day - this is a busy route - and a lot of traffic is waiting. She speeds in with her customary bow wave and docks stern-in to the linkspan. As at Tiree and Uig the tide is very low.

Only eighteen cars are loaded, including Andre, and she leaves late at 11.56 with three cars left on the pier. Strange, with some tighter packing they could have been accommodated, although space has to be left on the car deck for the manoeuvring of vehicles.

So this is our last ever sail on her and a brief one it is - only eighteen minutes on passage.

The car is taken up the hill above Mallaig harbour in time to film her final appearance on an Island Hop. We even hang around to photograph her arrival back in at Mallaig again an hour later. This time *Lochnevis* arrives in from the 'Small Isles' a few minutes ahead of her.

That's it. It's in the can, as they say in Holywood, and we can now go home. On the long drive south we hold the usual post mortem.

"Eventful," Gibbie describes Island Hop 2003. Despite the preceding years we still find new things to do. We agree that the highlight was the Tiree-Barra sailing. So what about next year? "What about the Swiss Lakes?" asks Ian.

"What about them?" Gibbie replies.

I say nothing, I have a cunning plan . . .

Postscript: Back home I hear there was an eclipse of the moon while we were away. Perhaps that's why the tides were so low.

Pioneer eventually returned to the Clyde on 20 August and continued in service on the Wemyss Bay-Rothesay and Gorock-Dunoon routes when required. She gave a special farewell excursion from Gourock to Tighnabruaich on 31 August and then surprisingly headed back to Malliag for further service on the Armadale and Small Isles routes. Her last ever day of service for CalMac was on Saturday 1 November, sailing to Rum, Muck, Eigg and Canna from Mallaig. She then headed back to the Clyde for lay-up. She was eventually sold for service off the west coast of Africa and left Scotland for the last time on Christmas Eve 2004.

Ferries arriving at Kirkwall
Favourite sunny spot on HEBRIDEAN ISLES

2004 Orcadian Daze

The Plan

QUITE SIMPLE, REALLY. Let's go to Orkney! After years of consideration we finally decided to include some Orcadian islands to our Island Hopping tally and to forsake Caledonian MacBrayne for Orkney Ferries, amongst others. There are lots of ferries in Orkney and most of them are operated by Orkney Ferries and most depart from Kirkwall to serve the many inhabited islands that make up the Orcadian archipelago.

There are also three links to Orkney from the Scottish mainland. Firstly there are the services run by Northlink from Aberdeen to Kirkwall (and Lerwick on Shetland), and from Scrabster (Caithness) to Stromness. Northlink operate three passenger ships on these two routes. Secondly there is a passenger-only service from John o'Groats to Burwick, on the south coast of the island of South Ronaldsay. Thirdly, and most interesting of all, is the service run by Pentland Ferries between Gill's Bay (Caithness) and St Margaret's Hope, on South Ronaldsay. This is interesting because the ships used on this route are ex-CalMac ships, namely Iona, now named Pentalina B, and *Claymore*. Both of these ships have featured in previous Island Hops.

Studying the respective timetables it became clear that with a car it would be possible to use both the Pentland Ferries route and the Scrabster-Stromness route to complete a wonderful circle. The problem was time.

It is a long sail from Aberdeen, and a long sail back. It is a long drive to Caithness, and a long drive back. And we have to keep the duration of the Island Hop within the constraints of four days. Then an idea we could fly to Orkney and hire a car. There is nothing in the Island Hop rule book that prevents us from using an aeroplane, in fact there isn't even an Island Hop rule book!

Another notion that ocurred during the planning stage was to visit the museum at Lyness on Hoy. Now Gibbie, especially, has a keen fascination, and excellent knowledge, of military history in general and the history of naval warfare in particular. And what better museum to visit, apart from perhaps the Imperial War Museum in London, than the naval museum at Lyness, on the very shores of Scapa Flow. He has never been there before, in fact I'm amazed that he has never received an official offer to come and run the place.

With several Orkney Ferries routes to choose from to fill the rest of our time it was not difficult to put an interesting itineraray together on this, our first ever Island Hop away from the Western Isles.

Day One - *Unfamiliar Territory*

It seems like sacrilege but we are taking a plane instead of a ship at the start of an Island Hop. This is, of course, a first. We have no option, unless we want to take ten days over our Island Hop instead of the usual three or four. Ten days would just not be practical, however, even ignoring the fact that none of us would be speaking to each other after that length of time in each other's company.

The plane is a Saab 340 and we are setting off from Edinburgh Airport on our Loganair flight to Kirkwall, the capital of Orkney. And remember, it's 'Orkney', not 'The Orkneys' nor 'The Orkney Isles'. The flight will touch down at Wick en route. It is a bumpy but not unpleasant ride north. And there is catering, but Gibbie is already making an official complaint, to the air-steward.

"What's that green stuff on my sandwich?" He asks abruptly.

"That's your salad, sir."

It is a strange thing, but Gibbie never stops the stewards aboard the ships ladelling 'green stuff' onto his plate, and yet he never touches it. "Why don't you tell them you don't want salad or peas, you never eat it?" I have often asked.

"It brightens up the plate," is his unexpected reply.

We should have a car waiting for us at Kirkwall Airport. It wasn't easy getting one but a local firm was eventually happy to oblige. I had been honest and explained that we wanted to take the car off the island on one of the days. "We don't usually allow that."

When I explained we were going to leave Orkney on the Stromness to Caithness ferry, drive along the coast for fifteen miles and then sail back to Orkney from another Caithness port, at Gill's Bay, there was a sufficient silence at the other end of the line for me to think we had been disconnected. "You want to do what? Why? Do you realise what it will cost?"

"Sshhh, yes, but don't tell my pals." A brief explanation of what Island Hopping is all about and his tone changed.

"Well that's okay. If you're that crackers then I'll have to say that's fine. If you're that daft you must be genuine." Needless to say a spotlessly clean, jade green, Ford Mondeo is waiting for us outside the airport terminal.

We step out of the car at a blustery Kirkwall Harbour and survey the nautical panorama that has so expeditiously appeared in front of us. No Oban Pier or Rothesay Harbour this time. This is different. The cold wind reminds us we're still in Scotland however.

There are four ferries tied up at the harbourside. Orkney Ferries run things up here, but by the look of things not too hectically on a Saturday afternoon. Numerous small sailing craft, a small coaster and a hotch potch of fishing boats add a more commercial flavour to the crowded basin. This is a working harbour, no doubt about that, and I can see that Gibbie and Ian are keenly interested.

To get the show on the road we plan to take two ferry trips this afternoon. Well they're in the itinerary so that means we have to go. First it's a return trip to the close-by island of Shapinsay, a twenty minute crossing from Kirkwall. We will have about an hour ashore there. Then, a bit later, we shall board a larger vessel for the sail out to the islands of Eday and Stronsay. On returning to Kirkwall we shall dash over to the other side of Mainland to our hotel for the night at Orkney's second conurbation - Stromness.

Our first Orcadian ship appears to be *Thorsvoe*. She was built in 1991 at Campbeltown and frequently replaces the regular ferry *Shapinsay*, which at the moment is away for annual overhaul to Buckie. The ticketman aboard the ship is offering concession fares - but only to Gibbie and Ian. I protest. "I'm actually seventy-three I just don't look my age!"

With a gravely rumble we reverse out from the slipway at 14.15 and spin around to head out from the jetty, with its trio of resting 'northern isles' ferries *Earl Sigurd*, *Earl Thorfinn* and *Varagen*. These three serve the more out flung islands of Westray, Papa Westray, Sanday, Eday, Stronsay and North Ronaldsay. They are sturdy looking ships with high bulwarks, their hulls painted in an attractive shade of dark blue. Their construction reflects the heavy winter seas which prevail in their northern domain.

Today it is calm, but breezy as we motor out. To our left, at the ferry terminal of Hatston, two miles out of Kirkwall, a cruise liner is berthed. She is instantly recognisable as *Funchal*, an ex-Fred Olsen Line ship. This is also the ferry terminal now for the two Northlink vessels which serve Orkney from Aberdeen - Hjaltland (the Icelandic name for Shetland) and Hrossay (the Old Norse name for Orkney). These ships sail from Aberdeen to Kirkwall and Lerwick in turn before returning to Aberdeen. One heads out to Orkney first and the other via Shetland. Sadly we will see neither on this trip as their arrival times are 23.30 at night and we are always tucked up in our beds by then. We see no point in seeing them if we can't get decent photographs. So we won't bother. Northlink have a third ship *Hamnavoe* which runs between Scrabster in Caithness to Stromness on Orkney Mainland. We certainly hope to see her later.

Shapinsay is basically a rectangular-shaped island lying five miles north of Kirkwall, but separated by only two miles from a spur of Orkney Mainland. Balfour Castle dominates the south-western corner, which we are now sailing past. The Balfour family originated in Fife but was given land on Shapinsay by the Bishop of Orkney in 1560. By the eighteenth century they owned a good bit of the island. Work began on the castle in 1847 and Balfours lived there until 1961. The village was laid out in the 1880s by Laird David Balfour. Okay, that's enough history for now.

The ferry slipway is at the northern extremity of the village, which basically consists of one street. It is mercifully sheltered from the westerly wind which is causing us to seek shelter on Thorsvoe.

Ian and I have a stroll along the deserted street and boost the local economy to the tune of the price of an ice lolly. Gibbie cannot get beyond the entrance to the castle as he has been accosted by a huge black cat. When we return to him twenty minutes later he is rolling on his back with his legs in the air - the cat that is, not Gibbie. Cats always seem to sense that Gibbie is a cat lover and forever treat him as one of them, and this panther is no exception. Gibbie responds to its open affection by pulling its tail. "Look they love this." Suddenly it drops over onto its side.

"You've killed it," I remark.

Back aboard the ship I engage an overalled crew member in general chit-chat about his ship. It is the first proper chance we've had to hear the melodic Orcadian brogue which to my ears resembles Welsh spoken by a Scandinavian. We are getting along fine until I blow it by asking if he is the engineer.

"No, certainly not, I'm the mate!"

"S-s-sorry."

"What's wrong with being an engineer?" Gibbie pipes up. "I'm one!"

Our sail on *Thorsvoe* has whet our appetite, but fortunately we only have half an hour back ashore before we are afloat again - just time to reposition the car for a fast get away when we return. We are now sailing out to the islands of Eday and Stronsay, but on which of the aforementioned trio will we be sailing? It turns out to be *Varagen* and we now have about four hours aboard her.

Varagen was acquired in 1991 and looks a bit different from the two sisters *Earl Sigurd* and *Earl Thorfinn*. She was built in 1989 for the ill-fated service from Gill's Bay to Burwick on the island of South Ronaldsay. This service was the brainchild of a new operator who wanted to set up in competition to P & O's services from Aberdeen - the services now run by Northlink. Some considered his choice of terminals ill advised. They were proved correct, for in September 1989 the Gill's Bay linkspan was severely damaged in a gale and this alternative 'short-route' to Orkney never came to fruition. And so Varagen was to join Earl Sigurd and Earl Thorfinn on services to the northern islands of Orkney instead. Ironically, as I've already mentioned, there now is a link from Gill's Bay to Orkney, but to St Margaret's Hope and not Burwick.

Up on the top deck of *Varagen* we find a sheltered spot and, for the second time in two hours, head out of Kirkwall. Gibbie and Ian take a tour of the ship and agree that they are glad that we are not spending the entire Island Hop on vessels such as these. Gibbie is missing *Isle of Mull*.

Once underway we head to the cafe on the starboard side to sample the culinary delights of Orkney Ferries. Mmm. Just tea and a biscuit for me please.

Eday is a seventy-five minute sail from Kirkwall and is an island I have never set foot on before. So I am keen to amend that this afternoon. It is a long, thin island, home to about 150 people and famous for the yellow sandstone which was used in the construction of parts of St Magnus Cathedral in Kirkwall. Most of Eday is rather bleak but we won't have time to see anything other than the south-eastern coast and the ferry terminal.

When we berth stern in at the short linkspan I stroll ashore so that my brief visit can be recorded on film. Then I almost do what Ian almost did on Coll many years ago - get left behind. Barriers are raised again and amid strange looks from the shore staff I quickly rush back aboard. *Varagen* heads due east now for Stronsay.

Out on deck, going with the wind, we spot porpoises dancing ahead of us in the surf, and overhead great skuas swing in purposeful arcs searching for hapless gulls to harry into giving up their last meal. At least they've had a meal - no such luck for us. The cafeteria is rather basic; there is a smashing soup machine though!

Stronsay approaches. The island is an interesting shape with arms and legs of land pointing everywhere. First we have to negotiate the narrow but well buoyed channel between it and its little sister Papa Stronsay.

At Stronsay Pier *Varagen* practically empties. There is a more recognisable village here, which is because only at Stronsay, of all the northern Orcadian islands, is the ferry terminal still sited at the island village. This is called Whitehall. I have been here before, when I brought my bike and cycling pal Sandy Stevens a couple of years ago. We cycled up and down all those arms and legs that day. But the three of us have no time to go ashore today, unfortunately, as the turn around times are neat. By neat I mean fast. There's no messing about and the ramp is up and we're heading back to Kirkwall as fast as we can say "this is saturday night, isn't it?"

We cannot remain out on deck for long as the wind is now sharp and the sky becoming more overcast and leaden. Worst of all - Gibbie's hair is getting blown all over the place - which is really annoying the other passengers. So we take a comfy seat inside the passenger lounge - well three comfy seats to be precise - where the TV is blaring out the usual diet of inane early Saturday evening television. Despite this, all seven occupants of the lounge - and that includes us - have their eyes fixed on it. Outside the weather is not so loud but equally dull. "Cabin air's so smart a dose," says the tannoy. "What?" I look at Ian for clarity.

"The cafeteria will shortly close," he translates.

The islands and deserted islets slip by as we push onwards back to Kirkwall. The little ship seems to be running faster - I think the crew are keen to get home so they can enjoy their Saturday night. Let's hope their not banking on anything worthwhile on telly.

Reunited with our car we are soon speeding westwards towards Stromness to enjoy what remains of our Saturday night.

I find Stromness a curious place. The second largest settlement on

Orkney it has a long waterfront, a very long waterfront, which is consistent with it being a busy port; in fact it was formerly a base for the Hudson Bay Company. Nowadays it serves as a ferry port for the ship from Scrabster, usually *Hamnavoe*. The main street is narrow and paved with large, grey, rectangular slabs, and seems to go on and on forever. Just as you think you're coming to the end it takes another half turn.

We drive around looking for our hotel. Unfortunately I cannot remember the name of it, which is a bit of an embarrassment really. I mean, just think about this. Imagine flying your good friends all the way up here, spending all afternoon on the ocean wave with them, arriving tired and starving at your final destination and then announcing at the eleventh hour - well about eight o'clock actually - that you cannot remember where you booked their beds for the night! It doesn't go down well. I try to defend myself by pointing out that I got the town right.

"It's somewhere here in Stromness."

So we spend half an hour on a somewhat bewildering tour of Stromness trying to find a hotel with a generally familiar name. Eventually Ian gets exasperated. "Come on Stuart, think! What is the hotel called?"

Put under such pressure it suddenly comes to me. "The Ferry Inn!"

"My how appropriate. And perhaps we'll find it near where the ferry is?" His good manners are suppressing his incredulity at my lack of lateral thinking.

"It's been a long day, I'm tired." It certainly has and we've still not eaten so after checking-in we have a quick stroll, or a slow sprint, along the one street looking for a suitable restaurant. Soon we are back at the Ferry Inn again. The halibut is very good.

Ian and I are sharing a room in the hotel annex, but after drifting off we are both awakened by much bellicose drunken screaming and shouting from the street outside. I had told Gibbie that if he had a dispute with the bill, or the band are too noisy, he should wait until morning!

Day Two - *On and Off and On Again*

It's an early start in the morning and I'm off to find the shower room with my pre-packaged personal bath mat under my arm. A nice touch, beats a free sewing kit any day. Washed and then breakfasted we are in the car joining the queue to board *Hamnavoe* by 08.30. She is a real ship and has been berthed at Stromness overnight. Like a trio of enthusiastic abdominal surgeons, we can't wait to get a look at her insides.

Hamnavoe is 112m long and has a gross tonnage of 8940. She has a normal sailing speed of nineteen knots. She was built at Aker Finnyards (Finland) for the Scrabster - Stromness route operated by Northlink but although launched in November 2001 she didn't commence service at Orkney until April 2003. Her name means 'safe haven' in Old Norse.

Security around the parking lanes and the terminal is conspicuous. None of the relaxed CalMac modus operandi here. Tickets are checked and re-checked before we are ushered to proceed onto the gaping car deck.

It turns out we are lucky bunnies. *Hamnavoe* has a problem with her propeller shafts and is heading for drydocking in Bremerhaven in Germany tomorrow. This is her penultimate sailing before she goes. All of our plans were made months ago and this is one of the highlights of the trip. We've made it by the skin of our teeth. When *Hamnavoe* is gone the sailings between Scrabster and Stromness will be by Northlink's freight vessel *Hascosay* - but for vehicles only. Passengers will be bused to the ferry terminals at Burwick (South Ronaldsay) and John O'Groats.

Hamnavoe is quite beautiful inside, more like a luxury cruise ship than a car ferry. The passenger accommodation is over two decks and includes a huge, stylish restaurant, a large bar and lounge, and a coffee bar, where the chairs and stools are wired to the floor. Yes the Pentland Firth has the reputation of being the roughest seaway in the UK. The shop and reception area would also not be out of place on a cruise ship.

The outside passenger accommodation is, however, limited to an area of rear deck. Just like one or two other ships I could name. There are very few seats for some reason and consequently the coach load of elderly passengers, which forms the bulk of this morning's complement, are wandering in a desultory fashion around the open space.

From this elevated platform we watch the linear Stromness slip past, as we head out of the channel, between Orkney Mainland and the island of Graemsay, on the start of our ninety minute passage to the Scottish mainland. Our route will take us around the north and west shores of the island of Hoy. This will take us past the sea cliffs of St. Johns Head. These cliffs are seriously impressive (almost 350 metres high), and just beyond is that momentous, mountaineering monolith, the rock stack Old Man of Hoy. The deep red sandstone cliffs positively glow when highlighted by the sun. But we have to use our imagination today as heavy clouds have strayed down over their tops, parting teasingly from time to time to offer us brief glimpses of the grassy summits.

The sea is bumpy and the westerly wind is whipping the wave crests horizontally up and over the sides of the ship. The clouds were trying to wring out their last drips of overnight rain, but we brave the elements to watch the dramatic scenery of Orkney's hilliest island creep slowly past.

"If only the sun was out," remarks Ian. But away ahead of the ship it is. The Scottish mainland is glistening in the morning sunshine way ahead of the plunging bow of the ship and it is evident that we will eventually sail out from under our bank of cloud. The sea becomes calmer the further south we sail. We descend for a coffee.

"Just how rough does it get up here?" I ask our cappuccino man.

"Very," he nods and heads off with a good impersonation of a roll-induced stagger.

Hamnavoe arrives fairly smartly into her berth at Scrabster. Much debate about what we do now as we have a couple of hours to kill before our sail back to Orkney from Gill's Bay, which is only fifteen miles along the road to the east. The agenda is to get the car up the cliff above Scrabster for a good photograph of *Hamnavoe*. From her deck we can see where we would like to be - there are some cottages high on the cliff above us, so there must be an access road.

We drive off and find a rough track that will get us to our vantage point. *Hamnavoe* will not be sailing for over an hour so we content ourselves with a picture of her sitting there at the pier, looking quite resplendent in her pale blue hull and white superstructure. We have been impressed by her. It is now a beautiful day and the joggers on the golden beach just below us are obviously having as much of a feel good factor as we are - just a touch more energy!

"Where will we go now?"

"There," Gibbie points straight out to sea. Illuminated by the sun the promontory of Dunnet Head is five miles away from us. "The most northern point on the British mainland," he explains with irrefutable authority. Okay, we're off.

Despite John O'Groats getting all the glory as being the most northern tip of the UK mainland, it is actually Dunnet Head. A look at the map will confirm it beats John in latitude by a mere two miles. It lies at the tip of an oval-shaped bulge which is reached by a B road just a few miles beyond Thurso. At the car park an inscribed block of granite confirms Dunnet Head's heady position.

There is of course a lighthouse, built in 1831 by Robert Stevenson, and a path leading to the top of some fairly splendid sea cliffs. We head along here and survey the seascape in front of us. Out to sea a lonely coaster, laden to the gunnels, inches westwards. Beyond her, five miles away, the *Hamnavoe* is pushing her way back to Stromness on the lunchtime sailing. We can even see the Old Man of Hoy poking up skywards above the cliffs of Hoy fifteen miles away.

Kittiwakes and fulmars fly out from the cliff ledges, engrossed in the business of feeding their young. A few puffins flutter by, way below us. A family with young children - a human one, that is - have set up their own little observation station on the path, complete with telescope and wooden box to stand on. Mum is scanning the cliffs intently. Suddenly she lets out a shriek which startles everyone around, plus a couple of fulmars.

"A peregrine!" She performs a dance of joy which would not have been out of place outside a tepee. We all get a look in the eyepiece and sure enough, perched nonchalantly on the edge of the cliff, two hundred metres or so away, is a male peregrine falcon, oblivious to the stir it's caused. The young Mum explains, once she's calmed down, that this is her first peregrine, a new 'life tick' despite many months of searching. Her enthusiasm is infectious. We cannot linger anymore, however; we have a

117

ship to catch and she is an old friend.

Claymore was actually the first ship that all three of us sailed together on an Island Hop. That was back in the misty haze of 1990 and we sailed from Islay to Oban on her. When she left CalMac she became the Campbeltown - Ballycastle ferry under the auspices of the ill-fated Argyll and Antrim Steam Packet Company; and we sailed on her on this route in 1998. Now, after her fair share of languishing, she is being operated by Pentland Ferries, who also own ex-CalMac ship *Iona*. They have one route - from Gill's Bay here in Caithness, to St. Margaret's Hope on South Ronaldsay. *Claymore* was always Gibbie's favourite ship, so he is looking forward to seeing what kind of condition she is in today. Hopefully just as good as Gibbie!

Gill's Bay is a further ten miles along the coast and on the way we pass the entrance to the Castle of May, a favourite residence of the late Queen Mother. The ferry terminal of Gill's Bay looks as though it was thrown together. A couple of disheveled Portakabins amid an untidy car park. We are early and in need of a cup-a-soup. My tomato and herb consomme gets stuck, while still in tablet form, in the bowels of the machine and takes much finger-probing, in the style of a proctologist, to free it.

"That's very clever," observes Ian, "where did you learn such digital dexterity?" It is an exercise I repeat twice before we can all dine.

Claymore can be seen rounding the south-west corner of the island of Stroma, which lies in the middle of the direct passage from South Ronaldsay. Back in her black hull livery, and with her red and black funnels, she looks almost like a CalMac ship again, and I can imagine I see a lump in Gibbie's throat. As she nears it becomes obvious that she has lost some of her poise and grace and is aging into the twilight of her career, like an old spinster who no longer cares about dressing for the occasion. Once on board her we can see that some of her paintwork is fading and her decor and upholstery looks tired. But she takes on a full load of vehicles and heads out into the sunny Pentland Firth purposefully like the *Claymore* of old. We have never before sailed on a ship which has had three different owners.

The contrast between the ferry terminals and the two ships we've sampled today could not be greater. The sleek, polished interior of *Hamnavoe* and the fading splendour of *Claymore* are in striking contrast. But who cares? Both are providing a good service, albeit at very different prices. They have given us a unique Island Hopping opportunity to sail on a circular route between the Scottish mainland and Orkney. I just wonder if anyone else has ever done this! I also wish that the car-hire chap could see us and his vehicle now, crammed onto the car deck.

We sample lunch in the cafeteria. Gibbie has another egg sandwich - he's had so many eggs on this trip I'd swear his mop of white hair now resembles feathers. In time honoured fashion the yolk spurts out from his roll and runs down his chin into a congealing amber wax. You'd think that in sixty-odd years of eating eggs he would have mastered control by now.

The one thing that always made *Claymore* a favourite for us was the forward deck with its view over the bow. From here we watch in silence as the abandoned villages on the islands of Stroma and Swona pass us by on our port side. Empty, hollow, roofless houses stare desolately across at us. Stroma was abandoned in the 1950s and Swona as recently as 1974.

Entering the southern reaches of Scapa Flow, between the islands of Flotta and South Ronaldsay, empty gun placements from WW II straddle the channel. As we turn around the western headland which guards the entrance to St. Margaret's Hope we spot *Pentalina B* (ex *Iona*) lying at the pier. We think *Claymore* is looking a touch jaded but *Pentalina B* looks in an even worse state. The bow has actually grounded on the shore and she lies at a strange angle.

Once ashore we take a closer look. Despite her initial posture she has been given a fresh lick of paint and it is intended that she will take over the service in the summer as she has the pace to provide four return trips daily instead of three. I don't recall ever seeing these two ships together before, when they were in CalMac colours, so it is odd to see them berthed together now.

We drive north now towards Kirkwall, thus completing the circle. This will take us over the islands of South Ronaldsay, Burray, Glimps Holm and Lambs Holm, which are linked like beads on a chain by causeways. These causeways, which carry the road right onto the Mainland over the four famous Churchill Barriers, were built to protect Scapa Flow from German attacks approaching from the east during WW II. As we shall see later it was a bit like shutting the stable door after the horse had bolted. On the last island before Mainland, tiny Lambs Holm, we stop to look inside the Italian Chapel.

When they weren't building the Churchill Barriers the 500 Italian prisoners-of-war on Lamb Holm built themselves a chapel. They were permitted to construct their chapel by positioning two Nissen huts end-to-end and with great resourcefulness constructed a little gem. A stone facade, painted in a smart creamy-white, was built onto the front end of the first Nissen hut and this makes it look like a real church. It was obviously put together with love and care and must have been a spiritual haven for the Italians. Such was the recognition of their pride in their work that in 1960 some of them were invited back to help restore the chapel. It still looks quite splendid today.

We reach Kirkwall about 18.00, and while my colleagues peruse the dinner menu, I take a stroll with my camera up the pier, telling them, "I'll be back in ten minutes." It is a grey but peaceful early evening; the wind has now died away completely. The lighthouse tender Pharos is moored at the head of the pier; we have often encountered her at Oban. Further down the pier a fishing boat is unloading nets full of the largest whelks I've ever seen. These are being taken by lorry and ferry to Macduff on the

Scottish mainland but are eventually bound for South Korea, where they are considered a delicacy.

Out to sea three ferries are making their way in convoy towards the harbour. I decide to skip the first course of dinner, set up camera and wait to film them all. First *Thorsvoe* arrives from Shapinsay, and then Earl *Thorfinn* and *Varagen* enter. By the time they have all berthed an hour has passed since I left Gibbie and Ian. Oops!

Day Three - *Scapa Flow*

We're off to a museum this morning - not something we commonly do on an Island Hop - but this is a special place and one earmarked as a must-see during the planning of our trip.

Lyness Museum is on the site of a famous British naval base on the eastern side of Hoy. It is dedicated to the history of Scapa Flow, particularly from both World Wars. I've been there before, but not Gibbie and Ian, who are keen to see it. To get there we are sailing from Houton, on Orkney Mainland, which is just a few miles east of Stromness and at the northern reaches of Scapa Flow.

Our ferry is *Hoy Head* and we sail off as foot passengers into a surprisingly cold and blustery wind. Aboard we are accompanied by a full load of cruisers from *Black Prince*, which is now anchored in Kirkwall Bay. Trying to find a warm corner on *Hoy Head* is not easy, but we eventually huddle in the smokers' lounge, where we ban Gibbie from lighting up. At least the soup machine works and our fingers thaw out as we clutch cardboard cups of what is loosely described as chicken soup. It has been a very 'soupy' Island Hop so far.

Lyness takes thirty-five minutes to reach and everyone herds off. It is clear that the contents of *Black Prince* are also heading for the museum, which is a mere stroll away. So we head straight for the cafe to secure our line of culinary advance. "When is that lot booked in for lunch?" I ask the pretty girl behind the counter.

"They're going back to their ship for lunch." Great - I don't think the cafe could cope with a queue of fifty strong.

We spend nearly three hours in the museum, with a break for lunch. The history of Scapa Flow is neatly laid out in chronological order in simple format. Scapa Flow covers 120 square miles and its name comes from the Norse world 'skalpeidfloi', meaning 'the fjord of the ship isthmus'. It has seen much action.

King Hakon Hakansson sailed into it with 120 longships in 1263 prior to heading south to play his part in the Battle of Largs.

At the tail end of the Napoleanic Wars the Martello Towers, round stone structures used as gun supports, were constructed at Hackness and Crockness on the southern approaches to Scapa Flow. These were built to protect Scapa from American privateers.

In WW I the British Home Fleet was based here and set up antisubmarine nets to link the islands around it. This did not prevent tragedies like *HMS Hampshire* being mined in June 1916 on the western side of Hoy, killing British Foreign Secretary Lord Kitchener. In July 1917 *HMS Vanguard* exploded out in Scapa Flow killing 800 sailors. During a dreadful storm in January 1918 two British destroyers, Opal and Marlborough, sailed blindly into cliffs on the east side of South Ronaldsay. There was only one survivor. Most famous of all was the sinking of the battleship *Royal Oak* - more of that later.

In June 1919 the seventy-four ships of the German Navy, held here in limbo since the end of WW I, were scuttled on the orders of Admiral von Reuter. The garrison of British ships had left early that day on exercises. The ships took five hours to sink. Nine Germans died and 1774 were made POW's. Fifty-two ships sank and twenty-two were beached. Much of their steel has been salvaged, as its low radioactive count is useful in body-monitor machines used in medicine (modern steel has absorbed nuclear fission products from the atmosphere). What remains of the German ships under the surface makes Scapa Flow a Mecca for recreatitional diving to this day.

And that leaves *Royal Oak*. In the early days of WW II German U-boat U47, captained by Gunther Prien, found a gap in the eastern defense of Scapa. She crept stealthily through the gap to torpedo the anchored British battleship. U47 escaped back out the way she came, but *Royal Oak* sank in thirteen minutes, with the loss of 833 sailors.

Prien was trying to find a gap around the blockships between Lambs Holm and Glimps Holm. Apparently one of his junior ratings pointed out that he was too far south and should try threading the needle between Lambs Holm and Mainland Orkney. He was persuaded to try further north. Here he found that the blockships nearest the Mainland shore had hinged outwards by the tide, and amazingly Prien found the gap. He sailed his U-boat through on the surface and escaped the same way. The result was a devastating blow to the Royal Navy but he was lucky - had he approached Scapa Flow from the south he would have encountered two British aircraft carriers instead.

The loss of *Royal Oak* convinced Churchill that the blockships were ineffective and he ordered the construction of the Barriers that bear his name. The intricacies and fine detail of the *Royal Oak* tragedy are related to us by one of the museum staff, whose grandfather served on battlecruiser *Lion* in WW I. He initially thinks we're part of the *Black Prince* complement, but I point out to him that I am too young.

Soon we have the museum to ourselves - and then the cafe, so we have that lunch break, which we share with a group of divers (that's people dressed in wet suits, not the ornithological kind). Another egg sandwich for Gibbie has Ian and I calling him 'the royal yolk'.

Before *Hoy Head* returns for us I take a stroll up the track that heads uphill from the museum. After tales of death and destruction it is a wonderful contrast to find the hillside alive with bird life. Curlews and chasing crows, a heron stalking a nearby pond, a cuckoo calling evocatively high on the hillside, and the coniferous plantation alive with the bouncing zing of goldcrests. Such abundant wildlife overlooking a place haunted by the destruction of the past.

At 14.05 *Hoy Head* takes us away from Lyress in blustery but sunnier conditions to the island of Flotta.

Flotta sits at the southern end of Scapa Flow and was an uninspiring, bucolic little island, until Europe's second largest oil terminal was built on it in 1974 and changed its countenance forever. Hundreds of miles of pipeline link it to the North Sea fields and a thriving community once more lives here. A tall gas flare serves as a beacon, demonstrating how a thriving industry can bring economic benefits to an island community and still merge harmoniously into the environment. It is also a useful landmark in locating the southern approaches of Scapa Flow.

The ferry exchanges a few passengers at Flotta and then heads north back up Scapa Flow towards Houton. Waves splash high over the ramp of the ferry and we head down below to keep warm. We are passing over the very spot where the German Fleet scuttled eighty-five years ago, but Scapa Flow looks peaceful now. Apart from *Hoy Head* there are a handful of diving boats around, most of them converted from fishing boats. These carry parties of well-equipped diving tourists, now apparently a more lucrative business than fishing.

We disembark at Houton and drive into Stromness looking for our next ferry. At the pier Hascosay has replaced the injured *Hamnavoe* and is getting ready to sail. She is carrying vehicles only - their passengers have to take the bus.

Our ferry is the little *Graemsay*, a small, sturdy passenger ferry built in 1996 at Ailsa, Troon. She resembles a neat little tug. Her cheery crew usher us aboard and we embark on a short trip which will take us to the island of Graemsay, onto North Hoy pier and then back again. I've promised my chums a bumpy ride and they're not going to be disappointed.

The tide seems to merge and conflict around the waters of Graemsay in a style reminiscent of Corryvreckan. We bump out of Stromness, past fishery protection vessel *Minna* and followed by *Hascosay*, which is sailing for Scrabster. We are not the only passengers just going along for the ride. Graemsay is a heart shaped island measuring a couple of miles across by one mile north to south. It is really like one big farm. Our call at the pier has to go down in Island Hop history as the briefest ever. As soon as I step ashore to take a photograph I am simultaneously beckoned back aboard again. "Just a quick photo," I reassure.

"Be quick," says the skipper, "and take your lens cap off."

We sail off again, circumnavigating the island. Over to the pier at North Hoy to exchange a few passengers very quickly and on again. Then it's back to Stromness around the west side of Graemsay. It is very bumpy and green water is shipped through the freeboards on the little open deck. Well I know the term is 'green water' but it looks the usual clear stuff to me.

At the confluence of the tides the boat lurches and we have to hold on tight. Overhead an arctic skua races after a gull at frantic speed and a group of puffins flutter purposefully out to sea.

We arrive back at Stromness windswept, cold and with hair all over the place, but with big smiles on our faces. We drive back to Kirkwall now and find the harbour full of yachts - many of them Norwegian. Bunting flutters wildly from their rigging. We find a little American diner and choose to eat there. The chilli is enormous and delicious, and still served with an Orcadian accent. Huddled around a roaring fire in our hotel bar we discuss everything from whisky to the emancipation of women in today's society. But then we've sampled a few tonight - the whisky I mean.

Day Four - *Three Isles Soaking*

Breakfast is at 08.30 and I arrive promptly. My two colleagues have arrived even more promptly - by twenty minutes - so I finish by dining alone, while Ian goes off to "check the plumbing" and Gibbie to "clean his teeth." Why doesn't he brush them like everyone else?

The island of Rousay is "the Egypt of the north" says my leaflet. Well we're off there this morning and I'm hoping we see some pyramids. We will also visit the islands of Egilsay and Wyre.

Before we head off to Tingwall for our ferry trip we have a wander around Kirkwall. Ian and I have a look inside St Magnus Cathedral which seems massive for a such a small town. The rich russet hue of its sandstone is what really impresses me. The stone came from nearby on Mainland and from the island of Eday. The cathedral was completed in 1137 and is the resting place for the bones of Saint Magnus (who was slain on the island of Egilsay). We take a closer look. At the entrance to the cathedral a huge restored stained-glass window reflects the Orkney way of life down the centuries. Inside the columns of red sandstone look squint! It is a most impressive building.

We drive under an overcast sky to Tingwall, which is about ten miles up the western side of Mainland. The rain goes on and off, as if it can't make up its mind whether to drown us or spare us. We arrive at Tingwall in plenty of time and discuss our route.

Eynhallow will take us to Rousay, where we will have an hour ashore, then over to Wyre, then Egilsay, back to Rousay, then back to Tingwall. These three islands, of which Rousay is by far the biggest, lie between the north-eastern shore of Orkney Mainland and the more far-flung islands of Westray and Eday. All three islands are rich in wildlife and historic sites, however Wyre is not much more than a green lump of rich farmland - measuring only one mile by two.

At the ticket office on the pier I check that the alleged cafe on Rousay will be open. I am reassured it will. Very important as there aren't many eating places around here. The ferry looks like a large landing-craft. Among the vehicles aboard is a trailer containing a huge black bull. He stares out at me with a huge, dark, intimidating eye. "He's a mean fellow that," says the crewman.

"Where's he going?"

"Wyre - to sow his oats."

I look at the bull again, and am surprised he's not got a smile on his face. The sea is also looking fierce today and it is a rough passage over to Rousay. Taking shelter in the cabin, looking out of the window at the sea, we could easily be in the North Atlantic. But then I suppose we are.

We take thirty minutes to get to Rousay. In the cabin we struggle hard not to stare at the only other occupant, who is sitting opposite us. A bulky chap with dark hair and a face that only a mother could love. We get off at Rousay and the ferry sets off on an extra run over to Wyre to deliver its fresh gene pool. We seek refuge in the cafe, which is indeed open.

Rousay is a very hilly island, and remarkably circular - with a diameter of four or five miles. About 200 people live here, and about ten per cent of them are in the cafe just now. But we get fed and are soon back on *Eynhallow*, heading now towards the more fertile Wyre (in more than one sense of the word - thanks to that bull). This is a ten minute journey. Then it's to Egilsay. One little schoolboy is delivered on Egilsay with no one waiting there in return.

Egilsay is another small island - three miles north-to-south and only one mile wide. The ruin of St Magnus Church stands like watch-tower near the centre of the island, just up from the ferry slipway. It was on this island that St Magnus was killed by his rival's cook in 1117. No he didn't die from food poisoning but by the axe!

The weather has really closed in now and it is impossible to step out on deck without getting a soaking from the many gallons of spray being thrown over the ship by the buffeting sea. It looks like a force seven or eight out there. The cabin of the ferry has a door leading out to the stern from where a flight of steep steps leads to the upper deck. I tentatively climb up and carefully put my head above the parapet, only to have the upper half of me completely drenched by a wave. I return to the cabin to let Gibbie and Ian have a good laugh at me. I don't think I have ever been as drookit on an Island Hop. It is totally miserable outside and we are canned up in this small lounge, unable to go out on deck, the only passengers and wondering why we are here. To make matters worse we have to sail over to Rousay again before returning to Tingwall.

124

We are glad to be reunited eventually with the car. No more sails now but still some photography to be completed. We decide to have a brief cultural tour of the island, and then catch a view of Hascosay from a good vantage point as she sets out from Stromness in the late afternoon.

We drive around the north and west of Mainland, pointing out such sites as Birsay, the Kitchener Monument on Marwick Head and Skara Brae. We just point them out of course, we don't actually visit them. At Skara Brae we come quite close, as close as a coffee and a biscuit in the cafe at the visitor centre. I've actually visited them all before, you see, whereas my two colleagues are just Philistines. Ian's comment proves the point, "There's a lot of stones in Orkney!"

Our final drive is to Stromness and then it is down at the shore by the golf course where we are in pole position to film Hascosay departing for the Scottish mainland. It is cold and blustery but the rain ceases for five minutes while the cameras are rolling. On the way back to Kirkwall we stop at the Ring of Brodgar to take in the 'stones'. It is our final piece of culture, we're well and truly stoned..

Day Four - *Plumbing Inspection*

Up at 06.15 for a 07.30 flight. We return the car to the airport and plop the keys in the box as requested. Not long after checking-in Ian's latest plumbing inspection is rudely interrupted by a tannoy requesting his immediate materialisation at baggage check-in.

"Eh - he's in the toilet."

"He is wanted for a random inspection," they say.

"Well I would put those rubber gloves away as I reckon you're too late." I didn't actually say that, of course, but told Ian I had. But he eventually gets clearance to travel, and so do the rest of us.

We get a final aerial glimpse of *Pentalina B* and *Claymore* before they vapourise into the clouds. Will we ever see these dear old ladies again?

Andy's Jag at Lochranza

2005 Small Isles, Long Isles and Steamboats

The Plan

C HOOSING A PLAN FOR ISLAND HOP 2005 was fairly straight forward. It was two years since we had sailed in the Western Isles, and a few things had changed since then. For a start, there were two new CalMac ships in service: Coruisk serving between Mallaig and Armadale, and Loch Portain across the Sound of *Harris* between *Harris* and Berneray. By sailing on the latter we would have the opportunity to journey the whole way down the Western Isles chain. The 'bridging' of these islands by the provision of inter-island ferries, without the need to sail via Skye or Oban, was completed in 2003. With the introduction of Loch Portain, across the Sound of *Harris*, and the resulting redeployment of Loch Bhrusda to the Sound of Barra, the ferry and causeway links between Lewis, in the north, and Vatersay in the south were complete. This route, and the new vessels in service, were opportunities too good to miss, and so achieving these objectives became the backbone of Island Hop 2005.

It was also eight years since we last sailed on Isle of Lewis; and we had never stayed overnight in Stornoway. So the finer details of the plan could be added. And there were two other new possibilities for us in our quest to add new experiences to Island Hopping. The completion of ramps on each of the Small Isles meant we could at last step onto one of those islands that we had never visited. Also, with time to kill on our last day we spotted an opportunity to sail on a real old steamer.

Day One - *Just Getting There*

We're off at 14.20, heading north up the familiar road. We have no sailings today. We have just to get to Mallaig. Unusually we are in Ian's car, and we should make the journey in under four hours - it was either that or taking seven hours in Gibbie's car! Ian is doing all the driving - it helps to relieve his tension. I've worried him by announcing that there will be an Island Hop Quiz during the course of this year's trip. We had one of those a few years ago. That time Ian failed so miserably that I wondered if he had used a doppleganger to accompany Gibbie and I around the Western Isles all these years, while he himself sat at home with his feet up. I rake through our archives and come up with a dozen or so questions on ships, islands, dates etc.

Gibbie relieves his strain by indulging in a long rambling story, delivered in Ronnie Corbett style, about the virtues of spending a summer holiday in Fife. His story has more tangents than a book of trigonometry tables but keeps us entertained for at least fifteen miles, before finishing in typical Gibbie candour.

"Aye Fife's nice, mind you I'd rather spend it on the Clyde!"

I stretch out along the back seat as we speed through Glen Coe. The mountains are not their usual gloomy selves but are highlighted by spring sunshine and consequently tower impressively above us.

Inevitably on the first day of an Island Hop my two engineering pals get locked in a nostalgic flashback about their days in the shipyards. Listening to them talking I wonder how we ever lost so much of that industry. But the conversation gets a bit too anatomical for my liking. "Remember you had that trouble with your stern gland, Gibbie."

There's a comfort stop at a very pleasant cafe at Ballachulish and then it's off again, brain tingling from a double espresso. Gibbie takes over the driving and keeps Ian on edge by boasting about his propensity of adding scrapes and scores to his own car. "When I got my new Citroen last August (Andre was traded in for about a fiver) my kids took bets on how soon I would put a bash on it. Number Two son was the most unkind with his guess of three months." Gibbie swerves slightly to avoid running into the back of the Fort William bus before continuing. " In fact it only took me forty-three days." Ian winces.

We get to Mallaig at 18.30 and Gibbie embeds the front valance of Ian's car onto the pavement right outside our hotel. "We're here!" He announces proudly.

We hump our considerable gear out of the boot. "Your boot could do with a wee refinement, Ian." Gibbie remarks.

"What did you have in mind, Gibbie? You've already shortened the front end of the car"

Mallaig speaks, if not reeks, of the sea. In close proximity there are the Marine Hotel, Mallaig Marine World, The Fisherman's Mission, The Fisherman's Co-op and, best of all, a sign announcing 'Jaffy's Kippers Seafood by Post'. The harbour is quiet. There is no wind and the promised rain has not materialised (probably because of the BBC's new dumbed-down weather maps, which do everything except tell us what the weather is going to do). Tomorrow's ferries are lying dormant at the pier, *Coruisk* and *Lochnevis*. I head back to the table for a little malt nightcap. Ian and Gibbie are one step ahead of me.

"You know," Ian starts, "some of my pals think our Annual Island Hop is just an excuse for a booze-up. I've told them that's nonsense." He's right - none of us can remember that ever happening.

Out of our panoramic window to the west the unmistakable aircraft-carrier contour of Eigg, and the Hawaiian outline of Rum are silhouetted by the orange glow from an evening sky unimpeded by cloud. Tomorrow looks as if it is going to be a nice day - and we're off to Honolulu!

Up not too early. Ian is ahead of the game and half way through breakfast already. Things are not going too well, however. He asked the waitress for tea and brown bread toast - and got white bread and coffee. Gibbie is late down. He hasn't brought an alarm clock with him and apparently needs one if he is forced to rise before 11.30.

Just as we hoped Mallaig is bathed in clear sunshine this morning and playing the part of the archetypal Hebridean port. The ferries are waiting at the harbour, the fishermen are slowly getting their act together and the train from Glasgow has arrived at the station, disgorging its load of backpackers and tourists bound for Rum or Skye. Down at the pier Ian is eyeing *Coruisk* disdainfully as she departs for Armadale. It is his first sight of her.

"Strange looking craft." Our first ship will be *Lochnevis*, but we have a few things to attend to before we sail at 10.15.

First we have to tell the CalMac staff that we have brought a different car to that booked on their computer, Ian attends to that. Next we have to purchase *Rover* tickets, Ian does that as well. And finally the car has to be parked away from the pier as we will be sailing on *Lochnevis* without it. So we let Ian attend to this as well. So Gibbie and I stand around and watch Ian scurrying around in circles and remark on how important it is to share duties on our Island Hop.

"Must get myself an alarm clock." Gibbie suddenly declares and off he goes. He returns looking very smug a few minutes later. "Got one. A cracker! £2.99, good, eh?"

Ian returns and we have a brief photo call above the pier, and then climb aboard Lochnevis for what will be a seven hour trip. This is definitely one of our favourite ships and today we are just a little excited, because not only will we be able to set foot on Rum, for the first time, but we will also have a decent bit of time ashore on Canna, which we only previously visited very briefly in 1996. The ship is busy, mostly with middle-aged chaps clad in beards and Barbour who we reckon, correctly, will be disembarking at Rum.

We depart three minutes early and head out gently onto a calm sea towards the Small Isles. It is good to be on the move at last. The ship will call at Rum first and then head out to Canna. The Rum revellers will have four hours on the island - enough time for a good hike. We shall stay aboard for Canna, where there will be an hour and a half stop-over - time for Ian and I to have a short hike and Gibbie to have a snooze.

The twin peaks of Askival and Hallival are dead ahead as we emerge from the cafeteria after our second breakfast. Turning into Loch Scresort, Kinloch Castle now lies dead ahead.

Kinloch Castle was built as a lavish and extravagent holiday home by George Bullough, the son of a wealthy MP who had made his fortune from the manufacture of milling machines in Lancashire. The Castle was constructed from red sandstone shipped in from Arran and was completed in 1902. The profligate internal fittings were enjoyed by guests ferried in by steam yacht. I'm not carping here, just being a little envious - we're arriving by CalMac ferry and don't even have time to set foot in the place!

Rum, and Kinloch Castle, were sold by the Bullough family to the Government in 1957 and are now owned by Scottish Natural Heritage. The Castle interior has faded somewhat from its original glamour but from the outside the building still holds considerable charm.

The excitement of stepping ashore on a new island is - well almost exciting. The new concrete ramp is situated on the left hand (south) side of the bay and easily accommodates *Lochnevis'* huge ramp. The land rises steeply above the jetty to merge with the deeply grooved mountains and cliffs of this wild and seemingly inhospitable island. The forty all-weather types walk off onto the island cheerfully and string themselves out along the track towards Kinloch. But our visit will be one of those infuriatingly ephemeral step-off-and-on jobs. We have to jump back on very quickly for the ship will not hang around. At last, after seventeen years of Island Hopping, we can say that we are finally on the Rum.

The clouds are on the Rum as well. The peaks of the island attract a veil of mist which only adds to the atmospheric mystique of this island. I was tempted to stay ashore and join the rest of the ramblers, but this is Island Hopping and the island of Canna beckons. The ship wheels out of the bay and turns northwards, back into the sunshine again.

Canna is owned and managed by the National Trust for Scotland. The island is only about four miles by one. The pier tiny and only a handful of visitors disembark today. They head off past the tiny church towards the small neat cafe. We follow along behind. The cafe is a cottage on the shore with tables and parasols outside. Not surprisingly it's full and the young woman in control is clearly doing her bit to help the intrepid tourist. We pass on the crab thermador, however, and settle for a coffee.

Canna Harbour is a haven for yachts due to it being almost completely encircled by the tidal island of Sanday to the south. Surprisingly there are no yachts here today - perhaps it's too early in the season. Instead there is nothing but tranquillity.

We walk round the bay to the point where Sanday touches Canna, if only at low tide. According to the map this two mile strip of an island has a footbridge connecting it to Canna. Can we claim another island? The answer is no. Like the Bridge at Remagen - it's gone! The narrow wooden structure has fallen into the channel between the two islands leaving a series of concrete supports standing redundant. A beach lies tantalisingly just out of reach on the other side. How do the residents of Sanday get across for a coffee, a crab thermador or anything else for that matter? We head back but take a short detour to the small bay at Coroghan where the remains of a tiny castle cling precariously onto the side of a huge rock.

Below it is a beautiful small beach of dark grey sand. At the side of the path leading back to the ship there is a tiny church and we stop to look inside. It is still in use as a place of worship and an open dish of collection coins lies unattended on a table. Only trustworthy tourists come to Canna.

Back onboard Lochnevis we wait to depart. The woman from the cafe arrives with great gusto to perform her alternative job. She zooms up astride a quad-bike and drives it right up to the side of the ship where she eases the ropes off the bollards. Then she's off again, back down the track to simmer another crab bisque.

Down for a bowl of CalMac broth. We now head back to Rum where most of the walkers and ramblers are awaiting the return of the ship. A tractor appears and proceeds to board the ship with a trailer full of bags of empty cans and bottles, heading for recycling on the mainland. For some reason most of the bottles are Budweiser. The onboard crane hoists the eight bags one at a time from the trailer, but progress is slow.

Time is neat now for once back at Mallaig we only have a forty minute leeway between this ship and the last sailing of the day of Coruisk. We need to be on that, and just as importantly, so does Ian's car. If we miss that sailing it will be a long, unpopular drive to Skye across the Skye Bridge. So when we are ten minutes the wrong side of our Rum departure time, with still no sign of the tractor and trailer disembarking, we give ourselves anxious looks. But soon we are finally away and we are confident there will be no further delays.

The sky is overcast now and it is cool out on deck. As we turn into Mallaig Harbour we can see *Coruisk* just leaving her berth at Armadale. She's coming to get us. Back ashore we have eaten fifteen minutes into our time but there is no panic. Ian collects the car and parks it in the queue for the final Armadale sailing of the day.

Coruisk is indeed a strange looking craft; she looks as if she's been made out of Lego. She was constructed as a dual purpose vessel - serving Armadale from Mallaig in summer and relieving the Upper Clyde ferries on the Wemyss Bay-Rothesay and Gourock-Dunoon routes in winter. It is a dual role that seems to be working very well. Not only does she have a dual purpose, she has a dual bow as well, and a dual stern. In fact when she's at sea it's difficult to tell whether she's coming or going. Now all of CalMac's Loch class ferries are double-ended, with ramps at either end and no discernable bow or stern. And they look okay, in my opinion. But Coruisk is a much bigger vessel and actually looks as if she has two bows. She doesn't look right to me. Gibbie and I have sailed on her on the Clyde but this is the first time we have sailed on her on an Island Hop.

We head out on time, stern first, although it could be bow first - it's difficult to tell. And there is hardly time to sip a coffee in her excellent passenger lounge before we are suddenly at the other side.

Once on Skye we have a long but enjoyable drive up to Uig for our overnight berth. Passing through the Cuillins, as we have done so many times, past Sconser where *Loch Striven* is taking her final sailing of the day to Raasay and through Portree with its usual bustle of tourists.

The evening is spent enjoying an excellent meal and sipping real ale at an inn at Uig, at the northern end of the island. We share the small lounge with two couples, who coincidentally happen to be Dutch. There's Ruud and Harriet from southern Holland, and a honeymooning couple from Alkmaar. It is a fun evening, at the end of which the honeymooners ask Ian and Gibbie to pose with them for a photograph. For some reason they don't want me in the frame - I'm asked to take the picture!

Day Three - *Thrice the Minch*

It's a real hearty breakfast this morning to which, perhaps surprisingly, the honeymoon couple are in attendance. Which is more than can be said for Gibbie. He eventually appears, muttering almost inaudibly. "£2.99 down the drain!"

This morning we are off to *Harris* onboard *Hebrides*. This will get us over to the Western Isles and once there - well I'll just tell it as it happens.

Outside it is cloudy and cool and, according to the forecast, showers can be expected. We chunter down the hill to the pier. Now here lies a major bone of contention with me. Namely piers. No longer can one amble aimlessly up a pier to watch the ferry arrive or cast an eye on the local fisherman or, God forbid, do a little fishing yourself. Largs Pier, for example, has recently been cordoned off, like a murder scene, to prevent anyone from accidentally wandering up for a closer look at the sea. Is this Health and Safety again? Do they think we are going to wander up to the end of a pier and throw ourselves off the end and then try to sue somebody? I find it all quite condescending that someone has decided to protect us from ourselves in this fashion. Why don't they cordon off railway platforms? Have you ever stood an unprotected metre from the edge of a platform when a train thunders through a station it has no intention of stopping at? That is a much more dangerous situation to find yourself in. Anyway, the point of all this is that Uig Pier is not just cordoned off but one is not even allowed to walk up it to board the ferry. You have to take the bus! Needless to say I break all the rules and am up there with my camera when *Hebrides* comes circling into the bay.

We take the car onboard the ship and ascend to the rear deck where we bump into Ruud and Harriet. We chat about tourism and football while *Hebrides* sets off for Tarbert on *Harris*. "You must all visit us in Holland," Ruud offers. A dangerous thing to say - we might all turn up at the same time. Ruud is a carpenter, making furniture for a living, and he and his blonde wife are off to see the beaches of *Harris*. I assure them they will not be disappointed.

Hebrides has been altered since we last sailed on her. Her upper deck at the stern has been extended aft to give more outdoor seating. This was done during her annual overhaul on the Clyde last winter and a similar amendment was made to her sister *Clansman* - a feature we should be able to appreciate on our planned sail from Barra in a couple of days time. Meanwhile we are enjoying this new facility for the sun is out and it is a very pleasant sail across the Little Minch.

We have second breakfast in the cafeteria, or in Gibbie's case first breakfast. He is still deeply traumatised by the failure of his alarm clock. "Do we go home via Mallaig? I could take it back."

Our arrival at Tarbert on *Harris* coincides with some serious sunshine. What happened to the showers? Must be those new weather maps.

We bid farewell to Ruud and Harriet. "Come and visit us, bring your family! We can go watch PSV Eindhoven."

"We've got nine kids between us, you know, not counting some grandchildren," replies Gibbie.

The plan now is to get up to Stornoway, but we are in no particular rush so pause to take in the amenities of Tarbert. This doesn't take very long. We drive away from Tarbert and East Loch very quickly becomes West Loch. There are many 'tarberts' in Scotland but this must be one of the narrowest. We begin our climb into the hills. In the middle of the loch the dark form and dorsal fin of a half submerged creature is spotted. A minke whale? It could be, its fin seems well astern on a body which is at least four metres long. As usual I am the only one who sees it.

Our route now will take us up the main road, through the glens and past the mountains of *Harris* to its larger neighbour Lewis. We immediately encounter major roadworks as the road is being upgraded and widened. This stretches along many miles and we are forced to stop frequently at temporary traffic-lights. We manage lingering looks at the spectacular scenery, even Ian who is supposed to be driving. Mountains devoid of any greenery but dappled in the sunshine stretch up on both sides and fold into high valleys that look impenetrable.

On the map I try to work out where *Harris* ends and Lewis begins, for this is not a geographic boundary in the usual sense. *Harris* and Lewis are counted as two separate islands, but the casual observer, who happens to look at a map, could be forgiven for thinking they are the same big island. It is more of a social and historical divide - and that is not easily found on the map I have in front of me.

Loch Seaforth cuts deeply into the flank of Harris/Lewis and it is the head of this loch that I believe designates the boundary. We stop the car to film our passing from one Western Isle to the next but the road has just been laid with loose chippings and Ian is worried that his nice black Honda will get sand-blasted by each vehicle that passes. I don't want to remind him of the front valance! So from the perspective of three Island Hoppers the boundary between Harris and Lewis is - well wherever we think it is. More importantly to us we are now on island number five of

132

the trip, and the sun has now battled through. This is particularly good news for we are planning to sail on Isle of Lewis this afternoon, across the Minch to Ullapool, and back again. It is the most exposed crossing on CalMac's network and some good weather would be appreciated. And it looks as if we're going to get it.

At Stornoway in good time for our sailing. We take a stroll down to the pier where CalMac's freighter *Muirneag* is lying idle. She will sail late tonight, but looks as though she will have to give way to allow our ship, Isle of Lewis, to berth. Much discussion between us about camera positions, sun positions and car positions when it suddenly dawns on us that we are at the wrong pier. A new one has been built since our last visit here and as we scamper along to set up cameras, yet again, Isle of Lewis arrives ahead of schedule at the head of the pier and almost makes the whole performance academic. I say 'almost' because Gibbie captures one of his 'sharp-end' specials and is consequently a happy man.

There's not just a new pier but a modern departure suite as well. This is the closest I've seen to a pier terminal that looks like an airport since our visit to Campbeltown and Ballycastle in 1998. Needless to say we cannot get anywhere near this pier either but have to wait until called. "Are you sure this is the pier and not Stornoway Airport?" asks Gibbie. "We don't want to be arriving back home half way through our trip."

We shuffle our way up the glass tube to the ship, behind yet another bus party. Not only can we not step onto the pier but we are now hermetically sealed from it. Mind you, if we were boarding Isle of Lewis in January we may well be pleased at that.

After what seems like an eternity we are onboard *Isle of Lewis*, and a very fine ship she is too. Having not been on her for eight years we refresh our memories with a wander around. Both her cafeteria and observation lounge are huge. And the reclining seats are filling up fast. But there is plenty of open deck space and from here we obtain a good look at the older pier, where not only Muirneag but the lighthouse tender Pole Star and a small tanker Border Heather are also moored.

We are off on time, as usual - you've got to hand it to CalMac when it comes to timekeeping. As soon as we have cleared the Eye peninsula we head for the cafeteria for a late lunch. To my delight the stewardess looks up at me while dishing out my chicken curry and states, "I know you. I've read *Full Cycle*." (my book on cycling around the Hebrides).

"Oh yes," I give her my beamy, JK Rowling smile.

"You're Sandy!"

"Eh no! He's the guy I cycled with....."

As we cross The Minch the sun disappears behind cloud and the ship rocks gently from side to side as a modest swell advances on our port side from the north. It is a soporific motion and so there's nothing else for it. Within five minutes both Ian and I are 'zizzing' in that big observation lounge. Gibbie takes off for a stroll on deck. He is wearing his red shoes today - there is a legend that the Isle of Lewis will one day sink into the sea (the island or the ship?), but those wearing red shoes will survive the experience. Gibbie is a cautious man. He's not the only one, as I stir from my slumbers I spot another pair of red shoes walking back and forth across the lounge. I follow surreptitiously to try to capture this chap's feet on camera.

I'm soon joined by a disgruntled Ian. His snooze was disrupted by a middle-aged couple depositing their very elderly relative into a seat beside him. Despite stern efforts to look as though he was sleeping she succeeded in striking up a conversation with him. "So tell me young man," she was obviously shortsighted as well, "why you come to the islands?"

"We just like the ships."

"Do you golf?"

"No, we just like the ships."

"Do you sail?"

"No, as I said, we just like the ships."

"Do you climb?"

Suppressing the desire to say "do we look as though we climb?" he returns, "We just like the ships!" Easing himself off his seat he bids her an abrupt farewell. "Just off to the cafeteria - for we also like the chips."

Up on deck the ship is turning into Loch Broom. We watch two fulmars following our wake. They turn this way and that, without hardly flapping a wing, but with wing tips barely an inch above the surf.

At Ullapool the ship lays up for almost an hour and as this is not an island we cannot be bothered disrupting CalMac's counting system by disembarking. So we return to the observation lounge to commandeer three reclining seats before the next bus party embarks - it's tiring work this island hopping!

We set sail again at 17.15 with a fresh load of passengers. Gibbie is by now sound asleep but a whisper of 'Glenmorrangie' in his shell-like has his legs wheeling in an attempt to hit the carpeted floor running.

Suddenly there's a 'bing-bong' over the ship's intercom. The captain announces that the crew are about to take part in an exercise and the 'fast-rescue-craft' (FRC) will shortly be launched on the port side of the ship. Off we go to watch - and off go the three lucky crew members who have the chance to whizz across the mouth of Loch Broom just for the sheer hell of it. I wish we could join them. They disappear from sight for a while, but after twenty minutes reappear on our starboard side and come around the stern of the ship to hook back on to their lifeline. This turns out to be more difficult than it looks and for a brief moment the inflatable and its contents are left dangling and rotating at the end of a wire, three metres above sea level. But soon they are back aboard and we are reassured that the ship's crew are well capable of dealing with any emergency arising - or at least just having a good fun ride on the FRC.

We cross The Minch for the third time today and complete our seven

134

hour sail on Isle of Lewis with a large dose of the feel-good factor gently pitching our way back to Stornoway. The town is lit up for our arrival by the evening sunshine and we watch it come closer through those large observation lounge windows. There is a peaceful atmosphere around us - and Gibbie is sleeping again! He seems to come on Island Hop just to hibernate.

We arrive back at 20.00, and as we step ashore and wander around the town we have the distinct impression that the whole place is asleep. We find our guesthouse and then seek a real ale pub to round off a perfect day. It takes a bit of time but we eventually locate one.

Unfortunately two sips of my beer has something stirring down below and I have to leave my two colleagues fairly expeditiously. I try to find my way back to the guesthouse but take a wrong turning and give myself an unintentional tour of backstreet Stornoway. By the time I find our lodgings I am feeling distinctly off-colour. I amble off to bed, resisting a strong temptation to scribble a Basil Fawltyesque note for my pals - requesting my breakfast be brought to me in the morning on either a teak, rosewood or mahoganey tea-tray. Perhaps I'm just tired or perhaps I have found Stornoway uninspiring but I can't wait to fall asleep. I soon have my wish.

Day Four - *Long Day on 'The Long Isle'*

Today we are going to pass through the chain of Western Isles, from Lewis in the north to Barra in the south. We are using inter-island ferries; across the Sound of *Harris* and the Sound of Barra. Sounds easy but we have 112 miles to drive as well. So let's get going.

Gibbie drives and we head back down the road we came up yesterday. Speeding along the empty highway through Lewis the landscape is one of bog, marsh, small coniferous plantation and lochans, many of which are populated with lone pairs of grey-lag geese. Further on the roadworks of *Harris* are a positive delight, for each time we pull up at the edge of the un-made-up road we have a chance to admire the scenery. And there is lots of it to admire. We have been up this way before (well just yesterday!) but we reckon it must have been raining for we cannot recall seeing how spectacularly beautiful *Harris* is, even although the highest peaks are still shrouded in low cloud today. The morning sunshine gives a silky depth to the layers of mountains forming the backdrop to Loch Seaforth. We even have time to poke our cameras out the car window. When the signal-man waves us onwards we shake our heads. No we want to stay longer. It's not like that when you're sitting stuck at roadworks on the M8.

From Tarbert we climb up and over the mountain pass and then along the shores of the most beautiful beaches in the Western Isles, if not the west coast of Scotland. As we stop again to take in the views a cuckoo calls from the hillside above us. It is a sound that always reminds me of our Island Hops; that, and the sound of Gibbie snoring! It is also the sound that reminds me of how mad we are doing this year after year. Positively 'cuckoo', and that bird agrees. But it's worth all the effort, even if just to see those beaches, which are positively luminous this morning.

Our next ferry terminal is Leverburgh, but we have trouble finding it. It is all my fault. I'm navigator and am literally leading us up the garden path - a *Harris* crofter's garden path to be precise. After a five point turn underneath his washing line we negotiate his bin, bump off the patio and squeeze between a couple of garden gnomes back onto the actual road. All in a day's driving for Gibbie really!

We eventually find Leverburgh, just in time to grab a coffee in the nice new restaurant by the slipway, and set up cameras before Loch Portain arrives. There is much building work going on at Leverburgh - in fact the whole place looks like a building site. A new breakwater is nearing completion, a marshalling yard is being tarmac'd and new pavements are being laid. I can hardly get back to the car without spilling my coffee.

Loch Portain is one of those double-ended jobs, and a new ship for all of us. She is much bigger than the previous vessel on this route, Loch Bhrusda, but certainly no prettier. She's not quite as unattractive as *Coruisk*, but there's not much in it. In fact to my eyes she is a cross between *Coruisk* and *Loch Buie*. Strangely she has no 'funnels', or even bits of hull, painted in CalMac colours, merely two CalMac 'badges' painted on her sides. Instead of funnels she sports two ugly grey mesh contructions with bare vent pipes extruding from them. Maybe they forget to put the funnels on? Even wee 'pretendy' ones would be nice.

A full load of vehicles, is taken aboard (this is an important CalMac route). We ascend to the passenger accommodation two levels up. It is a well appointed square-shaped lounge, running athwartships, with two unconnected deck areas - one at the front end and one at the rear (I hesitate to use bow and stern here). Here is an important identification guide to help you distinguish whether the ship is coming or going - one of these decks has yellow rubbish bins and the other blue! Today, as she departs the *Harris* side at 12.05, the yellows are leading the way.

Loch Portain was built by McTay Marine of Bromborough in 2003 and at 46.83m long, and with a maximum passenger complement of 201, she is undoubtedly ideal for the route. The crossing will take an hour. In fact she is heading for the island of Berneray, which is of course now linked to North Uist by a causeway. This route now effectively saves two separate hundred minute sailings via Uig on Skye as a means of crossing from *Harris* to the Uists. She may take an hour but the ferry terminals she's travelling between are only eight miles apart. The route is made tortuous by the submerged, and not so submerged, reefs dotted across the entire Sound of *Harris*. So just like our journey on Loch Bhrusda in previous years we zig-zag our way across to Berneray, weaving a fascinating pattern across the Sound. The three of us are interested by this but no-one else aboard seems to be - apart from the skipper, hopefully.

At Berneray I set up camera to film *Loch Portain* at the jetty. Five, well spaced-out bikers (distance wise I mean, not pharmacologically) come flying down the hill. Each in turn inclines to port to board the ferry. But the last one, who is a touch behind the others, zooms right across the adjacent causeway to North Uist. He soon realises his mistake, turns around and heads down the correct road. I then realise that I have been standing right in front of the sign for the ferry and obscuring the all important arrow.

I walk up the quarter mile to the one and only cafe. About half the ship's passenger complement is inside but fortunately Gibbie and Ian, who had gone on ahead, have ordered my tuna bake for me. The building of the causeway from North Uist has obviously made a difference to the small island of Berneray, or at least to the cafe's business. The previous times we've been here it has been closed.

Soon we're across the causeway ourselves and we speed, without stopping, down through the islands of North Uist, Grimsay, Benbecula and South Uist. On the causeway linking Grimsay with Benbecula we witness the damage caused by the violent storms and high tides earlier this year. Tragically, near here, five members of the same family were swept to their deaths when their car was overwhelmed by the sea. The damage to the wall of the causeway is extensive but on a calm serene day like today it is hard to imagine how tempestuous the sea can be, especially as we can hardly see it across the mud and sandy islets to our right.

We're heading for Ledag, at the southern end of South Uist, where yet another causeway has been built, leading to Eriskay. From there we will take the ferry across to Barra.

Time is short but I twist my colleagues' arms to take a short detour across the waist of South Uist to the south-west coast to see the tidal island of Orosay. Why? Well that's the question Ian and Gibbie ask too. There are lots of Orosays, Oronsays or Oransays on the west coast of Scotland (the name is synonymous with tidal island), but this one is a mere pimple stuck onto Uist by a little scratch of rocky sand. At high tide it reverts to a little round island. Ian and Gibbie don't mind the visit but the two mile-long bumpy track has taken years off Ian's car, and he says he is going to put in a claim for a new one to the Common Island Hopping Fund. On the plus side we see and hear a corn bunting singing its jangly song just a few metres from the car. This is now a rare and declining bird, but fortunately still fairly common in the low intensity farmed Western Isles.

We've crossed the causeway to Eriskay before (in the opposite direction in 2003) and sailed over to Ardmhor on Barra before, but this time it's a different vessel. It's *Loch Bhrusda* and I'm up on the hill overlooking the ferry point on Eriskay filming its arrival. The others are boarding the car onto it, and I have a mad dash down to board myself before it leaves without me. These ferries leave on time.

It is 16.25 when we sail away from the slipway on Eriskay, just a stone's throw from where Bonnie Prince Charlie landed in 1745 (that's the year - I have no idea what the time was) to start his rebellion. It is dull and cold now and we settle for a seat in the lounge for the forty minute crossing to Barra. When we drive off at the other side the sun reappears and we take the shortest route to Castlebay, which looks positively glorious. It's just a shame we've got to leave so soon.

At the planning stage I was hoping we could have an overnight here, but there is no morning ferry tomorrow, and in any case Gibbie is apprehensive about a repeat of his 2002 ceilidh experience! So we will pick up the 18.50 sailing to Oban tonight, in about an hour.

We reckon our ship back to Oban will be *Clansman*, and we're right. She rounds into the bay in a blaze of glory, pushing her characteristically huge bow wave in front of her.

Soon we're standing on her new rear deck watching Castlebay recede. "Sea conditions will be moderate to rough." Our captain informs us. Once out of the bay into The Minch it's like a millpond .He must be looking at those new BBC weather maps.

We spend a lot of time out on the rear of the ship. It is sheltered from the wind and we have the beautiful spectacle of the sun sinking slowly behind Barra, gradually sending the Western Isles chain into silhouette. After all the driving today it is such a peaceful scene that I struggle to tear myself away for dinner. I wait until the haze around the horizon obscures the distant islands and all I can see around me is sea. This is a scene I always enjoy, for when all around is seascape then with very little imagination you could be anywhere on the world's oceans. This could be the South China Sea!

Gannets, guillemots and fulmars continuously whizz past in different directions, their presence reminding me that this is the *Hebrides*. Many of them are carrying food for their young. I need some sustenance too so we descend to the cafeteria where we enjoy haddock and chips CalMac style beside a huge panoramic window looking out at The Minch beyond.

Afterwards a wander around the ship. We find a useful notice informing us that *Clansman* burns 0.7 pints of fuel per second. That's close to what my car achieves when my wife drives it.

Up to see the refurbished observation lounge. This has futuristic lighting and new low tables; the latter presumably for children. The low level of lighting gives such a peaceful atmosphere that I feel like joining the numerous supine figures crashed out around us. The curtains at the front of the lounge are drawn and the lights dimmed as, apparently, the angled forward window reflects glare up into the bridge. We drag ourselves back to the rear deck where we are passing a ship to port. This materialises out of the gathering gloom as Greenpeace's *Esperanza* (Spanish for 'hope'). She is a converted Russian trawler and is now heading west after a courtesy visit to the Clyde. She seems to be heading in the direction of Lochboisdale, or perhaps the open ocean beyond.

We are passing Ardnamurchan Lighthouse just as the sun is dipping into the sea, and so are soon in the sheltered waters of the Sound of Mull. It darkens quickly. Just beyond Craignure we pass a lit-up *Lord of the Isles* heading into that Mull pier on her late Friday night run.

"What on earth is that?" The barmaid asks me as she peers in puzzlement out of the window. I was just about to ask her the same question with regard to my beer.

"It's *Lord of the Isles* heading for Craignure." I tell her.

"Goodness, you know more about it than me."

I could tell her all about Island Hopping but it's getting late. Around us now, also heading for Oban it would appear, are a dozen yachts, showing ghostly white mast lights and red port lights. They appear out of the ether like ghost ships.

The late hour of our arrival back at Oban means that our landlord at our guesthouse has stayed up specially to let us in, by prior arrangement. It has been a long day, one of the longest continuous journeys of any Island Hop. Some 263 miles by land and sea. So it's straight to our beds, delighted that we don't have to go to a ceilidh.

Day Five - *Steamboats*

Open my curtain onto a beautiful morning in Oban. The ferries have shuffled around during the early hours. *Lord of the Isles* has returned from her overnight berth at Craignure and *Isle of Mull*, which was here last night, has gone. *Bruernish* sits idle at the pier and *Eigg* is just setting off for Lismore. Soon *Isle of Mull* can be seen wheeling into Obay Bay just as *LOTI* sets off for Lochboisdale, and the two pass photogenically just outside the window of our guesthouse. Outside a silver-haired procession of elderly ladies is emerging from Esplanade guest-houses and snaking its way in the direction of the shops. We are soon heading there ourselves, but we don't shop for long - we have date with an old lady of a different kind. We set off southwards - destination Loch Katrine.

At 105 years old the steamer *Sir Walter Scott* is certainly the oldest Island Hop ship we've ever sailed on, by quite a margin. Powered by a Matthew Paul triple-expansion engine *Sir Walter Scott* was built by William Denny of Dumbarton in 1900, which makes it even older than Gibbie. She is 110 feet long with a beam of 17 feet, and during the summer season she sails up and down Loch Katrine, the source of Glasgow's water. In order to prevent pollution of the loch she is coal fired and as we board this afternoon the fireman is stoking the black stuff energetically down into the bowels of the ship. It is a stunning afternoon as the little white steamer putters off on its hour long sail, with about sixty passengers: maw, paw, the weans, and Gibbie, Ian and I.

There are two saloons down below, one with a little shop, and plenty of deck space up top. At the stern, where we park ourselves, three swarthy looking men and one swarthy woman are lining up to take photographs of themselves, and so I gallantly step forward and offer to take a picture of all four of them. I think they are Spanish and see this as a perfect chance to practise language skills of considerable mediocrity.

"¿Quisieren ustedes una fotografia?"

"Si!"

I'm obviously on a winner. "¿De donde eres (where are you from)?" I ask the lady.

"East Kilbride!" She replies. We all laugh.

"Could you not make out the accent?" She continues. Politness prevents her from adding, "By the way your Spanish is awful!"

"Oh yes," I am trying to regain my poise. "But I couldn't make out if it was from St. Leonards or The Murray!" I continue our cruise speaking in English, but confine conversation to between Ian and Gibbie and myself. The little steamer turns to starboard and heads back to Trossachs Pier spewing dazzling white steam from an exhaust pipe just above water level. It looks as though we are going to run out of puff but of course we make it back. This is only the second steamer we have sailed on during our seventeen years of Island Hopping, but we are off now to see another.

Maid of the Loch last saw active service in 1981, and has been moored at Balloch Pier on Loch Lomond ever since. Fortunately she is now in the capable hands of enthusiasts, who are convinced that one day she will steam again. So if we cannot sail on her at least we can go and see her, and walk her decks. We'll count her as a 'new' ship for an Island Hop!

Ian has not seen the paddle-steamer, built by A & J Inglis in 1953, for twenty odd years but is pleasantly surprised how far her refurbishment has come on. Freshly painted with white hull and red and black funnel she now has several lounges restored tastefully, and can now offer catering and corporate facilities. Her twin-pistoned, triple-expansion engine is still in situ. Wouldn't it be wonderful if she could raise steam once more and paddle up and down Loch Lomond.

We have a quick coffee and end Island Hop 2005 aboard our second steamer in two hours. We cannot count her as one of our vessels, however, but otherwise we have sailed on eight ships this year - three of them new! Including islands linked by causeways we have reached, one way or another, eleven islands - and one of them was new. We have also driven 530 miles! And unknown to us at the time, this was the last Island Hop with just the three of us.

An hour later we are back in Glasgow. With the customary handshake Ian bids me farewell. "See you next year."

Gibbie? Well he just lives along the road, I'll probably bump into him next week.

The meeting of two old ladies, Millport

ISLE OF MULL, Oban

ISLE OF MULL, passing Kererra 2002

EIGG, before her stretch

2006 New Berths

The Plan

Various ideas had been muted for our eighteenth Island Hop, but by February (the month when the plans are usually being drawn up) I was still looking at a blank sheet of paper. Where was the inspiration?

We had considered travelling further afield, to such disparate places as: the Isle of Man, the Lake District, the Norwegian fjords, the lakes of Switzerland, Lake Tangyanika. But nothing inspiring leapt out of the pages of the numerous timetables that we had amassed, although I couldn't get my hands on the one for Lake Tangyanika. And then an idea suddenly hit me. A very simple idea. Forget the geographical theme or the nautical theme - why don't we try to stay overnight on islands where we have never had an overnight stay before. There are several of them, Gigha, Coll, Colonsay, Lismore or one of the Small Isles. After some checking we selected the first three. Each of these three islands has just one hotel. We could book ourselves into each hotel for one night and then weave as complex a pattern as possible between each island. We had visited these islands before but, apart from Gigha, we had never actually spent any time ashore, which is pretty pathetic considering all the years we have been doing this silly thing. So forget Norway or Switzerland, it's the west of Scotland yet again!

This idea went down favourably with my colleagues. Having ascertained that each of the hotels could accommodate us I spent a couple of nights locked in my room with CalMac's 2006 timetable. I came up with a route which, apart from enabling us to reach our overnight berths on Gigha, Coll and Colonsay (in that order), also allowed us to sail on the newest addition to CalMac's Clyde fleet - *Bute*.

Ian then almost put a spanner in the works by announcing that he may not be able to manage at all, as he required minor surgery to a delicate part of his anatomy. I would love to tell you where but have sworn a code of secrecy. Oh all right then - it was somewhere in Surrey.

Then just three weeks before our departure it was Gibbie's turn to induce some chaos to this strategy by announcing that his pal from Canada, an ex-pat named Bob Barr, was coming across The Pond for a holiday, and was keen to join us. Would the hotels be able to billet a fourth member of the party? The answer was a resounding yes. So The Three Stooges became the Gang of Four.

The addition of a fourth member to our elite Island Hopping party would certainly be refreshing. Bob was very welcome to join us. He flew into Glasgow on the Saturday, showed his wife Lilias the direction of Braehead Shopping Centre on Sunday and joined the three of as at Wemyss Bay Pier on the Monday, at the start of Island Hop 2006.

Day One - *Lord of the Glens and Dancing Ladies*

Sitting in the pouring rain in Gibbie's car at Wemyss Bay. Last week the weather throughout Scotland was wonderful. The forecast for this coming week is miserable. Apart from the four of us, and all our gear, we have a large black bin-bag full of various knick-knacks which Gibbie's wife, Janette, has instructed be deposited in a charity shop as far from Glasgow as possible. She is clearly worried, not without reason, that Gibbie will buy back some of his old clothes.

Today we are heading, eventually, for the ferry to Gigha, which leaves from the west side of Kintyre at Tayinloan. The purchase of a car Hopscotch ticket, in addition to our usual rover tickets, allows us a cost effective way of using the various Clyde ferry routes to weave our way by land and sea to the Kintyre peninsula. Even more cost effective as we now have Bob to share the expenses. Gibbie brings out his free-travel bus pass and wonders if this will enable him to complete his Island Hop without having to put his hand in his pocket. His photograph alone will preclude that - he looks as though he was suffering from some kind of syndrome the day the picture was taken.

We have never started an Island Hop at Wemyss Bay before. This has been such a famous and important Clyde pier for 110 years now and today it is still the main ferry port for sailings from the mainland to the Isle of Bute.

On the drive down we paused to have a look in James Watt Dock in Greenock. Here *Isle of Arran* was finishing off her annual overhaul. Perhaps we'll see her on passage during the next few days. Behind her, in Garvel Drydock was *Waverley*.

At Wemyss Bay two ships are usually in service. Today it is the new *Bute* (which commenced service in July 2005) and the somewhat old *Juno*. An eleventh hour study of their respective schedules had suggested that the 11.00 sailing would be taken by the new vessel. She had been our target, but an e-mail from a friend late last night had alerted me to the possible presence of the small cruise ship *Lord of the Glens* at Lochranza later this afternoon. Now, if we postponed the sail aboard Bute to our last day, and caught an earlier sailing to Rothesay today we would actually be able to incorporate a brief visit to Lochranza into our tight schedule. For this to work we would have to take the 10.15 sailing from Wemyss Bay. What's more, *Lord of the Glens* should actually be sitting at Rothesay right now. So, with a bit of luck, we could film her at the Bute pier and Lochranza. So instead of the 11.00 sailing from Wemyss Bay aboard *Bute* we find ourselves driving onto the open car deck of *Juno*. She departs on time at 10.15 across an uninteresting sea.

Juno has actually been a popular ship on past Island Hops. We have spent more time on her than the two other 'streakers', *Saturn* and *Jupiter*, combined. She is, however, undoubtedly in the twilight of her long Clyde career. Her sister *Jupiter* has been laid up, out of service, for eight months at Rosneath.

The commencement into service of *Bute*, and the imminent arrival of her sister ship Argyle, has heralded a new generation of Clyde car ferry and the writing is on the wall for the thirty-three year old twins *Juno* and *Jupiter*. So as we shuffle around her worn timber decks we eye her with sombre and tacit realisation that this may well be our last collective look at her. For Bob it's his first look at her. It is clear that over the next few days we are going to have fun pointing out the facts and features of the west coast ferry scene that the rest of us take for granted.

Half way across to Rothesay *Bute* speeds past us, sailing in the opposite direction. She looks so different from the ship we're on. But more on her later. As Rothesay Pier comes into view it is apparent that my source has been correct and *Lord of the Glens* is indeed moored at the southern end of the pier.

Lord of the Glens is a compact, modern, luxury cruise ship which sails out of Inverness. She operates a variety of cruises down the Caledonian Canal and out into the waters of Loch Linnhe to far flung places such as Tobermory or Portree. This is the closest we have ever seen her. Her dark blue hull and banded navy and white superstructure allow her to merge into the backdrop of Rothesay town on this drizzly, heavy-skied day. She could easily be overlooked. Our tight schedule only allows a brief photo call of her with *Juno* at the pier before we drive north to Rhubodach. If we are very lucky we may just meet up with her again at Lochranza in a few hours time.

So having crossed over to Bute the next target is to get off it as quickly as possible. By the time we reach Rhubodach, nine miles up the east coast of the island, the ferry *Loch Dunvegan* is arriving at our side. We drive straight onto her and almost before Bob realises it we are off Bute and onto the Cowal peninsula. We are heading now for the ferry at Portavadie, which will allow us to cross *Loch Fyne*. We believe there is a small cafe there, hope so - we are in need of a coffee.

"Jings lads, do you ever get to spend any time on these islands?" Bob is still coming to terms with the nuances of Island Hopping. It is a valid question but at least this year we will get a decent look at some of our islands. We also get a decent look at the beautiful scenery of this quiet corner of Scotland. It unfolds before us as Gibbie whirls his red Citroen around the single-track roads between Colintraive and Portavadie, scattering sheep in his haste to get us on the 12.45 sailing to Tarbert. My usual blase reassurances that we have plenty of time only cause him to furrow his brow deeper and depress the accelerator further.

We arrive at Portavadie in plenty of time and I walk around the car inspecting it for bits of wool. Ian props himself up against a telegraph pole, baseball cap at a jaunty angle on his head, and starts to text frantically on his new mobile phone. I say 'frantically' but it is more a case of one digit every ten seconds.

"You look very trendy, Ian," I comment.

"Can't get the hang of this bloody thing. Have you been sending me pervy texts?"

"Certainly not!"

"I can't get rid of them." He gives up and strides into the little cafe. I can't help but remark that he appears to be moving surprisingly freely despite his recent surgery.

"I asked my surgeon when I could start exercising. He said a little walking would be good for me straight away. He also said I could play golf in six weeks. Pretty clever, I thought, I couldn't play golf before my op." It's an old joke but it still has us laughing as we sip mugs of tea and watch the ferry approach.

Gibbie and I had a sail on this handy shortcut across *Loch Fyne* in early December last year. In winter the Tarbert-Portavadie vessel takes a daily deviation to Lochranza on Arran, and we decided to join it there - thus sailing Lochranza-Tarbert-Portavadie. On that day the vessel was *Loch Riddon*. The usual incumbent is Isle of Cumbrae. And it is she that is arriving at the slipway now. It is a twenty minute crossing and the sun now at least looks as though it is trying to break through.

Off at Tarbert, debating whether we have time to stop for lunch. Our nutritional advisor, Ian, says no. This is a title we bestowed on Ian many Island Hops ago and Bob takes it very seriously throughout the trip. For the next three days nothing passes his lips without asking Ian first.

So we press on, passing down the side of West Loch Tarbert now, and then crossing the narrow waist of Kintyre - more cursing from Gibbie about single-track roads. At Claonaig there is, as I am sure you all know by now, a ferry crossing to Lochranza on Arran.

We have sailed across this route many times, but I don't think I've given you a history lesson on it before. So here we go. The pier at Lochranza opened in 1888 and steamers called there, usually heading for Campbeltown, until 1971. The following year the steamer calls ended, a slipway was built and a car ferry service began across the Sound of Kilbrannan to Claonaig, on the east coast of Kintyre. Initially Island-class *Kilbrannan* served the route but she was soon superseded by *Rhum*, and then *Loch Ranza*, and now Loch Tarbert. But in June 2003 the pier re-opened and a real steamer - *Waverley* - regularly calls here once more. It's good to hear of a pier re-opening instead of the depressing news of one closing. Ian in particular is happy at that.

We can barely see Arran. The gloom and drizzle have descended again,

146

but least we are on schedule on what is becoming a hectic but intriguing day. The car gets abandoned here and we board *Loch Tarbert* as foot passengers. It is only 13.50 and we are sailing away on our fourth ferry.

Despite the weather Bob is loving it. Having left Scotland for Vancouver in 1966 he has made frequent return visits to his native Glasgow, but these lochs, hills and ferries are something he has not experienced in a long time. Being a fellow naval engineer (like both Ian and Gibbie) the conversation soon gets around to valve-gear, crankshafts and metrocentric heights, as it does every year!

I interrupt their marine ruminations to point out that through the gloom I can see a ship approaching on our port beam. It is indeed *Lord of the Glens*. I come over all smug at having predicted our rendezvous with her. They are suitably impressed, but I omit to tell them I phoned Rothesay harbourmaster last night for an update.

Loch Tarbert berths first and *Lord of the Glens* sits out for a few moments to allow the ferry to deposit her load, including us, and depart. The cruise ship then berths very gingerly. In fact very, very gingerly. After a very long time the stern rope is finally secured and a near vertical gangway run up the side of the ship.

A bus driver is hanging about impatiently waiting for the ship's complement. He is taking them to Brodick Castle. "They're an hour late," he mutters. "By the time they get off the ship the castle will be shut."

"Just take them to Lochranza Castle over there," I helpfully suggest. "They'll never know the difference." At last a dozen or so smiling Americans disembark, equally gingerly. They get on the bus eventually and all is well.

We are happy also. In addition to getting some very good pictures we get a chance to view the ship at close quarters. Apparently she is in the midst of a private charter taking in Greenock, Rothesay, Lochranza, Campbeltown and Port Ellen on Islay. I even have the audacity to ask if we can step aboard. This is politely refused. I don't blame the cruise organiser, I would refuse a bunch of scruffy old Island Hoppers as well. But we are happiest of all because there is a tiny carry-out cafe at Lochranza now, and so we stand on Lochranza Pier staring up at the *Lord of the Glens* munching cheese and ham sandwiches. Isn't it great that the pier has reopened?

We take a stroll around the village. Just adjacent to the bus terminus there is a headstone commemorating the loss of submarine *HMS/m Vandal*. She holds the unenviable record of having the shortest career of any Royal Navy submarine. She had only been completed at the Holy Loch four days before she disappeared while on exercise in the Kilbrannan Sound. She left Loch Ranza in the afternoon of Wednesday 24 February 1943 - and was never seen again. The reason for her loss is a mystery and it was 1995 before the wreck was identified - lying just a couple of miles off Lochranza at a depth of 300 feet. There are thirty-six names on the commemoration stone, and poignantly a photograph of one of the victims - o/seaman C J Menzies. This sad picture takes the smiles off our faces for a few moment.

When the ferry arrives back at 15.45 we board it and head back to Claonaig. The last leg now is the drive down to Tayinloan, about 15 miles away, and the Gigha ferry. If Gibbie puts the foot down we should just make the 17.00 sailing. He does and we do. *Loch Ranza* is the vessel. This causes confusion to poor Bob.

"Did we not just leave Lochranza?"

On the ferry Gibbie suddenly discovers that he has left home with his wife Janette's cash card. "Oh dear. I hope our new dining-room chairs didn't arrive today or I'm in deep trouble. She won't be able to pay for it. I'll phone when we get across."

It is a twenty minute crossing, our sixth sailing today. Gigha, as you may know, is Gaelic for "God's Island". Bob knew that. But Ian has got a bit mixed up - not for the first time, I have to say. Before coming up north for our trip he told a friend that this year it was likely that he was going to "God's Country". That left his friend believing that Ian's forthcoming surgery was a little more serious than he was letting on!

Dumping our bags at the hotel we take ourselves off to the South Pier where the ferry ties up for the night. We time it perfectly to get good pictures of *Loch Ranza*. Her three man crew (well - two men and a women actually) go through a series of activities to render their vessel safe for the night.

Gigha is now under the ownership of the islanders themselves. We get chatting to a handful of them this evening and they all admit to a new sense of confidence on the island. There are new houses being built in the village, a new halibut fish farm at the south-east and three wind turbines have sprouted since our last visit here. These are apparently called 'The Dancing Ladies'. Tonight two of them are doing the tango, but the third is having a rest.

The hotel is certainly busy and creates a nice atmosphere for our first ever night on Gigha. The evening is mild enough to allow us to stand around the hotel garden for a while, admiring the view across the Sound to Kintyre. It is such a peaceful scene.

Due to the recent introduction of the smoking ban (in public places) here in Scotland new, metallic ashtrays are sprouting up in beer gardens and outside hotels and pubs. The hotel garden on Gigha is no exception, one is luted to the garden wall by fresh cement into which some wit has imprinted 'keep puffin'.

"A man's got to do what a man's got to do," says Gibbie out of the blue. He shuffles off in trepidation to make a rare phone-call home. Ian and I can only remember him phoning home once before, and strangely that was from Gigha as well! Gibbie is gone a while. When he eventually reappears he is looking glum. "Guess what was delivered this morning?"

He pauses and looks wistfully across the water. "Has the last ferry left?"

"You know it has, Gibbie," I remind him. "It's tied up for the night, unless there is an emergency on the island."

"Do you think this would count as an emergency?" After a few seconds he adds, " she wanted to know if we've found a charity shop yet!"

Day Two - *Danna and The Stones*

We are up quite early. Gibbie tells us he awakens at 06.15 every morning. He doesn't get up - he just wakes up. He normally doesn't get up for another five hours. "Old habits die hard. Forty-seven years of setting my alarm to get up for work in the shipyards. Actually it should have been set for 06.45, but I could never work out how to reset it!" Bob announces that he gets up at 06.00 every morning, and either sits at his computer or makes his daily phone-calls.

"You should phone Gibbie," says Ian. "In fact you could phone me - I've been up half the night trying to work out how to delete my messages." I am glad to say I slept like a log.

Bob and I take a walk down to the shore where I give him his first ornithological lesson. A wren trills from the rocky shoreline, a whitethroat is bouncing about the nearby bushes, issuing its brief scratchy song, and a sedge warbler is heralding a new day with its discordant chattering from tall grass next to the road. It would be a beautifully calm morning, if it weren't for all these noisy birds! A sign on the church door requests that the door is closed tight because "swallows fly in and can't get out."

We join the others for breakfast. Bob orders a full Scottish breakfast with his egg 'over-easy'. I get into the North American theme and ask for mine 'sunny-side up.' The chef in the kitchen is pedestrian - and I don't mean he's gone for a walk. On second thoughts he might have done. Our ferry leaves in thirty minutes and we are just beginning to get a bit agitated when breakfast finally arrives. It is worth waiting for, but Bob's egg and my egg are identical. Serves us right - an egg's an egg!

Gibbie also wolfs into a hearty full breakfast, but Ian is more modest in his selection. Ian, always one to take good care of himself, looks as his own bowl of fresh fruit and natural yoghurt, and then peers enviously at Gibbie's plate. "If I pop my clogs before you there's no justice."

We race down to the ferry terminal to the awaiting *Loch Ranza*. This is where I discover I've chucked out the return ticket for the car. The young CalMac ticket-lady smilingly reassures me that she remembers us buying a return ticket yesterday afternoon. "But I still need to see it," she adds. I don't know whether she is joking or not so I spend the entire crossing hiding from her.

A veil of cloud is still obscuring the blue sky that we normally enjoy on our Island Hops. The visibility seems better, however, and it is certainly not cold. We have an interesting and varied day ahead of us. The most important target is the 15.00 sailing from Oban to Coll. We have to be at Oban by 14.30. As we have several hours to fill we can take in a few tourist hot spots on the way - and, hopefully, visit a spot where few tourists venture. But first we head for Crinan.

Surprisingly neither Bob nor Ian have ever seen the Crinan Canal. We drive to Ardrishaig at the eastern end of the canal and then follow its course as close as we can to the western end, at Crinan, seven miles away. Here the famous Para Handy puffer *Vital Spark* is lying in a disheveled state at an inner berth. Now that we are four Island Hoppers we have a laugh trying to allocate each of us to one of Neil Munro's famous crew. I'm Sunny Jim, of course, and there is no doubt that Gibbie would transfigure to Para Handy himself. Bob calls to Ian, "are you there, Dan?"

In a Crinan cafe, over coffee and curious flat scones called 'financiers', we watch a sleek, white yacht coming through the locks. It is now mostly pleasure craft such as this that use this canal shortcut, which saves a day and a half of sailing around both sides of the Kintyre peninsula. Just occasionally one of the smaller CalMac vessels uses the Canal when on its way to or from overhaul on the Clyde. I know that Gibbie once got a picture of Island class ferry *Kilbrannan* here. No such luck today.

From Crinan I take the wheel as we now set off on a mission to attain a 'new' island for this year's trip. I have to admit that this is all my idea. Gibbie and Ian are suitably taciturn about it and I suspect Bob is only showing interest out of politeness. We head off west from Crinan to areas where the tourist rarely ventures. So which island can we reach here? It's cheating really, for this is a tidal island linked by a small road bridge, which, according to my definition of what makes an island, means it is still a real island. By my book if it is completely surrounded by water at some stage of the tide then it is an island, whether it has a man-made link - a bridge, a causeway or a tunnel - or not. Otherwise neither Scalpay, Benbecula, Gometra, Eriskay nor Skye are islands. As we have never been there before, this is a new island for an Island Hop. It is called Danna, and it is a small square mile of island at the end of the narrow strip of land that forms the western shore of Loch Sween.

We drive through Tayvallich, which is supposedly the 'most beautiful village in Scotland'. Personally I don't think so. It is amazingly secluded and a superb yacht haven, but I'm quite fond of Saltcoats myself.

"STOP!" Shouts Gibbie.

I screech to a halt. "What is it?"

"Is that a charity shop there?"

"No, it's a craft shop, Gibbie."

Six miles on from Tayvallich we come across a narrow bridge at a particularly pleasant spot. On the other side is the low hump of Danna. We film our walking across the bridge like all- conquering Island Hoppers. Island number fifty-three after eighteen years. I'm sure you recognise that after eighteen years we're clutching at straws somewhat to attain 'new' islands. But as I've just explained, an island's an island!

I need hardly tell you that we don't stay long. Soon we're driving back towards Crinan. We take a left on a B-road heading north to Kilmartin and there, to Bob's delight, we visit the old church yard to look at some old stones. There is a sign which points us in the right direction. "To the Stones", it reads.

"Are we going to a concert?" I flippantly comment, but nobody gets my joke. These are not so much 'standing stones' - more 'lying flat' stones. But they depict the sword carvings of the Templar Knights. This is a subject which fascinates Bob, but which leaves Gibbie rather cold. The history of this part of Scotland has both mystical and mythical connotations for many people interested in the Temple of Solomon and masonic symbolism, but having given you that I will say no more. I'll take Mick, Keith and the lads anyday.

Our ferry connection at Oban is beckoning and I take the wheel again to continue on the last twenty odd miles to Oban, searching all the time, in vain, for a roadside charity shop.

We get there in plenty of time to dump the car and purchase a few necessities. We also get a decent look at the new CalMac terminal building at Oban Railway Pier. Opened just last year this is the first time we have had a decent look at it. It seems to be built mainly of glass, with a rather stylish lion logo engraved into the facade. It looks very nice and certainly feels very spacious, just a shame there is a 20p charge to use the toilets. I pick a cheaper option - at the risk of being charged with vagrancy.

After a fair bit of driving over the past two days it is good to leave the car behind and embark on a decent sized ship for once. We are sailing aboard *Clansman* at 15.00 to the island of Coll. Tomorrow we will return to Oban, spend a couple of hours ashore and then sail on *Lord of the Isles* for Colonsay. Poor Gibbie finds this very confusing, however. On reaching the gangway he is convinced we are going to Colonsay first. "Are you sure it's Coll today?" Ian and Bob take an arm each and guide him up the gangway. "Are you sure we're not supposed to be sailing on *LOTI*?"

Lord of the Isles is indeed entering Oban Bay, but she will be heading out to Lochboisdale later. Our ship, *Clansman*, keeps her sitting our for ten minutes until we eventually get underway. It gives us a great photo opportunity - passing so close to *Lord of the Isles* - as we wheel away from the pier. Also 'wheeling away' from her slipway is the Lismore ferry *Eigg*. Her sister, *Bruernish*, is dormant at the pier, as she has been for the last few Island Hop visits to Oban.

Our sail this afternoon will take us direct to Coll (the ship carries on to Tiree) up the Sound of Mull. It will take about three hours. We have, of course, seen the scenery so many times before but it never gets any less beautiful, and for Bob there are lots of delights. Sailing past the inbound *Isle of Mull*, passing Lismore Lighthouse and the dominating Duart

Castle, watching *Loch Fyne* scurry across our bows and pointing out Tobermory through the gathering mist. Just past Rhubh nan Gall lighthouse the cliffs on the Mull side rise up away to our left to form the curve of Bloody Bay. I whisper to Bob, "Ask Gibbie if he knows what this bay's called."

"What is this bay called, Gibbie?"

"Haven't a bloody clue."

"That's close enough." Bob gives his impish smile and returns to the panoramic view out of the front windows of *Clansman*'s observation lounge.

Over a beer in the bar Gibbie and Bob reminisce about their shipyard days and their fortnightly visits to Ibrox Park to watch Rangers play. On a recent trip back to Scotland a couple of years ago the two of them watched their team play in a league match. After many years living in Canada Bob's ear for broad Glaswegian was tested to the limit of comprehension when buying tickets.

"Why is the chap asking me if I have gonorrhoea?" He asked Gibbie in perplexity.

"He's not," replied Gibbie, "he's asking if you want to sit in the Govan Rear (stand)."

At Coll Pier the hotelier Kevin has kindly driven down to collect us and our bags. He frowns when the four of us assemble at his car. "Four! We have only three of you down for tonight."

"It's alright, I phoned last week to change the booking," Gibbie reassures him.

"But two of you might have to share. I don't mean a room, I mean a bed!" Ian and I look glance at each other and shake our heads in unison.

"That's okay," returns Gibbie, "we're just good friends."

As it happens there are two twin-rooms available and all is well. Ian and I take one of them and let the two old buddies take the other. They can reminisce about Rangers all night.

Before dinner Ian, Bob and I take an extended stroll out along the road leading west from the hotel. It follows the course of a long sea-water inlet and rises gently up to the heather moor and rough grazing of this sparely populated island.

Coll is very different from its more populous neighbour Tiree, and there is rumoured to be occasional strife between the two communities. Coll measures about twelve miles long by about three wide, and on the map, if you tilt it a bit and use a liberal amount of imagination, resembles a giant whale. The northern half is very rocky and barren, resembling a miniature *Harris* without the mountains. A feature it does share with *Harris* is its beautiful beaches, all on the west coast. We don't have enough time to reach any of these on our walk, but we get as far as Achamore Farm and get a good look at some of the moorland birdlife on the way. There are skylark, wheatears and meadow pipits in abundance, and a stunning pair of stonechats, which turn Ian and Bob into ecstatic David Attenboroughs. Bob has brought his camera with him and is constantly breaking off in a run to the edge of a field to capture an unsuspecting ewe or lamb on film. I don't want to discourage his enthusiasm but I can envisage that on his return to Canada he will discover that he has thirty-three pictures of the distant rear-end of two sheep.

We return to the hotel, which is at the northern extreme of the only village - Arinagour. This consists of the hotel, church, bistro, school, post-office and charity shop. CHARITY SHOP! We daren't tell Gibbie, his bag of goodies is still in the car at Oban.

We sit in the 'snug' trying to make the difficult decision on what to eat. I pick up the local fortnightly Coll/Tiree newspaper *An Tirisdeach*. There is no evidence of friction between the good people of Tiree and the Collachs here. There appears to be much mutual admiration and cooperation. Some funny adverts however. Someone has found a silver walking-stick and wants to return it to its rightful owner. Someone else (or perhaps the same person) wants to purchase a second hand deep-fat frier. In the same issue Argyll and Bute Council intimate that "All household waste can now be deposited on Coll free of charge." At last a sign of Tiristeach tyranny! It apparently includes washing-machines, cookers and fridges, but what about deep-fat friers? I have a vision of the ferry collecting Tiree's junk and offloading it on Coll.

Dinner is pretty sumptuous and we indulge ourselves, a little. We even have room for dessert. 'Spotted Dick' is one of the puddings on offer. Bob raises an eyebrow, "Oh, we're back at the Govan Rear again!"

Surprisingly there is also a real ale on tap, and some of us indulge in this as well. The lady of the hotel pulls me a beer and instantly mistakes me for an American 'yachtey' who had been in the restaurant earlier. She starts pulling my leg about yachting, Americanisms and George W Bush.

The bar is full of off-duty, part-time firemen, drinking 'lemonade'. Apparently there has been an exercise tonight. So tonight should be a good time to have a fire on Coll - or perhaps not.

Day Three - *Pig's Paradise*

It was a good night last night, somehow we can all tell that this morning. We are a bit quiet over breakfast. We're not alone - the lady of the hotel is a bit sheepish as she brings us our breakfast. Recalling her American jibes she looks horrified when she discovers that I am one of her guests.

"Terribly sorry, I've given you an extra rasher. Oh, and would you like a lift to the ferry as well? I'm actually taking the car over to Oban?"

We get a wee ride down to the pier, which is about a kilometre from the hotel, and stand and stare into the pea-soup haar for signs of *Clansman*'s arrival.

"I think the fog is clearing," says Bob. My goodness he's almost as optimistic as I am.

Inevitably we hear the ship before we can see her. She departs at 0845 with us all tucked aboard. She is heading now for Tiree. Coll has been fun - for us it's Colonsay next. We practically run into Tiree before we can see it. The gloom is a bit disappointing. The ship does not linger long and we now head direct to Oban - foghorn bellowing.

Bob returns to his favourite spot in the observation lounge, and Gibbie to his favourite spot in the 'zizz' lounge. After a while on deck Ian and I join Bob and find him chatting to an affable lady called Maureen who is returning from a few days teaching on Tiree. She is fascinated by our journey and our brand of island-hopping.

"So you must know the ships well, then." I nod in agreement.

"The lasagne, the macaroni-cheese" Gibbie appears and looks disappointed at having missed most of a good conversation. Maureen continues, "so it's a bit of a 'Last of the Summer Wine' only with ships." I don't think anyone has ever come up with such a perceptive view of us before.

The sun eventually appears when we are half way down the Sound of Mull. "Where have you been?" I shout angrily at it. We amble downstairs to the cafeteria for a quick soupy lunch and then it's up top to watch our approach to Oban.

The lighthouse tender *Pharos* is at her usual berth (she wasn't there yesterday). Nothing else of particular interest.

There is a significant crew change aboard *Clansman* on touching base. Half of the crew are now in their 'civvies' and looking forward to two weeks leave Their substitutes are first aboard when the gangway is connected. They must be keen to get to their stations for they are aboard even before any passenger disembarks.

We have a couple of hours before changing ships. We are all dispatched to do different chores. I am sent up Pulpit Hill to film the departing *Clansman* (to Barra) and the arriving *Isle of Mull*. To be honest I go willingly. But this favourite panoramic spot above the Railway Pier is gradually having its vista obscured by ever-expanding trees and shrubs. It is now difficult getting a clear camera shot of the pier. Next time I come here I shall bring secateurs with me. Either that or a chain saw.

I return to the pier and meet Gibbie. His chore has been to sit on the pier and eat oysters. He manages this easily enough but is disappointed that none of us was around at the time to watch him. Bob and Ian join us. They have been Good Samaritans, apparently. On the North Pier they encountered Mrs 'Coll Hotel's car - full of shopping, but with driver's door lying wide open. After a brief search of half of Argyll they find her in a cafe. She is appalled at leaving her car like that and rushes off to rescue it.

"Thanks chaps, you can come back and stay at the hotel any time."

154

"Goodness," says Ian, "normally we can't go back to anywhere we've been before."

On the pier waiting for the ship to arrive we are joined by a gentleman with his golf clubs. He was apparently aboard *Clansman* with us this morning. He is amateur golfer Ernie Payne and his mission is more eccentric and absurd than ours - to play a round of golf on every Scottish golf course. He was on Tiree this morning and is off to play Colonsay this afternoon. This whim commenced in 1983 at Muirfield. He has played 551 courses and claims there are just twenty-seven to go. Ernie claims his quest is unique. He tells us that he visited Iona once, without his clubs because he didn't know there was a course on the island.

"I'll just have to go back," he adds wistfully.

"We'll see you tonight in the hotel, then." I suggest.

"No, I'm only on the island for a couple of hours, I'll be sailing back to Oban tonight." We wish him well.

Lord of the Isles glides into the berth and we are onboard fairly sharply. This is the last week of *LOTI's* spring timetable. On Wednesdays she leaves Oban at 15.30 for Colonsay and on to Port Askaig on Islay. She then retraces her route back to Oban. From next week, until September, *LOTI* will undertake cruises at this time of the week and it will be *Hebridean Isles* that will take Islay and Colonsay traffic up to Oban. The all-the-way Kennacraig-Islay-Colonsay-Oban sailing has thus been reinstated by CalMac after a couple of year's absence.

So we sail at 15.30 and as soon as we leave the sun disappears. On our way south I take Bob out on deck and point out all the passing islands to him. I succeed in getting them all out of sequence - Luing becomes Easdale, Seil becomes the mainland. Have I never been here before? We pass inside of Inch Island and outside of the Garvellachs. I scan for the eagles with binoculars, but there is no sign. Plenty of kittiwakes and guillemots. The presence of the latter prompts Gibbie to head off to tell the entire ship's complement his favourite black kilowatt story. He tell's it so well.

A weather front was forecast for the late afternoon, and it is moving towards us as we sail south towards Colonsay. I am really disheartened by this. Have I really used up my nine 'weather' lives?

The ship is quiet. There are so many pleasant areas to sit on this ship so we keep moving around. Eventually we settle for the observation lounge, and watch the rain start to stream down the windows. The crew seem particularly chirpy and I ask one of them about the new airfield that is being constructed on Colonsay. He is not sure how much progress has being made but can tell me that it's being built near the golf course.

"It's a bit of a mess up there, the course is actually closed because of the excavation work." Closed! I can't bring myself to tell our golfing pal. Looks like that's another Hebridean island he's going to have to re-visit.

There's a surprise for us at Colonsay. *Lord of the Isles* swings around

155

to berth stern-in but it is clear that the linkspan is closed, due to maintenance. So the ship uses her port-side hoist and ramp to unload her vehicles. It is many years since I last watched a car ferry unload this way. It takes me back to the days of the early car ferries *Bute* and *Cowal*, I used to watch them with fascination at Rothesay, they seemed to take forever to shed their traffic. My Dad's Ford Anglia once broke down on the hoist turntable of Cowal and caused all sorts of havoc. It had to be towed off.

Here at Scalasaig Pier *LOTI* seems to be coping very well; her crew look as though they do this everyday. She is dropping off cars and vans from Oban and loading traffic for Port Askaig. She will, of course, be back in at the pier in a couple of hours. We could stay aboard for that return run to Islay but the deteriorating weather has dampened any enthusiasm for that.

Ian, Bob and I head off up the hill to the hotel, Gibbie seeks a lift, and is successful. Ernie, the golfer, strides out in the direction of the golf course - come airfield - come building site. With the rain now streaming down I can't help feeling sorry for him. And I never thought I'd hear myself say that about a golfer. Maybe he can play just the one hole.

It is a delight to be able to spend some time on Colonsay after all the brief calls we have made over the years. We have been allocated one big 'family room' tonight, for all four of us. This has been given the befitting appellation 'Pigs Paradise' (sic). How appropriate.

We have a very pleasant meal served by an enthusiastic posse of young antipodean staff. Then it is a quick dash back to Pigs Paradise to watch Barcelona beat Arsenal in the European Champions League Final. Soon we are four little pigs asleep in our beds.

Day Four - *Bute from Bute*

Have a walk before breakfast along a rough track leading up a grassy slope opposite the hotel. Unknown to me Bob is further up the hill, chasing the sheep with his Kodak again.

The goldfinches are out, jangling their metallic song. The sun is also out, but feebly. Will it last? The forecast is still not great. Hopefully our sail back to Oban will be bathed in sunshine.

We ordered our breakfasts last night. It leads to efficiency in the kitchen but Gibbie is late down, yet again. His scrambled egg on toast arrives and we all sit and look at it. Ian had decided against a cooked breakfast but can be seen to swither.

"Oh go on - have it," I goad.

So he does. Of course Gibbie arrives just as he is shovelling the last bit into his bearded face. Gibbie looks suspiciously at the three of us stuffing our faces. "Where's mine?"

Bob raises an eyebrow, "It's bad enough over-sleeping, but it could be worse. Someone could have eaten your breakfast!"

Unusually, this morning we have time to kill. That doesn't happen on many Island Hopping mornings. Our ship doesn't sail till noon. We contemplate cycling round the island - well one of us does - or even a taxi circumnavigation. In the end we sit on our backsides in the lounge and watch the sky darken.

Eventually we stroll down to the pier where the harbourmaster, Kevin Byrne, is organising things very well. He seems to be very understanding of everyone's needs. "Have you all got your tickets? Have you filled in your boarding cards? Did Gibbie get a lift down or did he walk?"

When the ship finally arrives Mr Byrne pedals up and down the pier giving and taking instructions. I admire his enthusiasm, and it adds to the general air of competence with which the pier staff and ship's crew unload and load *LOTI*. In fact she is away from the pier only thirteen minutes behind schedule. A delay that this ship, if any, can make up very easily on passage.

And so it's another grey passage back to Oban. A palid sun fails to impress, nor sustain its strength for long enough to atone for the disappointing weather this year. Bob seems happy with his experience but it is a shame he can't go back to Canada and rave about the sunshine. But then if he had, no-one would have believed him.

We have a committee meeting in the cafeteria, over a curry, to decide on the last leg of our trip. My target is to get back to Bute to sail on *Bute*; if you take my meaning. Gibbie's target is to find a charity shop for his bag. Ian suggests over the side of the ship with it.

We arrive back at Oban just after 14.00; entering the bay from the south just as *Isle of Mull* is slipping out to the north. At the pier a very smart looking *Hebridean Princess* is being cleaned and stored in readiness for another week of exclusive cruises. We hoi polloi are quite happy with our CalMac *Rover* tickets.

Once ashore I head off to do some last minute shopping while Gibbie and the others collect the car and go off to search, one last desperate time, for a charity shop. We agree to meet back at the car park in half an hour, but by coincidence I emerge from my pottery shop just as Gibbie emerges from his charity shop - next door!

We head now for Colintraive, a long drive via Taynuilt, Inveraray and Strachur. It is a quiet car load of Island Hoppers - we have that 'going-home'- feeling. We cross over to the Isle of Bute aboard *Loch Dunvegan*.

The 18.15 sailing from Rothesay will be by *Bute* - thus giving us our only 'new' ship this year. The departure of *Juno* from the pier at 17.30, just as we turn past Ardbeg, confirms that this will be the case. So it's a very indifferent haddock supper and a visit to the Victorian Lavatories to kill time. Bob is fascinated by the restored toilets, but cannot be persuaded to spend-a-penny. He says it's not the cost but his prostate that is to blame. It's actually 15p, which means it is cheaper that the toilets at CalMac's new Oban terminal. Ian can be persuaded, but then he usually can.

The new *Bute* goes down favourably with all of us. This is surely the shape of things to come as far as Clyde ferries are concerned. At least she looks like a ship, albeit a bit lofty looking. Gibbie is delighted that she has a view over-the-bow. I'm just delighted she looks nothing like *Coruisk*.

We brave it out on the rear deck, pretending we're still among the *Hebrides*. Fortunately we are going with the wind. *Bute* cuts across between Rothesay and Wemyss Bay very swiftly but slows considerably a good distance out from Wemyss Bay Pier. Here she berths nose in but the reason for her ultra cautious approach is a mystery.

So here we are back where we started three days ago. It is not often we begin and end at the same point. We head back to Glasgow, looking in at James Watt Dock again where *Isle of Arran* has gone - her position now occupied by *Jupiter*, which has been out of service for eight months.

So we have sailed the equivalent of 384 statute miles, got a new ship and a new island. And despite the gloomy weather it has been as good as any other Island Hop. So much so that we are all offering ideas for next year - some of them bordering on the outrageous. I will have to wait a year to find out, you will only have to turn the page.

Postscript: For the record Ian did not suggest throwing the charity bag over the side of *Lord of the Isles*. He is actually a very charitable person, a terrible litter-lout but a very charitable person. He would also like me to make clear that he did not have a fish supper in Rothesay. I believe it was a lettuce supper, but light on the chips. *Isle of Arran* had left the nest to join *Hebridean Isles* on the Islay route. *Jupiter* was in dock for overhaul prior to taking over the Gourock-Dunoon service from *Saturn*

Four Island Hoppers

2007 New Mode of Transport

The Plan

THIS YEAR I WANTED TO INTRODUCE a new form of transport to an Island Hop - the aeroplane. Why not connect two islands with a short flight? Benbecula to Barra seemed the logical option. The plane to Barra lands on a beach instead of a tarmac runway (but only when the tide is out!). And rumour has it that the beach will not be used as a runway for much longer. We'd better try it out. We did, of course, fly in one to Orkney in 2004. But that was just to get there. This inter-island link is different.

Another target was paddle-steamer *Waverley*'s extended run in the Western Isles during 2007. We had used her to link Skye with Oban five years ago, could we now make the link in the opposite direction? The paddler was due to visit the Island of Coll. Why not sail to Coll on the regular ferry, and then return to Oban on the paddle-steamer?

There were other attractions beckoning from the CalMac timetable. We had never sailed from Barra to Tiree before. We did it in reverse in 2003 on *Lord of the Isles*, but now we could sail directly between the two islands from west to east, this time aboard *Clansman*.

Finally there was a rumour that Cumbrae ferry *Loch Alainn* would be taking over the Eriskay sailings from *Loch Bhrusda* in the spring of 2007. Tempting. Compiling an itinerary was now easy.

There was a fly in the ointment. For the first time in nineteen years one of us had to call off at short notice. It wasn't me otherwise this chapter would be completely missing from your book. It was Ian. He had to step down due to family circumstances, but promised to return next year. Unless, of course, his replacement turned out to be more fun!

Gibbie came up with a substitute, but admitted his idea smacked of nepotism. His wee brother Andy, ten years his junior but a keen ship lover and yachtsman of considerable mediocrity, would love to step into Ian's deck shoes. We would certainly miss Ian, but Andy was welcomed aboard. So what could he bring to an Island Hop? Well a car for one thing.

Day One - *A Close Call on Coll*

Boy it's an early start! The earliest yet. Whose clever idea was this? Well mine actually. We're in Andy's car at 04.55, yes that's five-to-five in the morning, getting stopped at every set of traffic lights in the South Side of Glasgow. Why is it that when the roads are empty every light turns to red just as you approach? We eventually reach the motorway, narrowly avoiding an aberrant roe deer who seems as surprised to see us in the middle of Dumbreck Road as we are to see him.

Andy's Seat Toledo has us speeding nauseatingly on our way to Oban. I'm beginning to regret the early start. We have to have a very good reason for this, and of course we have. Our target is *Lord of the Isles*' early morning departure. She is due to leave Oban at 08.00 - and we cannot afford to miss her. I needn't have worried that we would, for I spill vertiginous and pale-faced onto Oban North Pier from the back seat of the Seat at 06.51. It's the first time we've done Oban in under two hours.

The dilemma we face this morning is simple. We are taking *Lord of the Isles* to Coll and Tiree and then back to Coll again, where we get off. We will then board *Waverley* an hour and a half later and return to Oban on her. Simple? Well no, actually. The weather is not looking too promising: westerly 25mph winds and a dreary-looking, restless sea. If *Waverley* cannot berth at Coll to pick us up we will be marooned there for a day and a half, with the resulting collapse of our Island Hopping plans. So do we disembark from *Lord of the Isles* and wait for *Waverley*? Our plans will sail away with her if she cannot berth. Or do we take the safe option and stay aboard *LOTI* back to Oban? Remember we will have a chance to sail on the paddler tomorrow.

Waverley is berthed at the North Pier. She is due to sail for Iona and Coll in a couple of hours. We look across her empty decks in the vain hope that someone will magically appear and promise us that she will definitely reach Coll this afternoon. But of course no one can pledge that, certainly not the Polish crewman giving the decks their first sweep of the morning.

If only we could have that assurance that *Waverley* will be able to berth at Coll. We could ask the captain, but the curtains on his cabin windows are still tightly closed.

"Why don't we ask the skipper of *Lord of the Isles* to ask the skipper of *Waverley* when we get out there," suggests Gibbie. "I'm sure they'll be in contact for an up to date weather report." It's not easy coming up with a good idea at seven in the morning but we all agree this sounds like one.

Out in the bay an inbound *Lord of the Isles* is passing an outbound *Isle of Mull*. We head round to the Railway Pier. Work is progressing on a second linkspan at the Oban Ferry Terminal. This will certainly ease congestion when it opens next year. No more queues of steamers waiting to offload; lots of future photographic opportunities.

Lord of the Isles sets off at 08.00 for Coll and Tiree, with us aboard and Andy's car deposited on a quiet Oban street. First call is a full breakfast in the restaurant. Stuffed with black pudding, Lorne sausage and fried eggs I head for the quiet lounge to catch up on some lost sleep. *LOTI* has the best 'quiet' lounge in the CalMac fleet. We call it the zizz lounge and with the gentle, soporific hiss of the air-conditioning vents in my ears I am soon dreaming of being stranded on a desert island.

At 09.45 I'm back on deck looking through bleary eyes at the open sea beyond the northerly entrance of the Sound of Mull. What is the swell like? There certainly is one. *Waverley* should be heading along the south coast of Mull towards Iona just now. I cannot see how she can comfortably do that this morning, judging from the rise and fall of the grey-green sea. If she abandons her Iona sail where will she go instead? Probably not Coll. I am not optimistic, and neither is one of the catering crew of *LOTI* whom I get chatting to out on deck. He used to work for *Waverley* Excursions and knows the paddler well. He doesn't think she will be able to call at Coll in these seas. It isn't exactly rough, but there is a definite swell running from the south-west and the wind is fairly strong. *Lord of the Isles* has no problem coping with any of this, of course. On the positive side the seas were much worse two days ago and the forecast predicts that the conditions will improve.

We take action on Gibbie's earlier idea and ask at the purser's office if there is radio contact between our ship and *Waverley*. I ask the chief steward if anyone on the bridge could help us. He responds by donning a pair of rubber gloves! "I'm just going up there to clear a toilet, I'll ask."

Iain McNeil is the second mate and he is down looking for me just a few minutes later. Surprisingly there has been no contact between the two ships but he suggests we ask the pier staff on the pier at Coll, as they will be likely to know if the paddler is on her way. We thank him for his advice. This means that one of us should go ashore at Coll on *LOTI's* outward bound visit there (*LOTI* will go on to Tiree and then return to Coll prior to *Waverley's* intended visit). I volunteer - well no-one else does. It is an Island Hopping fact that whenever a volunteer is required it is always me. I don't mind in this case for I can enjoy a good walk on Coll while *LOTI* is away to Tiree.

At Arinagour Pier on Coll there is a guest. Our old friend *Hebridean Princess* is berthed alongside the north face, bobbing gently in the swell. From the top deck of *Lord of the Isles* we get a great view of her.

LOTI berths stern-in and I disembark. Before she returns I will have found out if *Waverley* is likely to berth or not at the pier. We have arranged a signaling system to aid my two colleagues on *LOTI* when she returns. A wave of my arms horizontally means 'stay where you are, I'm coming back aboard, forget *Waverley*'. A vertical wave of one arm means 'get off and come ashore'. Both arms held vertically by my sides means 'I haven't a clue, get yourselves another volunteer in future'. Meanwhile, as *Lord of the Isles* pulls away from the pier I'm merely just waving good-bye to Gibbie and Andy and causing them great confusion by doing so.

The rain turns heavy so I pull my jacket around my ears and head uphill to the village of Arinagour. It is only a year since I was last here and I would love to get right across to the west side of the island this time, but it's three miles away and I only have two hours. If only someone would take pity on me and offer me a lift.

I don't have to wait long (you rarely do in the Western Isles). A LandRover draws up and I accept the kind offer of a lift to Gallanach Farm on the west side of the island. My driver is one of the rope-handlers who helped tie up *Lord of the Isles*. He is also a shopkeeper, Scottish Power repairman and police radio operator. "Don't need to worry much about that last one - we have no crime. In fact we have no police either."

I leave the road just past the farm and cross over a fence into a field bounded by a crest of sand-dunes at the far end. The field is full of sheep. Wading through knee-deep maram grass I reach the top of the dunes and discover that beyond - there is another crest of dunes! After fifteen minutes I reach the beautiful sandy beach of Bagh an Trailleich.

The beach is empty, but for me and several gulls and oystercatchers. The sun has now put in an extended appearance between the showers and by the time I reach the water's edge I am very warm. It is only half past eleven, not yet midday. I was in Glasgow this morning!

I cannot linger as I have a three and a half mile walk back to the pier, and only ninety minutes to do it in.

So I set off along the beach and ultimately find an easier way of getting back onto the road. I then have a fair canter back to Arinagour, but by the time I get there the heavens have opened and I am soaking!

I cram into the waiting-room down at the pier. This is full of what seems like an entire class of schoolchildren. But I also spot one of the rope-handlers who was on the pier earlier. She's still wearing a large red hat. I ask her (yes, her) if she knows anything about *Waverley*.

"Yes she's out there just now somewhere. I think she's intending to come in."

'Think' is not good enough for me, however. Looking out into the murkiness that now covers the sea I am still not confident that the paddler will be able to berth at the pier. Hebridean Princess is still bobbing up and down. We cannot take the chance of *Waverley* coming alongside but not being able to berth.

Lord of the Isles appears out of the mist and suddenly, just behind her, *Waverley* can be seen, almost like a spirit emerging from the gloom. She is there - and then she is gone. Seemingly vaporized. Did I imagine her, is she really out there?

The combination of the swell, the pelting rain and my indecision make my mind up for me, if you see what I mean. I will signal to Gibbie and Andy to stay aboard *Lord of the Isles*, and we will return to Oban aboard her. There they are, craning their necks over the side trying to see me on the pier. I can't remember what the signal was but wave my arms anyway. Soon I am with them. They never saw *Waverley*, she seems to have headed down the east coast of Coll towards Tiree. We sail off towards the entrance to the Sound of Mull, cosy and unanimous that we have made the correct decision.

The sea is definitely calming down and the wind dropping; mind you, we are now sailing ahead of both. Up on the top deck of the ship we plan the rest of the day. By not taking *Waverley* back to Oban we have gained a little time. Time enough to add another sailing to what is without doubt already the most attenuated day of any Island Hop.

We are now due in at Oban at 16.30, which means we can catch the 18.00 sailing to Craignure by *Isle of Mull*. Despite having been an incumbent of so many Island Hops it is actually four years since we last sailed on her. So a return crossing, with dinner aboard, will do nicely, thank you. And then my mobile phone rings.

It is a call from my daughter Fiona. My mother-in-law has just passed away. Clare's Mum was eighty-six and despite her recent decline in health this is still a bit of a shock. What will I do? The remainder of the sail back to Oban involves several phone calls home. The consensus is that I continue the journey. There is no point in me rushing home tomorrow.

Before catching *Isle of Mull* we have time to move the car to a more suitable spot and check into our guesthouse. Our host sighs when we request at early breakfast, on account of us having to be on the North Pier at 08.30 tomorrow morning. "More of you steamer nutters, that's seven of you guys I have! Continental breakfast buffet at half seven."

He shows us into a small room with one double bed and two bunk beds. This has to accommodate the three of us. I immediately bag the top bunk. Andy takes the lower, as it is sixty-five years since he last shared a bed with his brother.

Back down at the pier to watch *Isle of Mull* berthing. Three young lads on the pier are begging Gibbie to part with a cigarette, or three. "No!" Responds Gibbie gruffly. "You're too wee. It'll stunt your growth. Look at me - I used to be six foot seven!"

"But you've got Senior Service, they're strong."

"Yes, but I get them on prescription."

Isle of Mull has been refurbished since our last sail in 2003. She is looking very nice. The cafeteria has been restyled and there seems to be new carpets everywhere - well except the deck! We have a very pleasant meal. As we finish Andy demonstrates why he is known as Mr Tidy. His plate is so spotless it looks as though it won't need washed, his knife and fork laid neatly side by side, and all his little condiment containers (and there are many - for he has a savoury tooth) are sorted into a neat little pile. I remark on this. "Oh yes," he proudly acknowledges, "when I've finished an in-flight meal the air-hostess cannot tell if I've opened it or not."

After leaving Craignure we take to the capacious upper deck to see if we can see *Waverley* coming down the Sound of Mull behind us. According to her proposed schedule she should be. Sure enough, either my timing or her timing is perfect for there she is steaming into our wake. Unfortunately just as my camera appears the sun disappears and precludes what could have been a nice picture. *Isle of Mull* berths at the Railway

Pier and *Waverley* at the North Pier. We walk around to find out how her day went.

Waverley apparently cancelled her trip to Iona this morning and instead sailed up the Sound of Mull, her Master still debating whether to approach Coll or not. She cruised down towards the Gunna Sound, to allow *Lord of the Isles* to berth, and finally did manage to berth at Coll. She even managed a cruise for some of the 'Collachs', returning to the pier and then back down the Sound to Oban. So we could have taken her inbound from Coll - but I don't regret our earlier decision.

Many of her disembarking passengers are well-kent faces to us. Before long we are meeting up with them in Auley's Bar, surrounded by pictures of our beloved ships. On eventually disembarking from the bar we are followed back to our 'digs' by some of them. Yes, it seems that most of the paddler's complement is staying at the our guesthouse.

By the time I crawl up the ladder into my bunk the first day of Island Hop 2007 has lasted twenty hours. That must be some kind of record.

Day Two - *Paddling the Sound*

In the middle of the night I had to answer a call of nature, and on my way down the ladder I stepped on Andy's head. It doesn't stop him from crooning Barry Manilow songs at six-thirty in the morning, however. Perhaps he is exacting revenge. Gibbie is particularly unimpressed. Chastised for his rendition of Mandy, Andy dons what looks like six pullovers and totters off to see if he can waken the rest of the guesthouse.

The breakfast room resembles the dining saloon of *Waverley* - the same faces present. After breakfast we all set off in convoy along the waterfront of Oban to *Waverley*'s berth at the North Pier. There are no big CalMac ships around this morning - they're all away on duty elsewhere.

The sun is trying hard to penetrate the thin veil of cloud. The paddler has already raised steam and her paddle-wheels are turning over very slowly, as if twitching to get underway. Dozens of 'the usual suspects' are boarding the ship. But the numbers are not great as this will be a one-way sailing by *Waverley* - she will not be returning to Oban today. This is, in effect, a positioning cruise for her, but it suits us perfectly as a means of linking Oban with Skye, without the need of a car. From Oban *Waverley* will sail up the Sound of Mull and out into the Sea of the *Hebrides* towards Eigg. She will then head north to Armadale on Skye and then cross to Mallaig. Although we are ultimately heading for Armadale we intend disembarking at Mallaig and crossing back to Skye on CalMac's *Coruisk*. This will be the first time we have crossed between the two piers on different ships, on the same day.

While we head up through Skye by bus *Waverley* will be undertaking a cruise to Inverie, from Mallaig, and sailing up to Kyle of Lochalsh for the night. It seems as though both she and we three Island Hoppers have a wonderful day ahead of us.

As we reverse out of Oban Gibbie produces a mobile-phone from his pocket. He has been keeping its presence a secret as he normally berates them. I find him hiding behind one of *Waverley's* funnels, texting his wife. How cute! By the time he succeeds in sending his text we are off Craignure.

On board there are dozens of people we know - regular *Waverley* enthusiasts. One of them is Hans Freund, a German friend of Gibbie who we met on Island Hop 2002. Hans lives in Switzerland and has come over to Scotland just to spend ten days sailing on his favourite paddler. Off Craignure we pass *Isle of Mull*, her bulk filling the dining-room windows of *Waverley* as I tackle my second breakfast of bacon, eggs and sausage - well the first one was only a 'continental' breakfast!

The sun is now dominating and I'm up on the bridge filming the view from skipper Luke Davis' perspective. He seems to be enjoying himself, guiding the world's last sea-going paddle-steamer up the Sound of Mull. The lack of noise and vibration is immediately noticeable up here. It is as if we are gliding across the surface of the water. By the time we reach the northern limit of the Sound, however, the gliding has stopped. Out on the open water a moderate sea is advancing on us from the west and rocking the old ship gracefully from side to side. It is a wonderful movement which demonstrates the fine sea-going qualities of *Waverley*, a facet of the steamer that the Saturday punter to Dunoon or Rothesay is not entirely aware of. She is undoubtedly a superb sea boat and copes harmoniously with the three metre swell crossing her port bow. Ardnamurchan lighthouse passes to starboard, Skye lies away to the north and *Waverley's* bow points to the west. I climb up to her upper deck and enjoy the thrill of a half empty ship, like a private yacht, steaming steadfastly out into the Sea of the *Hebrides*.

Eventually we wheel to starboard and allow the running sea to push us from behind, onwards towards the island of Muck. We pass very close to the island, but not as close as we'd like to CalMac's *Lochnevis*, which is heading to Muck. Soon, even closer, is the south coast of Eigg. We steam past the long continuous cliffs of The Struidh, affording me (and probably the rest of us) the closest possible view of Eigg's impressive cliffs.

We are now heading north-east towards the Point of Sleat, the most southerly point on Skye. Many miles to port the island of Soay is visible.

I call home and am reassured that all is as well as can be there - no need for me to jump ship at Mallaig (which I had considered). My mother-in-law was a keen fan of the Clyde steamers and a seasoned sailor aboard many of them. She sailed many times aboard this very ship, but her favourite was *Eagle III*. I think she would have approved of me continuing my journey.

Armadale approaches, and here the 83 passengers aboard *Waverley* are joined by 300 schoolchildren. They are having an educational school trip aboard the steamer - and what a good way to get your education.

There is another visitor in the bay the little cruise ship *Explorer* is anchored off the pier. She undertakes cruises almost anywhere, occasionally to the *Hebrides* and Western Isles. These cruises often have a theme. What might it be today, I wonder, 'paddle-steamer spotting'?

We decide to stay aboard for the short hop across to Mallaig, a decision which we come close to regretting. The ship wallows from side to side as she crosses a fairly turbulent Sound of Sleat. The children are herded into little flocks by their ever-smiling teachers. They are all on their best behaviour - and so are the children. The rocking motion sends them into raptures, they are positively cooing with glee.

Approaching Mallaig the skipper slows *Waverley* down to a crawl; the rope-men on the bow and starboard sponson are ready with their heaving-lines. But the wind catches the ship and she starts to veer towards the rock guarding the harbour entrance. *Waverley* backs away - well away. Andy and I look at each other. Maybe she'll abandon the call at Mallaig and head straight to Inverie. What will we do then? Just as I'm beginning to wish we had got off at Armadale the telegraph rings loud and forward we go again, a little more assertively this time. When we pass the rock to starboard I know we have reached the point of no return. With no little skill the steamer's bow is brought within easy heaving distance of the knuckle of the pier, where several shore crew are making encouraging signals to the skipper. The bow line is cast and then the sponson rope also. We glide into the shelter of the harbour. Another hundred passengers on sunny Mallaig Pier are delighted that they will be able to get their cruise after all, and we are delighted we can get off and continue our Island Hop.

Waverley slips away astern a few minutes later. I spot Hans standing between the funnels waving at me. "Bye Hans!"

Three young lads leaning on the rail of the sponson think this is funny. "Byeee Hands," they wave in unison.

Not to be out done I shout back to Hans, " auf Wiedersehen." Three little mimics hanging on the rail shout in unison, "auf Wiedersehen!"

Waverley is no sooner gone when *Coruisk* rushes in confidently. There is only a handful of passengers, including us, in the passenger lounge of *Coruisk* for her 15.05 sailing. The other two form an attractive looking couple who look Slavic.

"Where do you think they're from?" I ask my colleagues. "I bet they're Latvian."

"Sweden," says Andy.

"Govanhill!" Says Gibbie.

I must find out. Within a couple of minutes I've got chatting to them and have discovered they are anxious to find castles on Skye. After consultation with my map I point them in the direction of Dunvegan Castle. "Oh and where have you come from?"

"I am from Poland," the chap replies, "she is Russian."

All five passengers spill out onto Armadale pier. According to my timetable the bus to Portree is due in ten minutes. When our fellow travellers see us waiting at the bus stop they form a queue behind us. Half an hour passes and we are still all there.

"Are you sure about this, Stuart?" Gibbie asks hesitantly.

The answer is quite clearly 'no'. I ask at the CalMac office about the bus. It seems I've screwed up and mis-read the timetable (not for the first time). There is no bus - well not for a couple of hours. So I order a taxi. We should still be able to get to Portree in time for our next bus. But the Pole and the Russian? Their castle quest is in tatters. They head off for a walk. At least they are still smiling.

The ever observant Gibbie has been casting his mind back to previous trips. "This isn't the first time we've been stranded at Armadale with no means of securing our line of advance, is it Stuart?"

"Eh no."

"And I seem to think that trip involved *Waverley* as well!"

"I've been so occupied with just getting us here that I forgot to check the bus times."

Hanging around Armadale induces boredom. Gibbie latches onto a middle-aged English couple who seem to be hanging around for no other reason than to see if our bus turns up. Andy chats up the CalMac crew. I spend the time annoying and tormenting two local collie dogs who are fighting over a soggy stick. One has an unmistakable dog-in-manger attitude. It clearly doesn't want the stick but can't bear the other showing any interest in it. When it eventually sinks its fangs into the other's flank I realise it's time to end this game. It could be my flank next. Anyway - our taxi has finally arrived.

We board our taxi, a full hour after first stepping ashore at Armadale. The Slavs reappear and head back to the pier to rejoin *Coruisk*. The collies head back to the shore. And the English couple? They appear to be rooted to the spot, either that or they cannot drag themselves away from Gibbie.

Our taxi-driver is a Glaswegian called Wullie. On seeing him drive up one of the pier crew whoops with delight. "It's Wullie, he must have got out of jail and his license back. And he's cleaned the blood off the front of his cab." But his comments are clearly for our ears.

The taxi has three rows of seats. "Can I sit beside Wullie?" Asks Andy as he jumps in. I don't mind - I make for the rear. Gibbie finally gives his English couple a reprieve and wanders over.

"Can I sit beside Wullie?" He asks. Wullie obviously feels an important man and consequently opens the throttle full - and keeps it there all the way to Portree. He also keeps up a cheery banter all the way. He informs us that he supplements his income by working at the local hospital. Andy jumps at this.

"Do you take your passengers there?"

We originally asked Wullie to take us all the way to Uig, our overnight base tonight, but we are covering the ground so fast that I realise that although Portree is twenty miles away we are going to get there before our planned second bus connection leaves.

So we step out shaken and somewhat stirred onto the square in Portree. "Thanks for the flight, Wullie," I find myself saying.

Andy joins in. "The next time I rob a bank I want you to be my get-away man."

"Thanks chaps, it's been a pleasure. Anytime you're back on Skye."

Before stepping onto the bus I have to finish my ice-cream cone; the driver just gave two young lads a row for drinking from a can aboard his bus. We set off at a more sedate speed and, after a few detours across several supermarket car parks, we are dropped right outside the front door of the Ferry Inn at Uig.

After a refreshing beer it's straight into the scallops and roast beef, although not on the same plate. Gibbie manages to scare both of the young waitresses with his new swept-straight-back and gelled-down hairstyle. "Don't you think I look like Al Pacino?"

It is so mild and calm tonight in Uig that we sit outside the inn, sipping a malt and listening to a Pavarotti of a song thrush belting it out in a tree above us. He really is in fine form. So is Andy, he is trying to imitate it. It is such a pleasant evening that we seem loathe to turn in for the night. The thrush stops and a tawny owl starts - the night shift taking over. As the light fades our pier for our next sailing tomorrow is jutting out into the bay way below us, empty and quiet.

Day Three - *Flight of Fancy*

Barry Manilow is Andy Williams this morning. Andy Williams at 07.15! And I'm three rooms and two corridors away.

Our hosts are exceptionally nice people. Apart from the lovely breakfast we are offered a lift down to the pier. Unfortunately this cannot be extended to up the pier as well. It is a long haul for Gibbie as he makes his way up the *Hebrides'* longest pier to board our next ship, *Hebrides*. Just to add a cruel stroke of irony a service bus overtakes Gibbie just as he reaches the ship. He would normally take this in his stride, excuse the pun, but he is feeling a little rough this morning, and he is annoyed with his wee brother.

"I'm not sharing with you again. Wakening me up singing like that every morning." I cannot bring myself to tell him that he is sharing a room with him tonight as well. Well someone has to, and it ain't going to be me!

Today should be interesting. We are heading for Lochmaddy, on North Uist, whereupon we will catch a bus (if I've got my times right and it turns up) to Benbecula. "So you're traversing the Long Isle again," I hear you muttering. "Well we're not. Yes, we are heading for Barra, but this time we are taking a plane." We are booked on the afternoon flight from Benbecula to Barra. Never done that before!

With Captain Andy McCrindle in command *Hebrides* slips her mooring ropes and heads sedately out into Uig Bay, bang on 09.40.

The forecast is favourable today. It is dull but mild, and the wind is light. The air is very clear but dappled with cotton-wool clouds which threaten showers. However the sun is due to appear this afternoon, which we all hope for, as we want good visibility for our flight.

In the morning light the western facing headlands of Skye look as if they have been fashioned from velvet. Looking south there are layers of them jutting out into the Little Minch. As we sail out onto its calm waters we seem to be leaving the shower clouds behind. Their grey curtain is split by an intense, angled shaft of light.

The crew of *Hebrides* seem to take particular pride in their ship. During the crossing they are out washing the deck. It looks clean enough to me already. Gibbie is also out on deck, fiddling intensely with his phone.

"What's past tense for texting?"

"You needn't know," Andy pipes up unkindly, " you never manage to send one."

The sailing over to North Uist is a joy. *Hebrides* is a very comfortable ship, the scenery stunning and the weather getting better the further west we sail. The ship is carrying a fair selection of yesterday's *Waverley* compliment. They are obviously suffering from some kind of 'paddle-steamer fatigue', a condition that can only be relieved by having a sail on a diesel-engined car-ferry. So they are off on a circular tour of North Uist and *Harris*, using the Sound of *Harris* ferry *Loch Portain*. They are also expecting a bus to meet them.

At Lochmaddy there is a bus, and a driver, but neither seem in any hurry to move. Fortunately we are in no rush. So we have one of those 'hanging-around' moments that have graced many an Island Hop. The folk on the tour head off on their own bus and we have nothing else to do but sit around in the sun and film *Hebrides* departing.

Eventually our driver wakes up, gives us a nod and we're off to Benbecula. Strange, yesterday our timetabled bus never showed up, and today we have a bus that seems to be operating to a timetable of its own.

We head out across the watery peat bogs of North Uist. The whole scene is awash with sunshine, which augers well for our flight later this afternoon. The greens and browns of the land, and the blues and mauves of the tidal pools and lochs merge intricately. Today, in the sunshine, the landscape is a delicately blended palate of colour, but in winter it must look bleak.

At Benbecula Airport we have a couple of hours to kill before our flight; yet more time to kill. I head off to find the nearest beach. It borders the airfield itself. Like most beaches around the Western Isles there is nobody on it. A look at the shoreline confirms that the tide is in fact receding, an important fact as we will soon be landing on the beach at Barra, and that will be somewhat easier if the tide is out.

Our Twin Otter has a grand total of eight passengers today for the twenty minute flight down the length of South Uist and across the Sound of Barra. Run by Loganair for British Airways this plane started at Glasgow this morning and has already called at Barra - on an Island Hop of its own in effect.

The co-pilot is bent double in the tiny cabin as he gives us a safety briefing in a rich Glaswegian accent. We then get a grandstand view over the shoulders of the crew as we taxi to the end of the runway. The plane, at full throttle, lifts abruptly into the clear Hebridean air after just a few seconds.

We soar above the shimmering lochs of Benbecula and turn eastwards to cruise at a mere twelve hundred feet above the rocky shores of South Uist. I know this because I can see the altimeter. We are privileged to see this eastern coast, devoid of human settlement, for the first time. No roads run along this shore and no ferry sails along this part of the island. We are getting an eagle's-eye view.

Lochboisdale appears below, shame *Clansman* isn't sitting at the pier. The beach of Traigh Mor on Barra can be seen through the cockpit window and as the captain throttles back to start the descent the plane almost seems to stop in mid-air. Now we feel as though we are gliding, down to a very soft landing on the beach. When we come to a standstill the lady across the aisle from me finally takes her hands down from her face.

"This is not my idea of flying!" The beach at Traigh Mor is not sand but very fine shell (it is as known as the cockle-shell beach) and a perfect surface on which to land a plane. But for how much longer? There are plans to build a runway here on Barra. Why bother? I ask. As long as the tide is out this seems to be a perfectly adequate arrangement. The beach was first used as a runway in June 1933, with the first scheduled flight taking off in August 1936. Now there are around fourteen hundred take-offs and landings annually.

All the passengers have to get off now. Those continuing on to Glasgow have to check-in again. The pilots, in the meantime, head off for a coffee - well a seventeen minute flight has probably left them feeling drained.

To my colleagues' concern I have made absolutely no arrangements on how we are going to get the six miles from the airport to Castlebay. "Let's just hang around, watch the plane take-off and see what happens," is the best I can come up with. In fact I was hoping for a bus, yet again! But fortune favours the unprepared, for we are not the only ones watching the Twin Otter take off.

Flora McKinnon is a very smart looking eighty year old and is waving her cousin off from the island. She very kindly offers the three of us a lift into town. Not content with that she even takes us the 'tourist' route, around the west side of the island. "There is no biss meeting this flight," she reveals.

Castlebay looks quite serene this late afternoon. We discover that Kismuil Castle, out in the bay, is now run by Historic Scotland and therefore open to visitors; their motorboat is just returning to the pier on it's last run of the day. We earmark this as an option for tomorrow - the chance to take in a new island.

The other vessel at Castlebay Pier is the lifeboat, a Severn class - the largest class of lifeboat. We chat to the engineer who has come down to tinker with the engine. Well that's all engineers do, isn't it? Upon our prompting he gives us a quick resume of recent rescues. Gibbie has numerous technical questions for him. I have a much simpler one.

"You ever sea-sick?" I ask him.

"Never."

Over dinner we watch *Clansman* come and go at the pier. She disgorges two Barratlantic lorries and loads approximately three passengers.

While setting down the rhubarb crumble and custard our waitress, a very pleasant lady in her forties, proudly tells us that she is heading to Glasgow at the weekend, to run the ladies' 10k race. She hopes to complete the run in under an hour. Gibbie's mouth drops open at this - so he pops another spoonful of crumble into it.

"Under an hour! It would take me that just to get my trainers on." He is so astonished by this that only the intervention of Andy stops him from pouring custard into his coffee. Which is only fair, as it was Andy who swapped the cream jug for the custard jug in the first place.

Day Four - *Sparky's Magic Island*

The last time we spent the night in Castlebay we badly misbehaved ourselves. Not this time last night we only partly misbehaved ourselves. Andy is doing his best to sound like Kiri Te Kanawa this morning, punctuated with a bit of Scots Guards, if you can imagine that! Gibbie seems happy that this is the last day.

So we are thankfully very refreshed as we assemble in the dining-room, only to find it full of Nova Scotians on a heritage trail. It makes for a noisy breakfast; made even more interesting when one of them thinks I'm the waiter.

"Sorry I cannot help you," I have to tell the lady, "But I'm from Barcelona."

We find ourselves down at the post office at 08.45, boarding the bus to Ardmhor, where the Eriskay ferry leaves from. The plan is to spend a few hours on the island and then get back to Castlebay in time for a trip to Kismuil and then, more importantly, our sailing aboard *Clansman* back to Oban.

The bus takes us around the east coast, this time, thus completing our circumnavigation of Barra. *Loch Bhrusda*, soon to be replaced by *Loch Alainn*, is full of our Canadian friends. One pear-shaped lady, clad in a long, bright yellow cape, is a 'dead-ringer' for Big Bird from Sesame Street. Her general shape lends itself to the general, overall impression.

"They'll be no trouble spotting her if she falls overboard," observes Andy.

It is a dull but pleasant enough sail over to Eriskay. The name Eriskay is derived from the Norse word Eirchr, which means Eric. But no-one seems to know now who Eric was. The island has a population of around 140, a fairly high density for such a small island. It did not suffer the depopulation of so many islands during the clearances, when crofters were forced off the land to make way for sheep. Eriskay was considered too barren for sheep and in fact its population actually grew due to immigration from the neighbouring islands of Hellisay and South Uist.

We are hoping that there will be a bus meeting the ferry at the Eriskay side. If there is it will be my first bus success this trip. If not Gibbie then will have to sit on some Canadian chick's knee - for they have a bus meeting them. Given that choice Andy and I decide to head off along the beach towards the local hostelry Am Politician. Gibbie? Well we last see him being hauled up into the bus by two long, yellow arms.

It is a beautiful stretch of beach leading to the village. This was the shore from which Bonnie Prince Charlie disembarked from the French ship *D'Outeille* in 1745. Today the main interest is a pair of common terns chasing a dark phase arctic skua. Just a few metres offshore there is a solitary great northern diver.

We reach the road and soon find Gibbie. He's standing outside the pub, waiting for it to open (we've been here before!). To kill time we head on through the village, closely followed now by a black-and-white collie, who we later discover is called Sparky. He soon takes the lead and the four of us head uphill to the church, peeing at every second fence post. A small terrier entrapped in a nearby garden takes umbrage at this and barks furiously at the collie. Sparky responds by peeing at the gate of his garden - the ultimate canine insult.

Sparky is a star, no more so than when he demonstrates how to cross a cattle-grid on four legs. Andy is so impressed that it is all he can do to stop himself from getting down on all fours and trying it for himself. Determined to film Sparky's exploit I motion to our friendly collie to repeat the feat. He rushes towards me enthusiastically, and then jumps up and runs along the adjacent wall, before dropping back down to me, thus avoiding the cattle-grid. Not daft these collies. But the next time he does it for real and Andy is ecstatic.

The barman in the Am Politician today is Stephen, and he pours us a nice lunch. The pub opened in 1988 and is a very welcome feature of this lovely island. A conservatory has been added and up on the roof the resident blackbird is on her nest.

Gibbie enters into conversation with a chap in the airy lounge. As luck would have it he is an off-duty CalMac crewman. He very kindly offers Gibbie a lift back to the ferry in half an hour's time. So how about that? CalMac serving their passengers even in their own time. So Gibbie has secured his line of advance in his usual style.

Andy and I set off back along the beach again, closely followed by Sparky who seems to think he's now an Island Hopper as well. Andy is quite concerned by this, seemingly certain that he is going to get himself lost. Lost! On Eriskay? Despite Andy instructing him to 'go home' Sparky is determined he's going to the ferry terminal as well. When we reach the road, however, a couple of hundred metres from the ferry, he gives up. As we sail off, heading back to a gloomy looking Barra, we can see his animated black-and-white form making his way back along the beach in short runs interrupted by pee stops. There is a tear in Andy's eye. "He never looked back once."

Loch Bhrusda is a very quiet little ship on the way back. Her future is uncertain as *Loch Alainn* is due to replace her on the Barra-Eriskay route as soon as she herself is replaced by the brand new Loch Shira. Loch Bhrusda may then become spare.

Just a few hundred metres off Eriskay's south-western shore is *Hebridean Princess*, last seen at Coll a couple of days ago. She is at anchor, her passengers probably ashore on the island - new friends for Sparky. I point this out to Andy.

"Tart!" He mutters.

At Ardmhor there is a bus-full of Irish tourists waiting to board the ferry. The skipper blares his klaxon when the bus fails to move forward. But the bus driver cannot get the engine started. Anxious looks for a few minutes but eventually the start button is found and all is well.

"Where's our bus?" Asks Gibbie with a noticeably questioning tone to his voice. I know my track record on acquiring a bus has not been too good on this trip. I am immediately rescued by its timeous appearance.

Back at Castlebay we have a coffee in the cafe down by the pier. By the time we finish the ferry-boat from Kismuil has berthed at our side, so we get aboard. Castle Kismuil, and the island it completely occupies, is like something from an Enid Blyton book. The Castle, belonging to the MacNeil clan, is a rabbit-warren of narrow corridors, passageways and small rooms. There is a central courtyard, which I find surprising as I imagined the castle to be solid.

There is a little shop within the castle and Andy feels the need to part with some cash. His eye is drawn to a neatly wrapped soap bearing the name 'velvet antlers'.

"Very appropriate for my wife," he announces.

"Why is that?" The lady behind the counter asks.

"Cos I always call her 'dear'."

In true Island Hop style we spend as little time on the island as it is practically possible to spend. The ferryman looks bemused as we step back on board his boat. "That you already?"

But we have a ferry to catch. *Clansman* is due in at Castlebay in fifteen minutes and our bags are still up at the hotel. As usual she is right on schedule and so we do not have a lot of spare time.

She is not the only ship in the bay. We are being followed by cruise ships this trip, for *Explorer* is anchored just off the pier. A fleet of rubber-hulled inflatables are ferrying her eager passengers ashore. What a joy it is to see these being thrown up and down when they cross *Clansman's* considerable wake.

Our ship is heading for Oban, but will sail direct to Tiree first. This is the first time we have sailed direct between Barra and Tiree. She will then continue on to Coll, thus completing an interesting circle for us.

I spend the first hour out on the ship's rear deck. There is a three metre sea coming at the ship from the south, hitting her starboard side. She takes this very comfortably and the rocking motion is very pleasant. How many times have we stood out on deck crossing the Minch like this?

The narrow gap of the Gunna Sound approaches. The waters around here are treacherous, due to shallow water and reefs, but *Clansman* powers on regardless. Well perhaps not regardless, I would give her skipper more credit than that.

Over on the Tiree side I spot the unmistakable fins of a basking shark, about a hundred metres from the ship. Both dorsal and tail fins cut the surface at the same time, this is what makes them unmistakable. Suddenly there is another, then another. Soon we can see five of these great docile beasts, heading out from the shallows into the Atlantic.

The ship swings to starboard and soon we are off Tiree. We daren't risk disembarking - the schedules are now so tight that the ship would sail without us. A handful of cars board, plus a wagon load of sheep, each with a one-way ticket to the mainland.

After Tiree we head downstairs for dinner. The large picture windows of *Clansman* demonstrate their worth. The sun streams in over the sea and, after a long day outdoors, gives us a wonderful glow.

As we finish our CalMac steak pie (which I thoroughly recommend) Coll Pier is sliding past our window. We get a close up view of the berthing dolphin where the lady with the CalMac hard hat demonstrates that women can haul in ropes just as well as men.

It's the last leg now - sailing back down the Sound of Mull. A serene atmosphere now descends the ship. The throbbing of *Clansman's* diesels is soporific and I fear I will succumb to fatigue unless I step out onto the deck.

Up top my ears become immune to the engine noise, all I can hear now is the swish of the waters passing the ship. The sun is finally sinking lethargically behind Coll and Ardnamurchan, uplighting a bank of low cloud with a deep amber. Ahead a shower cloud is waiting to ambush us.

We swing into Oban at ten o' clock. As usual it has all been great fun. We've certainly missed Ian, and I bet he has missed us. As for Andy - well how can we refuse him another Island Hop ticket next year? Even though his singing is dreadful.

All that faces us now is the unexciting drive home. Unexciting? Well all is well until we run out of petrol at Duck Bay Marina on Loch Lomondside at five minutes past midnight! It's not Andy's fault, it's the car's. We believed Andy when we drove past the last petrol station in Oban that his Seat could travel "a hundred miles on quarter of a tank of petrol."

Cheers Andy, sorry Gibbie and I didn't share the cost of the tow to Dumbarton with you.

Postscipt: Sadly *Explorer* struck ice while on an Antarctic cruise six months later and sank. Fortunately without any loss of life.

MAID OF THE LOCH, 2005

2008 Keeping the Best for Last

The Plan

THIS WAS EASY. It is almost unbelievable but we are about to embark on our twentieth Island Hop. And we reckon it could be our last. My idea was simple - let's try to follow the route of the first Island Hop that the three of us did, back in 1990 (Ian did not join Gibbie and I until that year). We could compare the ships we sailed on then, on the routes we took all those years ago, with the current fleet. And we could use a bit of embellishment.

Two routes have disappeared: Kyle of Lochalsh - Kyleakin; and the cruise from Kyle of Lochalsh to Mallaig, by *Lochmor*. The former has gone because of the construction of the Skye Bridge and the latter because of the replacement of the passenger-only *Lochmor* by a car-ferry. Neither of these changes was a set back, however, as we could leave Skye via the Armadale-Mallaig ferry.

Now for the embellishment. When planning the actual route I could see an opportunity to sail on no less than three 'new' ships - all of them on the Clyde. By setting off very early we could also sail to Dunoon on one vessel and back on another, and to Rothesay on one vessel and back on another. Furthermore we could cross to Arran on one ship, and sail away from it on another. In 1990 the Island Hop started with the Ardrossan - Brodick sailing, so we had to include this route.

CalMac's Gourock-Dunoon service has been under a political cloud for a few years now. Nobody, especially the politicians, knows if it will continue in its present form for much longer - and that despite the recent construction of a new breakwater and linkspan at Dunoon. So this may be the last chance for us to utilise this route, to sail on the ageing *Jupiter* between the two piers, and to sail on two different vessels, from Gourock to Dunoon. *Jupiter* has been operating the hourly vehicle and passenger service to Dunoon for many months now. She is now CalMac's oldest ship, and with her route in doubt and her sister *Juno* in mothballs at Rosneath the writing is on the wall for her. The other vessel serving Dunoon is *Ali Cat*, a catamaran which has been chartered by CalMac for a few years now to take the additional peak time sailings to Dunoon.

Another opportunity sprang to mind. Back in 1991 we used the Wednesday service to Colonsay to sail from Oban to Kennacraig, but we have never tried this in reverse.

So there was enough material there to ensure that we could end our Island Hopping saga with a bang! But we would need a car, so let's take

Andy's, so we can bang his. We also needed a Car *Rover* ticket, only the second time we've indulged in this. We could not achieve the 'embellishments' without one.

Andy is delighted to be asked back - especially after running out of petrol last year! But we're not bitter. And so with the return of Ian the four of us were straining at the leash on the morning of Tuesday 13 May 2008 - the start of Island Hop 2008.

Day One - *Double Measures*

It's 06.50 and we're not as much 'straining at the leash' as staggering like zombies into the car outside my house. Boy I hate early starts, but as usual I've no-one to blame except myself. It was my idea to be down at Gourock in time for the 07.50 foot-passenger only sailing to Dunoon. Most of our sailings today will be doubles - ie over on one ship and back on another, and we start with this Dunoon crossing.

We've never sailed on *Ali Cat* before on an Island Hop - she is our first 'new' ship - and she's arriving at Gourock Pier at exactly the same time as we are. She's had a leisurely sail over from Dunoon, on her 06.20 run; we've had a mad dash in Andy's Jaguar to get here on time. But we've made it, and off we bob on the short crossing to Dunoon.

The weather forecast for the week ahead is very encouraging but at the moment the easterly wind though light is surprisingly cold. Any time spent out on the little foredeck has to be brief. There are about twenty other passengers aboard, all off to work on the Argyll side of the Clyde presumably. I bet none are embarking on anything as mad as we are - we'll have about twenty-five minutes at Dunoon before sailing back to Gourock! This time on *Jupiter*. But hold on a minute - what's this we see? The 'streaker' on the main Dunoon roster, which we can see about to pass us in mid channel, is *Saturn* and not that other planet!

It transpires that *Jupiter* was taken out of service yesterday afternoon for overhaul and inspection. *Saturn* was re-activated from her lay-up at Rosneath (where she lay beside the redundant *Juno*) and pressed into her first spell of service on the Dunoon run for many months.

"So it's only eight in the morning and the Island Hop itinerary is wrong already," Ian complains. Welcome back Ian.

At Dunoon we are delighted to see that the Rock Cafe is open. This was an institution for me and my children. From which you can correctly deduce that whenever I dragged them onto any ferry bound for Dunoon we would always end up in there - for a roll and sausage. In fact I dragged my two younger children, Fiona and Tony, there just a few months ago. They came kicking and screaming - ridiculous behaviour for a nineteen and seventeen year old! Despite only having twenty minutes before our return sailing to Gourock we have time for - a roll and sausage!

Gibbie has not joined us in the cafe for he's met someone he knows on the pier and refuses to move. Andy calls him on his mobile. "Gibbie, we're in the Rock Cafe, do you want a roll and sausage?" There is no reply. Gibbie and mobiles have a suspicous and uneasy relationship with each other. Andy buys him a roll and sausage anyway. On returning to the pier Gibbie's reaction is predictable.

"I wondered where you went. Hope you've got brown sauce on it."

Saturn slides in to Dunoon Pier and we hop aboard. She will be heading to Arran in about three weeks to take up her role as second Ardrossan - Brodick ferry, to Caledonian Isles. As the ship has been out of action for a while a team of 'snaggers', in matching CalMac Ferries overhauls, are wandering around the car deck with spanners in their hands, tightening bolts, fixing pipes and sticking the side ramps back on again. Right now *Saturn* is taking us back to Gourock. She's also taking a team of Rangers fans. They are heading ultimately for Manchester to play Zenit St Petersberg in the UEFA Cup Final. Like all good football fans they look as though they don't have a jacket between them.

We pick up the car at Gourock and head around the bend and south towards Wemyss Bay. Round about Inverkip the sun quite dramatically emerges and our next ship, Bute, berths in all her glory. This time we are taking the car over, but our visit to the Isle of Bute will be brief for we are taking the next ferry back, as this will be *Argyle*. This will give us two different ships, of which *Argyle* is new for us.

As we wait to board *Bute* Gibbie produces his mobile and spends the next ten minutes trying to access his voice-mail. "Someone wants to know if I want a roll and sausage."

His wee brother, Andy, is more interested in the black-and-white ducks swimming just offshore from the pier. "Look! Are those eiderdowns?" Well he's nearly right.

As the male eider chase their brown, nondescript partners around they utter a curious salacious, and ever so slightly perverse "mmMMm". A large herring gull swoops down close to us with a starfish in its capacious beak. It has great trouble deciding what to do with it, as if undecided on which arm to tackle first.

Aboard *Bute* a posse of CalMac staff are being shown round the ship. In their dark suits and sunglasses they look like the Gourock Mafia. Their lapel badges give them away - they're all Port Assistants, whatever that is.

Rothesay Pier doesn't just resemble a building site, it is one. Huge new gangways are in place and a new linkspan is operational, but the inner harbour looks as if 633 squadron has just visited it. We cannot make out whether this huge whole in the ground is being excavated or filled in. From the length of time that the works here have been going on perhaps it's both. "Dig that hole, right, now fill it in again!"

We speed off to Craigmore tearoom - it's closed. So Andy drives us on a tour of the island. We turn up Canada Hill and wind down The

Serpentine. Oh what fun can be had in Rothesay in less than an hour.

Soon we're on our second new ship of the trip - Argyle - where the seats on the upper deck face aft instead of forward (as on her sister). There are other differences but I cannot be bothered telling you them - in case you think I'm a complete anorak! Another cup of tea and we're off at Wemyss Bay and heading down to Largs. Here, would you believe it, is yet another new ship for us.

Loch Shira is just about to depart. There is some confusion about our car ticket but we are eventually beckoned aboard. It's just gone 12.45 and we are boarding ship number five. Phew, this trip will be exhausting if we keep this pace up.

Loch Shira was launched in December 2006 at Ferguson's yard in Port Glasgow - I should know, I was there! She is the new Largs-Cumbrae ferry and is a giant. She seems far too big for the service she finds herself on, but then traffic to Cumbrae has built up considerably over the years and no doubt her capacity is justified. Today she is being backed up by *Loch Riddon* which sits motionlessly at the pier.

Loch Shira reminds me of *Loch Portain*, just a little smaller. All her traffic disembarks at Cumbrae and turns left. We go right, around the far side of sunny Cumbrae. It's always sunny here, isn't it? The firth on the far side is empty, not a single ship. Kilchattan Bay on Bute, the island we have just left, winks across to us in the early afternoon sun and on Arran, our next island, the 'sleeping warrior' is in his usual repose*

I cannot recall ever circling Cumbrae in a car. On foot, by bicycle and by ship, but never by car. It doesn't take long. We pass through Millport without stopping and we are soon boarding Loch Shira again. We get strange looks from the crewmen who study the car with a look of uncertain recognition.

Back at Largs Ian ignores all our pleas to find somewhere to eat and insists we take a tour of the town he wants to find all the houses he has lived in here. So we're up one street and down another looking at little white bungalows. It would seem that Ian has had more houses than a habitual bingo winner. "It was that one, no it was the one next door, no we're on the wrong street, can we turn left back down Haco Street."

On to Ardrossan now, eventually, where before our sailing to Brodick we decide to sample some traditional North Ayrshire fare. We find this at Fisher's Fine Foods. And it lives up to its pronouncement. We have a buffet of its finest, sitting on a wall opposite it.

The queue of cars waiting for *Caledonian Isles* is lengthy, but we are booked aboard; in fact we are booked on several crossings during the forthcoming days. Next to us a chap on a motorbike has an alsation riding pillion. On closer examination it's either stuffed or a cuddly toy. Whatever it is it's life size.

*The 'sleeping warrior' is the distant shape formed from the mountains of the northern rim of Glen Sannox on Arran. From a certain perspective, especially around the Largs, Fairlie, Seamill area, the outline resembles a human face and upper body lying supine, facing north. This is known as the 'sleeping warrior'. From 'his' size let's hope he never wakens up!

As we wait to board Andy plays his rumpy-pumpy brass band music, so consequently it is a relief when the queue starts to move forward.

This route was the first crossing on that 1990 Island Hop, but the ship is different. Eighteen years ago it was *Isle of Arran* that took Gibbie and Ian to Brodick (I joined them later). Nowadays even the bulky *Caley Isles* cannot always cope with the summer traffic - thus the redeployment of *Saturn*. Today the ship is busy but far from full. We sit out on the rear deck, sheltered from the easterly breeze and enjoying the sun's rays. All too soon we are in Brodick Bay, where a small tanker *Kraslava* is lying at anchor. Back down to the car deck and we're off and heading north now, up Arran's beautiful east coast.

After Sannox the road climbs steadily 199 metres up to the Boguillie, the pass above Lochranza. Having pedalled up her so many times it's great to be driven up and not look at each approaching rise in the road with dread.

Just as in 1990 Lochranza is the target. From there *Loch Tarbert* crosses to the Kintyre peninsula. Back then it was *Loch Ranza* but she is now the regular Gigha ferry. Three semi-wild red deer munch grass nervously at the side of the road near the ferry slipway. We've met these beasties before, the closest I've ever come to a bit of live venison. *Loch Tarbert* sets off at 17.15 for Claonaig, with Andy's jag and the four of us aboard. She is our last ship of the day, the pace will slow down from now on.

I am particularly fond of this crossing. Gibbie cannot understand why, but I have some happy memories of pitching across the Kilbrannan Sound on various vessels: *Rhum, Loch Riddon, Loch Ranza* and Isle of Cumbrae. We've certainly used this useful route on several Island Hops.

Today the sea is calm and Ian and I sit on one side of *Loch Tarbert's* upper deck and Gibbie and Andy on the other, to help balance the ship. We make friendly gestures to each other. Today's early start is beginning to its toll and soon our side of the ship is snoozing.

From Claonaig it is only a dozen miles to Tarbert, where our beds for the night are booked. As chance would have it *Isle of Arran* is just about to depart Kennacraig on the 18.00 sailing to Islay as we are passing. We zoom up to take a closer look and cause some consternation among the CalMac shore staff who think we are a late arrival for the sailing. The ship's ramp is already up so it's as well we're not.

Two ships serve Islay from Kennacraig *Isle of Arran* and *Hebridean Isles*. We will join the latter tomorrow.

At Tarbert the air is still and peaceful. So is our restaurant a little later on, until poor Ian is harangued by an irate elderly lady accusing him of talking too loudly over his Cullen Skink. She clutches her handbag and remonstrates loudly with him. For a moment it looks as though she is going to hit him with it. Much to the disapointment of the rest of us she doesn't. The quiet spoken Ian is quite taken aback by all this and needs two Bunnahabhains to calm him down.

Another early start. I'm up at 06.15 because Ken Dodd is singing through the wall from the room next door. Poor Gibbie is not a 'morning' person but is having to share a room with Andy who is. That's why Gibbie is sharing with him, Ian and I refuse to.

A continental breakfast is waiting outside the door. I almost stand on it when I step out to test the weather. I've been given such an enormous spoon that I don't know whether to pour the cornflakes into it instead of the bowl.

I have a wander around Tarbert. The sun is out but the air is still cool. The Portavadie ferry Isle of Cumbrae is tied up in the harbour and some heavy trucks are already roaring up the hill on the road to Glasgow. When their rumble dies away and peace returns a cuckoo can be heard announcing a new day.

Gibbie is paying the hotel bill. "Do you take direct debit?"

"Why, are you coming back every month," is the owner's reply.

Our next ship leaves from Kennacraig six miles away at 07.45 and we are soon on our way. We will be sailing from Kennacraig to Oban aboard *Hebridean Isles*, and will not be disembarking at Port Askaig nor Colonsay. I am wondering just how enthusiastically the crew loading the ship will react to this, as careful positioning of the traffic for the two islands is necessary in order that each car is pointing in the right direction when they disembark. Not many people are as daft as we are. I mean anyone with any sense would drive from Kennacraig to Oban! But as it turns out someone else is as daft as us, for there is another car making the same request. The advantage is that we get waved past all the busy car lanes and loaded first. After a three-point turn on the vacuous car deck the four of us are at the head of the cafeteria queue for a real breakfast.

Now a CalMac full breakfast is something to really look forward to. I could have one for breakfast, lunch and dinner. So it's the full 'horror', with extra black pudding, and then up to Ian's favourite spot on the sheltered afterdeck. Sailing 'with the wind' this indeed proves to be the place-to-be and the suncream is out by 08.30.

West Loch Tarbert has to be one of the most beautiful lochs in Scotland. I can't put my finger on it - I just think it's lovely. The ship purrs down it, seemingly without effort. It's just a shame I don't get to see the whole length of it - by the time we're halfway down I'm in the 'zizz' lounge zizzing. Two early starts on consecutive days, who plans this?

When I'm next up on deck McArthur's Head, the southern entrance to the Sound of Islay, is ahead. We are sailing into this narrow strait between Islay and Jura and both islands are closing in on either side. Ahead the Jura ferry holds our ship up as she crosses over to Feolin. We slow to a crawl and then pick our way carefully onto Port Askaig Pier. Gibbie and I remark that the ship hugs the shore as close as we've ever seen.

In 1990 it was *Claymore* that took us on this popular route. I much prefer *Hebridean Isles* but I suspect Gibbie misses his old favourite. A year earlier, on the very first Island Hop before Ian joined us, it was Glen Sannox which took Gibbie and I from Port Askaig to Oban. That seems a very long time ago.

Port Askaig is still under reconstruction - although it looks a lot better than Rothesay. A substantial slice of the hillside behind the handful of buildings that make up this tiny port has been excavated away to create space for a marshalling yard. This space was badly needed, of that there is no doubt, but I feel that much of the character of Port Askaig has been scooped away along with all those tons of rock and soil. The little shop now stands forlornly on its own - surrounded by car park. The buildings on the actual pier look as though they are being restored, so perhaps Port Askaig will soon regain some of its character.

I'd love to get off the ship and spend some real time on Islay - it is my favourite island - but of course this is Island Hopping and it is the journey which is important, not the arrival, as someone once said.

Two huge lorries drag themselves off the ferry and up the gradient. From their struggle it would seem that they are not empty but carrying grain, perhaps to the maltings at Port Ellen. Whisky production is booming on Islay and not only are all the distilleries functional again but an old one, Port Charlotte, recently reopened in 2007, and a brand new one, at Kilchoman, commenced production in 2006. Both *Hebridean Isles* and *Isle of Arran* served Islay throughout last winter to help cope with the increased export from the island.

Whisky is a subject which oftens crops up on an Island Hop. This is partly because we frequently find ourselves sailing among some of the whisky producing islands but also because collectively we once tried one. We each have our favourites. Gibbie likes Bowmore, Ian likes Bunnahabhain and Andy is a Glenlivet man. Me? I'm not keen on it - divulging my favourite, I mean. But for the record the bottle of 17 year old Ardbeg on my shelf at home is the one which never seems to gather dust. Enough of this - it's still morning, for goodness sake!

On up the Sound of Islay towards Colonsay. About twenty dogs have joined the ship at Port Askaig. I can hardly walk about the deck without stepping on one. Fortunately most of them have brought their owners with them, and we've got to step over some of them as well. Andy is delighted by this - he loves dogs. One mention of the name 'Sparky' is enough to bring a tear to each eye. As he makes his way around the ship he pauses to pat, stroke and generally annoy every one of them - and he annoys some of the dogs as well. Andy owns a Dachshund called 'Bertie' and at regular intervals during our trip the rest of us hear him mutter, "I wonder what Bertie's doing just now. He'll be missing his Dad."

We're soon at Colonsay. Another exchange of passengers. Many of those who joined the ship at Islay get off here. Most of these have bikes and look as if they off on a circumnavigation of the island. The rest are off to walk their dogs.

The ropes are off and we are away at 11.40. CalMac's time-keeping is impeccable. So is the weather. The sky is completely blue and the sea perfectly calm. Once clear of Colonsay there isn't even so much as a slight swell to rock the ship - we could be sailing on Hoggonfield Loch it's so calm. It is also high tide and our skipper announces that on our way to Oban we will be sailing inside the Garvellachs (normally we have sailed to the outside or west of this distinctive island group).

Ian suggests a bowl of soup for lunch and we drag ourselves away from the deck. But the mince pie looks so enticing that we empty *Heb Isles'* servery clean out of it. As he shovels down the last forkful Gibbie comments "I thought we were having soup?"

Abeam of the Garvellachs now. Several small fishing boats go about their business on the Scarba side. Close in to the islands themselves a small cruiser shows its passengers off to some local seals.

We discuss what we are likely to see and what we will do when we get to Oban. Oban has a second linkspan now so it will be interesting to see which ship uses which at this busy time of the week for Oban's ferries. I consult the timetable to work out which vessels will be due in at Oban during our time there. By the time we arrive *Clansman* should be heading out and *Lord of the Isles* and *Isle of Mull* heading in. This could be my first chance to photograph ships at both linkspans. As we enter Oban Bay it is clear that my plans will have to be jettisoned. For reasons as yet unclear to us only one linkspan is operational, and we are in a queue!

Clansman has indeed just left but *Isle of Mull* is ahead of us and takes precedence. We sit out in the bay, our skipper apologising sincerly to us for the delay. In comes *Lord of the Isles* and she takes her place behind us in the queue. Anyone on Oban Esplanade would be getting a terrific photograph of all this.

It takes ten minutes for us to eventually berth, be we are in no rush. I run up Pulpit Hill with my camera to watch what happens next. Below me both lighthouse tenders *Pharos* and *Pole Star* are moored together and *Raasay* lies idle.

After unloading *Hebridean Isles* moves out into the middle of the bay to let *Lord of the Isles* berth. In between Eigg sets off for Lismore. As *LOTI* is now off duty for a while she berths at the North Pier and lets *Hebridean Isles* move back in to the linkspan. We've witnessed this kind of frenetic activity at Oban many times before, but it never gets less fascinating. My photograph of ships at both linkspans, however, will have to wait - til they're both operational.

I descend to the pier where *Raasay* is berthed and for almost an hour sit in the sun at the edge watching a small fishing boat unload. The two fishermen have been trying to catch shellfish on the far side of Kerrera. Their reward for a whole morning's work is a quarter of a tub of prawns.

They're not happy bunnies, neither are the prawns presumably, but undeterred they load up with cans of fuel and set off out into the bay again.

When *Isle of Mull* comes wheeling into the other end of the bay I remember that I've got three friends somewhere on the Railway Pier! In twenty minutes we're taking *Isle of Mull* over to Craignure. Back in 1990 Gibbie, Ian and I disembarked from *Claymore* at Oban and shortly after sailed on *Lord of the Isles* out to Lochboisdale in South Uist. We cannot do that this year as the Outer Isles sailing now leaves Oban before the Colonsay sailing arrives; hence Craignure. We will spend the night on Mull, re-cross to Oban in the morning and sail out to South Uist tomorrow - and it will be *Lord of the Isles* again.

The car goes onto the ship and it's upstairs to the upper deck to enjoy our sail over to Mull. There we meet an English couple looking forward to for their visit ever to the island. "Have you been there before?" They ask me.

I'm embarrassed to tell them just how many times - even if I knew!

They are off to view the wildlife of Mull, and are hoping especially to see white-tailed eagles and otters. They're heading to the right place - Mull has several of both. It is encouraging that so many visitors now come to Mull to see its wonderful beasties in their natural environment. Whether it's eagles, otters or whales there are now many tours and excursions available to allow the visitor to observe the wildlife to the full.

We are not planning in searching for any wildlife tonight - we will be searching for a TV to watch tonight's UEFA Cup Final between Rangers and Zenit St Petersburg. As we drive off the ship Andy is practising his Rangers songs. He's hoping for a good win tonight - I'm just hoping that the accommodation I've booked at Craignure has a telly. It doesn't! Well not in the bar anyway. Fortunately both our rooms have, and we are spared a drive to Tobermory.

Craignure is drenched in sunshine and we spend a very pleasant late afternoon sitting out in the beer garden, sipping tea. "This is the best weather we've ever had," declares Ian. And who are we to disagree.

A cheeky male blackbird lands on our table and perches within a foot of me. Once our meal arrives it becomes apparent that this bird is tame enough, and brave enough, to take chips from our hand. He keeps returning for more. I admire his resourcefulness but he really should have a re-think about his diet. He could eat Gibbie's greens - he doesn't!

When *Isle of Mull* returns to Craignure later she berths for the night as *Clansman* and *Lord of the Isles* will be filling up all the parking spaces at Oban.

We finally drag ourselves away from the midges, go up to the room which Ian and I are sharing tonight and park ourselves in front of our fifteen- inch telly. The UEFA Cup Final begins - and the less said about that the better.

Andy isn't singing this morning. We can all guess why. Down at breakfast we are joined by the couple from the bedroom next door. I feel we should apologise to them for all our shouting last night. However it turns out that they were out till late watching short-eared owls. Wish I'd joined them.

This morning were driving to Fionnphort - to photograph a ferry. Not to ride on one, just to photograph one. I announced this clever idea to my colleagues last night. "A round trip of seventy-four miles just to take a picture of the *Loch Buie*!" Gibbie has a somewhat sceptical inflection to his voice, not without some justification.

"That's the point. It isn't *Loch Buie* that's there, she's broken down. It's *Loch Linnhe*, and I don't have a picture of her there. We've bags of time, we don't sail out of Craignure until 13.00."

So the others reluctantly agree. In fact I challenged them to come up with a better idea on how to spend our morning. And none of them could.

I set off on foot. I just fancy a walk - it's a beautiful morning. I don't mean I'm going to walk the whole way, the others will give me a twenty minute head start and then follow in the car. At least they'd better! I can imaging them saying,

"Naw, let him go himself, it was his idea, we'll just sit here in the sun until our 13.00 sailing."

As it happens I cover a full two miles and have reached Lochdon before the blue jag pulls up alongside me. It's the usual stop-start journey along the single-track road. Although I offer to drive Andy seems happy doing it. He's perked up a bit, now singing Rolf Harris' 'Two Little Boys', but making up his own words. He gives a near relentless commentary on every passing car, breaking every five minutes to ask, "Can we see Iona yet?"

Soon we can and to my embarrassment the usual ferry *Loch Buie* is back in action! Last week she had a problem with one of her ramps but repairs must have been expeditious for here she is arriving at the slipway at Fionnphort - and she won't be sailing again for an hour. We don't have an hour so we can't even have a sail on her. As Andy has never been to Iona he is disappointed. In retrospect I should have realised yesterday that she was back, for *Raasay* was laid up at Oban Pier and she would have been called into action while *Loch Buie* was being repaired. So we have a cup of tea and drive all the way back to Craignure. Sorry chaps.

We wait in the queue for *Isle of Mull* and get chatting to Port Assistant Andrew Hickford, who recognises our little group as the Away with the Ferries nutters. He informs us that due to gangway problems at Oban *Isle of Mull* will be berthing the wrong-way-in here at Craignure. That's stern-in instead of bow-in. Gibbie rummages for his camera to capture a new angle of one of his favourite ships. While this is going on Andy and I continue our Laurel and Hardy routine - we keep getting our baseball caps mixed up, he catches me wearing his again.

I'm sorry to leave Craignure. A tinge of sadness suddenly descends on me as the ship turns to starboard to head for Oban. It has been fun here, and the sun is still shining. Downstairs for lunch. Gibbie and Andy are now suffering the consequences of having shared a room for two nights now - their supping soup at separate tables in the cafeteria. Where is that brotherly love?

At Oban we have another of those hanging-around spells. Gibbie comes up with a good idea. *Lord of the Isles* is sailing in from Colonsay, why don't we drive down to the Kerrera narrows to film her sailing in. That gets the vote and we set up cameras opposite the Kerrera ferry slipway. The wee motor boat is doing good business, and no wonder. It is a glorious day and the island is popular with walkers.

We sit beside the car for half an hour watching eider chase each other on the still waters below. They're making those pervy noises again.

Suddenly *Lord of the Isles* glides into view and we get our pictures. When she next sails, to Lochboisdale, we will be aboard her.

Back at Oban Gibbie gets the car into the correct queue for our next sailing while Ian, Andy and I go in search of - whatever Oban has to offer. We do not linger in case Gibbie has to drive the car aboard. Half an hour later we find him sitting on the bonnet of the car The car is dwarfed by a huge coach filled with bubbling, excited silver-haired trekkers. There is a casual and relaxed atmosphere on the pier as we sit waiting for *LOTI* to lower her ramp. A crewman addles up, slaps his hands together and with undisguised enthusiasm announces: "right guys, we're off, let's get going!"

A very smart silver-grey Rolls Royce drives aboard just ahead of us. As its contents clamber out grandad in the back seat throws open his door and embeds it in an overflow pipe on the car deck. It takes a fair bit of to-and-fro'ing to disengage it and then Grandad is marched upstairs to the observation lounge out of harm's way.

The contents of the coach have obviously been on *Lord of the Isles* before, for they have sprinted - and I don't exaggerate her - up three flights of stairs, with commendable agility, to the upper deck seating, which they then monopolise. We're not exactly tardy in getting up there ourselves but we have to resort to shoving a couple of old ladies out the way to procure our own seats.

"Don't worry," says Ian, "as soon as we get underway into that easterly breeze they'll head downstairs for a heat." He's been here before as well. We've hardly moved off the pier when he nudges me. "Look, there's the first fleece coming out."

The Lismore ferry *Eigg* is heading into Oban, but sailing outside of Maiden Island. This is due to the falling tide and means she passes very close to *Lord of the Isles*.

We are back on our 1990 Island Hop route again, sailing out to Lochboisdale, and remarkably on the same ship. Interestingly we will be arriving in daylight, which after much discussion we agree we've never done before. On our sailing to Lochboisdale in 1990 we arrived in gloomy conditions, and in 1995, when we sailed there aboard Iona from Mallaig, it was pitch dark. Sailing up the Sound of Mull, off Craignure, it is the four of us who are descending to the lounges for a heat. Although still sunny the breeze coming down the sound towards us is cool. Well done coach party, how could we have underestimated you so?

Downstairs I overhear the coach driver telling the ship's catering officer that his party intend eating between five and six o'clock. So we will have to avoid that hour when we ourselves dine. But before dinner Andy comes up with an interesting idea. Why don't we get ourselves up on the bridge?

After a bit of negotiating with the very helpful assistant purser, John Wilson, Andy and I are given the nod (the other two are already nodding in the zizz lounge) and ascend by means of hidden doors and secret staircases into the glass capsule that is *LOTI*'s bridge. Here the view all around is simply superb.

David Allen is the Mate and a very courteous fellow he is too. He gives us a quick resume of the ship's controls. Andy is particularly interested in the 'fins' - stabilisers to you and me. "What if you forget they are out and come alongside a pier. Could you not rip them off?"

I know it's a stupid question but David has the answer. "Apart from that big red sign telling you they are out the thruster controls won't work until the stabilisers are retracted."

The ship is well beyond Mull and Ardnamurchan Point into the Sea of the *Hebrides*. The sky is cobalt blue and our destination South Uist a mere smudge on the horizon. The sea looks empty but David points out one other vessel on the ship's radar. A small fishing boat, about a mile away to our left, is gathering in its net. He invites us to look through his binoculars to watch the way in which it circles to gather in its catch.

"At least we have company," I remark.

"I had different company half an hour ago," says David. "I saw a minke whale, just a few hundred yards off the starboard side. It only surfaced once, and I think I was the only one who saw it."

With difficulty we drag ourselves back downstairs. In the cafeteria the choices are limited. The steward is apologetic. "The coach party have almost cleaned as out. We didn't even know they were coming." In the bar there is a huddle around the television set. The former Celtic player Tommy Burns has died. A dozen passengers sit silently watching the screen in sombre mood.

The barmaid is 'Daisy' - a blonde Latvian. Ian and Andy get chatting to her, so much so that my beer is warm by the time they drag themselves back to where Gibbie and I are sitting. Daisy's fiancee is also at sea. "He's is an engineer."

"I wouldn't stick with him," says Andy. "Look how he'll turn out." He points to Ian and Gibbie.

Our approach to Lochboisdale is superb. Remember, we've never seen this in daylight. The channel into the actual loch is surprisingly narrow. The surface of the water, the low hills ahead of us and the handful of buildings around the pier have been turned into delectable shades of chocolate by the setting sun. It has been a beautiful sail and we are almost reluctant to leave the ship. But we do, and content ourselves by watching her glide away from Lochboisdale Pier ten minutes after her arrival. She is off to Barra now, but we should see her again in the morning.

Over a nightcap in the hotel bar we discuss tomorrow's plans. Basically we have to be up at Lochmaddy in North Uist for 11.20. With the car it won't take long to get up there; we could have a long lie - it would make a change. But Andy comes up with the daftest idea that has ever been mooted on an Island Hop.

"Why don't we go over to Eriskay to see Sparky?"

Gibbie looks at him as if he has just suggested that we all hold hands and jump off the end of the pier.

"Who the hell is Sparky?" Asks Ian, slightly intrigued.

"The dug we met on Eriskay last year."

"Oh I remember it on the Island Hop video."

Andy persists. "We've got time, if we're quick. I'm sure he'll remember me." Unable to agree to a concensus we decide to sleep on it. And that should be easier tonight for this time we all have our own rooms.

Day Four - *And Finally . . .*

Something quite extraordinary happens at breakfast - Gibbie is down first! But he looks agitated. "I have an announcement to make," he announces.

Ian, Andy and I look at each other. What's coming, I wonder? He doesn't want to go to Eriskay perhaps. Or something more profound, like I'm not going Island Hopping anymore. The rest of us stop eating, forkfuls of scrambled egg poised motionless over platefuls of bacon and sausage. "Well?" Ian asks.

Gibbie breaks the tension. "I've left my pyjamas at the guesthouse in Craignure!"

The three of us heave sighs of relief - and then start laughing. "What's Janette going to say? She only bought me them three weeks ago - from Marks and Spencer!"

"The owner will destroy them, Gibbie, pour parafin over them and set them alight, no doubt." Ian isn't being helpful.

"I know," mutters Gibbie. "I hope he doesn't look in the pockets."

Outside *Lord of the Isles* has returned from Barra and is disgorging traffic. We assemble beside the car. Despite Andy's daft idea last night we decide to go to Eriskay. Time is tight but it should certainly be a laugh. But I feel I have to point something out to Andy.

"Look, we know where Sparky lives but can you imagine the scenario.

We drive up, he's not there, so you have to knock the door and ask if Sparky's coming out to play. It's going to seem a trifle odd, Andy."

He is undeterred. "I'll knock the door, I don't mind."

"Well none of the rest of us are going to do it."

"I can't believe we're doing this," says Gibbie.

So instead of turning right for Lochmaddy we bear left to head down to the causeway that links South Uist with Eriskay. It is nine miles from the hotel, plus nine miles back, plus forty miles to Lochmaddy. And we have to be there in ninety minutes time. About twenty minutes later we're sitting in the car outside the house of a black-and-white collie. It's elderly owner is mowing the lawn and drawing us curious looks. A moment later Sparky's head appears above the garden fence and Andy is in seventh heaven. It is left to Gibbie to explain his brother's strange behaviour to the elderly gentleman while Andy and Sparky have the kind of reunion that would bring a tear to the eye and hasn't been seen since the days of Lassie.

"We're from Glasgow," says Gibbie apologetically, as if that explains everything.

"Look! He remembers me!" Shouts his brother.

Andy steals a football from a nearby garden and he and his canine friend embark on a rather one-sided game of football. After the first tackle the ball is burst. Andy hands two pound coins to Sparky's owner. "I don't want Sparky to get the blame." Pathetic isn't it!

"Come on Andy, we've got to go!" I almost have to yell at him.

"See you next year, Sparky," mumbles Andy.

And go we do - but not directly back across the causeway. My terms for coming to Eriskay were to film the arrival of the ferry from Ardmhor on Barra. This is a different vessel from last year - namely *Loch Alainn*, the former Cumbrae ferry. She deposed *Loch Bhrusda* up here a few weeks ago and this is our first chance to photograph her. From a lofty position above the slipway we are in perfect time to capture her arrival. Then it's into the car and a hasty departure north.

The road to North Uist is thankfully quiet. The school run is over and *LOTI's* traffic has dissipated. Back in 1990 we took the bus on this leg as we had no car with us. The ship sailing from Lochmaddy to Uig back then was *Hebridean Isles*. Today it is *Hebrides*.

The drive from Eriskay to Lochmaddy takes just sixty-five minutes and we make the check-in time with ten minutes to spare; there's nothing more exciting than adding a bit of pace on an Island Hop. Gibbie couldn't disagree more.

Hebrides unloads a considerable amount of freight traffic. Eight large articulated lorries haul themselves up the linkspan, causing the ship to lurch as they manouevre on the car-deck.

As we sail out of Loch nam Madadh we are treated to a wonderful sight. A white-tailed eagle sits on a rock on the hillside above the ship, surveying its territory. It is a monster of a bird. Huge and powerful, bigger even than the golden eagle, whch also breeds around here. After becoming extinct in Britain around the time of the First World War white-tailed eagles were reintroduced to several Scottish islands in a planned programme which started in the 1970s. Now around thirty-five pairs breed in the west coast of Scotland and they are becoming a more familiar sight.

It is yet another lovely crossing but we spend most of it under the covered starboard deck trying to film our Annual Toast. We set up various cameras. By the time Gibbie is ready to give his eulogy on another ten years of Island Hopping about half the ship's crew is sitting amongst us. They are obviously on a break and watch in taciturn amusement at our antics. Gibbie tries to set up his camera for a self-timed exposure of the four of us. Each time his camera seemingly fails to function. He examines it more closely and discovers he's recorded twenty-three different pictures of us. In several his image can be seen either approaching the camera with a disdainful look on his face or his lurching away from it, his backside hiding the rest of us as he 'races' back to pole position. The recording of Gibbie's final words to our videocamera is even more comical. At one point one of the crew walks inadvertently in front of the lens.

Gibbie is stoic and his speech is a poignant moment. We are all aware that this is not only going to be the last Island Hop of the series, but may be the last Island Hop we ever do. We've done twenty now - we cannot go on forever. How much more energy will we have for this in the future? Only time will tell.

We have a quick coffee in the cafeteria and get chatting to newly weds Christie and Carmelita. They are returning from honeymoon on North Uist. It transpires that they have read Away with the Ferries which makes them instantly likeable people and assures them of a mention in this book.

This Island Hop isn't over yet, however. Once Hebrides berths we head off down through Skye to Mallaig. In 1990 there was no Skye Bridge and Gibbie, Ian and I crossed from Kyleakin to Kyle of Lochalsh where we picked up Lochmor. In those days Lochmor was CalMac's only surviving passenger-only vessel. She served the Small Isles of Rum, Muck, Eigg and Canna but on certain days undertook a cruise from Mallaig up to Kyle of Lochalsh and back again. Not long after our one-way journey in May 1990 this cruise was discontinued, which is a bit of a shame really. Today we will return to the mainland on Coruisk, which sails from Armadale to Mallaig. At Portree we stop off for a fancy fish supper. By 'fancy' I mean expensive. But nice.

Further south clouds are condensing over the peaks of the Cuillins, making them look like a row of smouldering volcanoes. We speed onwards - after all, it is Andy who is driving!

At Mallaig. It would have been nice to end our Island Hop, or even Island Hopping, with a glamorous ship. One which has style, charisma and neat trim lines. But we're stuck with Coruisk. And let's face it Coruisk has none of these attributes. But she's the twelfth ship of this year's Island Hop - so at least that's something. Right now she is struggling to berth at Armadale linkspan. A crosswind is causing her to drift sideways. This I can see very well for I am standing looking directly onto her front-end (note that I avoid using the term 'bow'). But she gets in eventually. Before we get aboard a veritable vintage vanguard of classic Jaguars roars off the car deck. There are eight of them. At least they have style, charisma and neat lines. Andy wants to follow them in his own 'classic' Jag.

"You can't, Andy. We've got to go home." We sail off towards Mallaig where, of course, our 1990 Island Hop also ended.

A melancholy envelopes me as I stare out of the lounge window at the approaching harbour. I usually feel a touch sad at the end of each trip, but this feels like the end of an era. Twenty years of Island Hopping has produced some wonderful memories: the ships, the islands, the scenery, the camaraderie, the laughs. Many of these pass ephemerally through my mind now as I sit watching Mallaig get nearer and nearer. Like the last grains of sand running out of an hourglass the last stretch of sea is slowly closing as the ship approaches the harbour wall. In twenty years of Island Hopping we've sailed on, or strutted the decks of, seventy-one vessels. We've visited fifty-four islands. And this ship is the last. Now it is all over.

I look round and catch Gibbie's eye. He just nods. "As one era ends, Stuart, another begins." I'm sure he's right - he usually is . . .

The Final Toast, aboard HEBRIDES, 2008

191

Islands in order visited 1999–2008.
New islands shown in bold.

Cumbrae	Seil	**Lambs Holm**
Kerrera	Tiree	**Hoy**
Mull	Eriskay	**Flotta**
Barra	South Uist	**Graemsay**
Skye	Benbecula	**Rousay**
North Uist	Grimsay	**Wyre**
Harris	**Baleshare**	**Egilsay**
Bute	**Orkney Mainland**	**Rum**
Islay	**Shapinsay**	Canna
Arran	**Eday**	Lewis
Raasay	**Stronsay**	Beneray
Colonsay	**South Ronaldsay**	Coll
Gigha	**Burray**	**Danna**
Iona	**Glimps Holm**	**Kismuil Island**

Ships in order sailed 1999–2008.
New ships shown in bold, ships within brackets did not sail.

Waverley	*Pioneer*	*Varagen*
Balmoral	*Loch Alainn*	*Hamnavoe*
Loch Riddon	*Isle of Cumbrae*	*Claymore*
Jupiter	*Isle of Arran*	*Hoy Head*
'Kerrera Ferry'	*Loch Tarbert*	*Graemsay*
Isle of Mull	*Caledonian Isles*	*Eynhallow*
Lord of the Isles	*Loch Striven*	*Coruisk*
Hebridean Isles	*Hebrides*	*Isle of Lewis*
Loch Bhrusda	*Loch Linnhe*	*Loch Portain*
(Kenilworth)	*Loch Fyne*	*Sir Walter Scott*
Rover	*Loch Ranza*	*(Maid of the Loch)*
Sound of Sleat	*Lochnevis*	*Bute*
Saturn	*Clansman*	*Ali Cat*
Juno	*Loch Buie*	*Argyle*
Loch Dunvegan	*Thorsvoe*	*Loch Shira*